ISO 9000 CERTIFICATION

and

TOTAL QUALITY MANAGEMENT

Second Edition

Publisher/Distributor:

STANDARDS-QUALITY MANAGEMENT GROUP
P.O. Box 30051, 250 Greenbank Road
NEPEAN, Ontario, Canada K2H 8X0
Tel. 613-820-2445   Fax. 613-820-1739

ISO 9000 CERTIFICATION

and

TOTAL QUALITY MANAGEMENT

SECOND EDITION

Subhash C. Puri

Standards-Quality Management Group
Ottawa-Nepean, Ontario, Canada

Canadian Cataloguing in Publication Data

Puri, Subhash C.
    ISO 9000 certification and total quality management

2nd ed.
Includes bibliographical references and index.
ISBN 0-9695927-0-1-X

    1. Quality control--Standards. 2. Total quality management.
I. Standards-Quality Management Group. II. Title.

TS156.6.P87 1995   658.5'62   C93-090495-8

ISBN   0-9695927-1-X

First Edition
    First Printing: April, 1992
    Second Printing: October, 1992
Second Edition
    First Printing: January, 1995

Cover design by: Saidul R. Mahomed
                    Qualitymark Editora
                    Rio de Janeiro, Brazil

 Printed on acid-free recycled paper

Dedication

To my wife: **Shashi**
and daughters: **Pamela and Anuradha**
for their patience, understanding and support

CONTENTS

Chapter 4: ISO 9000 (1994) Quality Standards   47

Quality and Standardization
Quality System Standards
International Organization for Standardization (ISO)
The ISO 9000 Series
Revision (1994): ISO 9000 Series
Premise of ISO 9000 Series
Three-Tier Model: ISO 9001, 9002, 9003
Adoption of ISO 9000 Series
Quality Standards - Further Developments
Other Quality Related Standards/Guides
Availability of Standards
ISO 9000 Certification/Registration

PART 2: THE QUALITY MANAGEMENT

Chapter 5: Developing a TQM Model   69

Introduction
Self-Developed/Self-Directed TQM System
The 7-Step TQM Model
Phases of TQM Implementation
Process Improvement Plan
TQM: The Product Profile
TQM: The Finale

Chapter 6: The Personal TQM   89

The Paradigm Shift
Personal TQM
Quality Leadership
Team Approach to Quality
People Empowerment

Chapter 7: TQM Model via ISO 9004-1   99

Introduction
Premise of ISO 9004-1 (1994)
ISO 9004-1: TQM Model
TQM: The Management Profile
TQM Implementation via ISO 9004-1

PART 4: THE QUALITY APPLICATIONS

PART 5: THE QUALITY IMPROVEMENT

FOREWORD

For a long time, I have upheld the premise that there are three fundamentally important attributes a person must inculcate in order to actualize the full richness and affability of life: Knowledge (awareness, understanding), Strength (physical/mental/moral/ethical/social), Beauty (appreciative proactive mindset). To succeed, an organization must have complete understanding of its market positioning and possess requisite technological and manpower capabilities. It must have strength to make a commitment to its vision and purpose supported by an empowered workforce. It must also imbibe a sense of excellence and ethical operability.

Having been managing a large organization for a long time in a competitive marketplace, I can now see my axioms becoming a virtual reality. Today's business mandate is "competitive marketability" and the success depends on producing more, more cheaply, and consistently better. When everything else is equal in competition, **Quality** provides the winning edge. At Albany International, we have been cognizant of this reality for a long time and we have adequately responded to the market demands by instituting effective Total Quality Assurance systems and by achieving ISO 9001 Quality System certification.

In his book, Subhash Puri provides a magnificent description of marketplace realities and needs and he outlines the appropriate methods for addressing these issues. We have made extensive use of the first edition of his book, as well as we had the opportunity of working with him as our external consultant. The first edition of his book has also been translated in the Portuguese language and is widely used in Brazil.

This second highly enlarged and enriched edition of his book is virtually all encompassing and commendable. Written with upmost tenacity, the book clearly manifests the experiential ability of the author to present a rather complex subject in the most simplistic and user-friendly manner. The author should be congratulated and complimented on his dedication and valuable contribution to the field of quality.

Ernoe Eger
General Director and CEO
Albany International, Brazil

FOREWORD

From my visits throughout the world in recent years, I can say categorically that amongst business, government, producers and consumers there is unprecedented interest world-wide in superior levels of quality for goods and services. There is rapidly increasing recognition that managing for optimum quality is not only desirable but also imperative. It means for the producer better profitability with increased productivity, lower costs, less waste, enhanced competitiveness; for the consumer, greater satisfaction and better value; for governments, an essential element in strengthening the economies of their countries. I attribute the drive for quality improvement to several factors:

- *the lowering and removing of barriers to trade between nations, and hence a more competitive world,*
- *management realization in recent years about providing the kind of leadership necessary for higher levels of quality performance,*
- *the development of new tools to help achieve quality performance,*
- *minimizing the cost-burden of carrying inventory through quality performance.*

To provide organizations - industrial, commercial or government - with quality system standards and guidelines, the International Organization for Standardization developed the ISO 9000 series of international standards. First published in 1987 and revised in 1994, these standards are sweeping the world and should be used without change, without additions or deletions.

In his book "ISO 9000 Certification and Total Quality Management", Subhash Puri lays out easy-to-follow, step-by-step procedures for implementing quality systems and for fulfilling external quality assurance requirements by qualifying for registration to the appropriate ISO 9000 standard.

The author has earned an enviable reputation for his contributions to the appreciation and understanding of quality management and quality assurance through several books and professional papers over the last two decades. This new publication is a valuable addition to the series and the author should be congratulated for his comprehensive and timely book on the subject.

Roy A. Phillips, CM. B.A.Sc., P.Eng.
ISO President (1989-91)

PREFACE

"The quality revolution continues..."

Three years ago, I wrote the first edition of this book when the clamour for ISO 9000 certification had just begun. There was hardly any book on the subject, and virtually no book addressed, simultaneously, the combined subjects of Total Quality Management (TQM) and ISO 9000 certification. In fact, even today I know of no other book jointly covering both topics. Yet, I strongly believe that these two subjects are virtually inseparable. The book has been very well received and applauded for its simplicity, clarity, and practicality of style and presentation. I carefully avoided the long-winded and novelistic style of presentation but rather attempted to elucidate the subject through a listing format permitting instantaneous hands-on application of the methods.

Enormous changes have transpired since the publication of the first edition. The ISO 9000 standards have now achieved global acceptance. The series has been revised and several new guidance standards have been incorporated. Conformance to ISO 9000 is virtually a business mandate of the 1990s and this trend is likely to continue well beyond the year 2000.

Over and above the desire to improve quality and achieve excellence, today's business world is continuously experiencing many other paradigmatic shifts in their operability framework. One such major paradigm shift is what I would like to annotate as the "People Revolution". The workplace is becoming increasingly democratized and people are being challenged and innovated through empowerment to strive for excellence.

This work is a revised and enlarged version of the first edition, dedicated to capturing and accommodating these evolving concepts and methodologies. From the former fourteen chapters, this edition comprises twenty six chapters, attempting to address a whole spectrum of issues and methodologies around the field of quality system implementation and certification. For instance, in line with the prevailing conceptual framework of empowerment and process ownership, a new paradigm of "Personal TQM" has been introduced and discussed. In addition, included are many more workable strategies and roadmaps for quality system implementation/certification which I had occasion to develop and use during my extensive consultation work with various international companies around the world. My hope is that these hands-on guidelines will provide a suitable working framework for implementing sustainable quality systems.

Finally, great care has been taken to ensure that the simplicity, clarity and style enjoyed by the first edition equally pervades this new work. Throughout the book, however, the emphasis is on creativity, innovation, and process ownership. Models and systems are sustainable only when they are people-developed, people-owned, people-empowered and people-driven. Therein lies the focus of the years 2000+!

Ottawa, Canada   **Subhash C. Puri**
January, 1995

ACKNOWLEDGEMENTS

The fabric of our society is intricately interwoven. Interdependence is an integral part of human life. We live and learn by sharing throughout our lives. Sharing provides enormous pleasure, dividends and opportunity for growth. No author can be so boastful and presumptuous as to believe that something utterly original can be created in isolation. It is only through uninhibited interaction and influence of writings and conversations with friends, colleagues, and professionals that a person gains an experiential insight and wisdom into the subject. This book is a clear example of such a collaborative effort.

The book is a direct result of many years of hand-on experience of consulting, teaching, seminars, keynote addresses, and standardization committee work. During the course of my consulting work, while I was instrumental in providing meaningful professional input into the process of quality system implementation in many organizations, the whole exercise, in turn, also provided me with enormous wealth of intellectual and experiential insight into the business world. I would, therefore, like to express my gratitude to the following persons whose interaction had a profound impact on my thought processes: Vince DiTullio, Jim Fulford, William Harvey, Karin McCullough, Barbara Tisdale, Mike Royo, Doug Lechleiter, Mike Wormwald, Cesar Rebelo, Julian Moser, Jim Hebert, Donald Roberts, Alex Leask, Larry Moffatt, and Richard Goddard.

I would also like to express my thanks to Roy A. Philips and Ernoe Eger for their continued support and admiration for my professional understanding of the subject, and for writing the foreword for my book. My heartfelt gratitude goes to my many friends and colleagues for their continued support and inspiration: William Forbes, Nand Gupta, Baljit Nagpal, Patricia Kopp, Om Kaura, Roger Trudel, Subhash Chander, Saidul R. Mohamed, Ashok Malhotra, Shyam Banik, and Mohan Mankotia. Sincere thanks to Sylvie Olsen and Diane Goulet for their devoted assistance in the preparation of the book. I also wish to thank all the authors and associations who gave me permission to use excerpts and references from their publications.

Lastly, no undertaking in my life would have been meaningfully successful without the perpetual love, care, support and patience of my wife Shashi and my daughters Pamela and Anuradha.

Subhash C. Puri

THE PARADIGM OF SUCCESS

VISION 2000+

◆ THE REALISM AND THE RESOLVE

Reality can manifest itself in a variety of ways - as concrete objects, abstract entities or cognitive schemata. Somewhere in this grand scheme of perceptual and non-perceptual materialization, there is a fundamental business reality - the reality of a common mission - "**Success**". *Success* translates itself into different configurations for different organization types. For manufacturing companies, success means profitability and continued growth. For private sector service organizations, success entails into profitability, credibility and survivability. For public sector agencies, success implies fulfilling the mandate in the most effective manner.

What are the typical characteristics of success? What does an organization have to do to be successful? Success is a multi-faceted entity and it requires a multi-dimensional activity span. Organizations cannot simply produce products and services, the way they want and expect to be successful. They have to satisfy the needs, demands and expectations of those for whom they are in business - the customers. Today's customer is intelligent, demanding and a comparative buyer.

In searching for the key characteristics of success, it is evident that only those organizations in the private sector would be competitively most successful that can consistently provide products and services which have, as a minimum, the following fundamental attributes:

- **Technological superiority**
- **Quality excellence**
- **Competitive pricing**
- **Customer satisfaction**

What are the determinants of success? How does one measure a company's health? Typically, there are three factors that can identify a company's standing: Aggressiveness, Maturity, and Knowledge.

An introspective analysis vis-à-vis these three factors can provide a fairly good idea how to measure and enhance a company's health.

Aggressiveness

- What is your company's market share?
- What is the market share of your competitors?
- Do competitors have greater market share? If so, why and how?
- Why can't your company augment its market share?
- How can your company increase its market share?
- How aggressively does your company pursue its marketability?
- How dynamically does your company undertake continuous environmental scanning and gap-analysis?
- How aggressively does your company reach the customer and satisfy the market demands?

Maturity

- Leadership maturity
- Infrastructural maturity
- Decision-making maturity
- Maturity for introspective analysis
- Empowerment maturity
- Maturity for change management
- Technological maturity
- Production maturity
- Quality maturity
- Customer-perceived market maturity/credibility

Knowledge

- Basic integrated knowledge
- Technical knowledge
- Special skills

Ideally, a successful enterprise would have an optimal and balanced mix of these three attributes: aggressiveness, maturity and knowledge. A disproportionate mix can certainly cause problems in terms of company's marketability and survivability. For example, if a company is overly aggressive but lacks in maturity and knowledge, it may soon find itself displaying a perception of being intrusive, unethical, lacking in substance, and, therefore, being undependable and untrustworthy. On the other hand, if a company is mature and knowledgeable only but lacks in assertiveness, it may hold enough credibility and respect, but it cannot achieve marketability/profitability success.

In general, the shape of a successful organization has the following distinctive features:

- Management is involved and committed
- Organizational framework is flat and horizontal
- Functional operability is transparent
- Organization is customer-driven
- Constancy of purpose is a mandate
- Quality excellence is a key focus
- Working in partnership is a mission
- Teamwork is a way of life
- People empowerment is a commitment
- Continuous improvement is an obsession

If we can pin-point the one singularly most important ingredient in the recipe for success, it would be **"Quality"**. Quality is the key to higher productivity and profitability. When everything else is equal in competition, quality provides that additional "winning-success" edge. Some of the essential elements requisite to the realization of the mission are as follows:

- Continuous Environmental Scanning
  - Keeping track of marketplace changes/realities
  - Understanding customer requirements/expectations
  - Developing competitor's profile
- Organizational Introspective Analysis
  - Evaluating company's operational framework
  - Identifying company's capabilities
  - Implementing effective quality systems

Let us just peep into the business world and observe how the managers are grappling with the rate of change and the marketplace realities.

Change is all around us. We are continuously immersed in it. Change is inevitable. There is little or no escape from it. The global order is changing faster than we can comprehend. The rapidity and voluminosity with which change is encompassing in almost every conceivable aspect of our lives - technological, political, economic, and social, is profoundly superabundant. In fact, the amount of change witnessed in this century alone far exceeds the cumulative changes which have occurred over the past several centuries. Probably, the most significant change we are facing today is change itself.

Moving in rapid succession, we have come a full circle around. Starting from the age of human endeavour - the stone age, and moving through the ages of agriculture, property ownership, capital intensiveness, and technological advancement, we are back to the age of human capacity, undertaking, endeavour and commitment.

In a volatile environment such as this, the corporate boardrooms are frantically busy in evolving strategies to cope with change. The agenda is familiar: "How to evolve or augment the organization's infrastructure and systems in order to accomplish the mission". The dilemma that is new for the managers at every stage of each era is,

"What methods, models or means to expend, that are commensurate with the focus, constraints and prevailing circumstances of the era, in order to achieve the desired results in the most effective manner".

It would be neither clement nor perspicacious to pass a judgement value and declare either way that the answer to this question is simple or formidable. Instead, it would be more germane and appropriate to discuss:

- The viability of the decision-making process
- The approach to selecting a simple, proper and effective strategy

Undoubtedly, the pressures, constraints and circumstances of the times exert enormous influence on the strategic decision-making processes as well as on the mood of the corporate boardrooms. In flourishing economic times, there is laughter and friendship in the boardrooms and you can even expect coffee and lunches as part of the agenda. On the other hand, when competitive pressures are high and economies are down, there can be bloodshed all over the boardroom walls and you may be expected to bring your own coffee from the vending machine. For this intriguing scenario, I would like to annotate a corporate boardroom as follows:

Corporate Boardroom: Deft Definition

"A post-office between the worker and the God"

- With the right stamp, you may become a CEO (Chief Executive Officer)
- With the wrong stamp, you may become unemployed.

Unfortunately, at this point in time, the world economic order is in turmoil and global competition is intensely fierce. Consequently, there is enormous pressure and responsibility on the shoulders of managers to make quick and appropriate decisions. However, it is also at this juncture when the probability of making bad judgement and decisions becomes extremely high. Working under extreme survivability pressures, managers may be forced to develop quick-fix strategies to overcome the impending productivity problems in the fastest possible manner. At the time of making such decisions, the strategy may seem to be a genuine effort and the only right option available. However, decisions with failure-prone beginnings like these, cannot result into anything but panic, instability and further aggravation and demoralization of the workplace.

What is fundamentally important for any strategic planning exercise is to have a clear picture of the marketplace realities, operational requirements, constraints and competitive positioning. Following are some of the generic distinctive features of today's marketplace:

- The world economy is in a state of interim dormancy.
- Markets are unsettled and volatile.
- Profits are down and financial resources are relatively deficient.
- Competition is high - both, within the domestic markets as well as between the international markets.
- Rate of technological developments/innovations is faster than the assimilation capacity/capability of organizations.
- Workplace is becoming increasingly democratized and the organizational infrastructure more horizontal.
- Customer awareness and expectations are high in terms of product/service quality, competitive pricing, and satisfaction.
- Changes in societal infrastructure are transpiring at an accelerated pace and are affecting every aspect of human life.

What type of business plan would be a cure-all for all the ills in our incessantly changing environment such as this? The market place overwhelmingly abounds in recipes, models, theories and gurus on the subject of quality-productivity enhancement. The problem, therefore, is not one of scarcity but of abundance and selecting the most appropriate strategy.

Quality experts like Deming, Juran, Crosby, Feigenbaum, Ishikawa, etc. have provided thought-provoking philosophies and methodologies for quality improvement. Their theories have exerted profound influence on business operability, the echoes and impact of which can still be strongly felt in all manufacturing circles. While these theories were most aptly conducive for the business environment of the 70's and 80's and while we can still derive enormous business sense out of these, what needs to be done is further augmentation and refinement of these ideas vis-à-vis time-dependent developments and changes. The impending environment of the year 2000 and beyond calls for something more new, more challenging and rejuvenating - a total re-engineering of present systems. We need something that I wish to annotate as "Total Quality Business Transformation (TQBT)".

What is "Total Quality Business Transformation (TQBT)" - it is the paradigm for success - a survival kit containing a mixture of divested realities, experiential opulence, churlish reminders, candid criticisms, and workable suggestions. TQBT is a layered quality model that provides an integrated approach to developing and implementing a self-directed whole system - a system that encompasses all requisite aspects of managing business and at the same time possesses the flexibility and capability of accommodating changing marketplace needs.

TQBT → Organization TQM + Process TQM + Personal TQM

The basic premise of TQBT revolves around the following key activities:

- TQBT: Implementing a quality culture
- Organization TQM: Implementing a total quality system
- Process TQM: Process-by-process enhancement system
- Personal TQM: A self-superimposed personal excellence mandate

Table 1 presents the umbrella axioms of TQBT. The guiding principles of the system have been amply elucidated throughout the remainder of this book.

Table 1: Total Quality Business Transformation (TQBT) Vision 2000+

TQBT AXIOMS	
Axiom #1:	*Dynamic Customer Orientation*
Axiom #2:	*Participative Management*
Axiom #3:	*Infrastructural Stability*
Axiom #4:	*Self-Directed Organization*
Axiom #5:	*Operational Framework Flexibility*
Axiom #6:	*Integrated Systems Approach*
Axiom #7:	*System Effectiveness Measurability*
Axiom #8:	*Process Enhancement Focus*
Axiom #9:	*Genuine Employee Emphasis*
Axiom #10:	*Continuous Reengineering*
Axiom #11:	*Proactive Change Management*
Axiom #12:	*Total Excellence Mindset*

The business world is constantly changing. To achieve success, you have to constantly evolve, change and adapt your strategies, systems, products and culture to the shocks and forces of time. If you do so, you will bedevil your competitors by maximizing your current strengths and developing new strengths as change occurs. To succeed, you have to persistently disturb the present. The paradigms of the quiet past shall not work in the turbulent future. With new demands, we must think and act anew. Success is certainly not beyond anybody's reach. Making your business an enviable success requires an enviable dedication.

◆ THE MANAGING OF MANAGEMENT

Before embarking on developing quality systems, it is imperative to be cognizant of the fundamental system management principles. The success of any model or system, howsoever viable, is virtually dependent on its effective management. There are certain recurring and fundamental system management principles which every enterprise must utilize to support management of any function, irrespective of its objectives, the size of the organization or the level within the organization. These principles are common to most management system models and can be applied in any specific context, such as quality management, ISO 9000 certification, team management, etc. This section provides quidelines on how these principles can be effectively applied in the management of systems.

The most simplistic and essential set of inter-linked management system principles that an organization must entrench into its operational framework include the following:

- **Mission**
- **Accountability**
- **Competency**
- **Knowledge**

Knowledge **(4)**	**Mission** **(1)**
Competency **(3)**	**Accountability** **(2)**

MISSION

- The enterprise must have a mission, a purpose - the reason for its existence. People must clearly understand the organization's mandate and their role in the overall game plan. The mission must be shared and valued by everyone collectively.
- The organization must create a vision also - a projection of the mission for the longer-term perspective.
- Commensurate with the mission and purpose, the organization should identify its policy, operational principles, code of ethics, and responsibilities.
- Policy is translated into objectives and goals that sets the parameters of desired action. A strategic plan must be developed to provide direction for the achievement of objectives. The policy and objectives must be congruent with the customers' needs and the company's internal capabilities.

ACCOUNTABILITY

- The organization must manifest its commitment and accountability to its policy and objectives.
- Accountability is evidenced through the establishment of proper infrastructure and delineation of appropriate responsibilities.
- A management system must be designed and developed that clearly identifies the processes and operational actions requisite to meeting the objectives.
- Accountability in the organization must come from both ends: management as well as individual employees. While it is the organization's responsibility to provide appropriate resources and suitable working environment for people to produce high quality products and services, it is also the responsibility of every individual worker to inculcate a high performance mindset and operate in a coordinated and integrated manner to produce optimum results.

COMPETENCY

- The objectives cannot be achieved unless the organization has requisite capabilities and competency. Some of the entities required are: knowledge, skills, technology, physical and financial resources, information systems, operational procedures and processes, disciplined methodologies, measuring and monitoring systems, and analytical capabilities.
- Effective leadership is required to provide appropriate direction and support.
- Managers must be competent in managing change.
- People empowerment and operational transparency can provide strong functional support for achieving the stated objectives.

KNOWLEDGE

- Continuous training and development must be an integral part of the organization's agenda and philosophy.
- People should be provided sufficient training to monitor and control their processes continuously.
- The systems should be self-correcting and self-sufficient to allow for the identification of problems, with a built-in corrective/preventive mechanism, and a focus on continuous improvement.

In closing, it should be noted that this prologue was only meant to generate a dialogue and a mindset. It was not meant to provide any details but only a preamble to the mental preparedness for utilizing the more comprehensive coverage of the subject in the remainder of this book.

PART ONE

THE

QUALITY

FOCUS

1

THE QUALITY IMPERATIVE

◆ QUALITY-PRODUCTIVITY ERA

Within the industrialized infrastructure of at least the developed countries, the 90's constitute what is being called a Quality-Productivity Era. Quality seems to be the single most profoundly sought and aggressively pursued entity in the manufacturing as well as in the service world today.

Product quality was really not a big issue a few decades ago, because the producers of finished products were a few industrialized countries only and whatever they produced was either consumed and utilized internally or could be conveniently sold to the majority of non-producing, developing countries.

The global order has changed considerably. The world market of today is steadily shrinking and is becoming intensely competitive. There are many more producers than ever before. With the rapid growth of scientific knowledge and advanced technology, the newly emerging producers, being labor-intensive, are able to compete favorably with the highly industrialized capital-intensive producers. In some cases, they are even capable of surpassing them in terms of volume, variety and low-cost production, if not in quality.

There is almost a universal concordance that the most essential factors for survival and growth, for an enterprise in a highly competitive environment such as this, are: high quality, increased productivity, cost-effectiveness and customer satisfaction. Quality is the key to pride, productivity and profitability. It is the basic entity that differentiates between an excellent company and a mediocre company.

◆ MARKET-DRIVEN QUALITY

Pursuit for quality is virtually market-driven. Changes in the environment exert enormous influences on the nature and extent of market operability. It is, therefore, imperative that the strategic planning framework for improving quality be commensurate with the market environment. What are the key factors influencing today's environment? Let us look at these in terms of five elements: the markets, products, producer, consumer, and regulatory/standards agency.

Markets

- It is a highly entrepreneurial, highly competitive world market today.
- Quality volatility is high due to the differential between labour-intensiveness and capital-intensiveness.
- Markets are dichotomously indecisive - attempting to diminish trade barriers while still upholding the protectionistic stance.
- Quality, competitive pricing and constancy of purpose holds the key to marketability.

Products

- Products are continuously increasing in complexity, variety and volume.
- Market-driven pressures on product lines include: high quality, innovativeness, economic competitiveness and affordability, conformance to regulatory and other requirements, safety and reliability.

Producer

- Producers are under continuous pressure to cope with the multiplicity of product lines, complexity and variety of products, regulatory requirements, and consumer expectations.
- There is a constant struggle for profitability, credibility and continued market share.
- Financial constraints and human resources volatility are high.

Consumer

- Consumer awareness for quality, safety, and competitive pricing is very high.
- Consumers are increasingly demanding variety, innovativeness, product dependability, better post-sales service and warranties.

Regulatory/Standards Agency

- Greater emphasis is being placed on standardized procedures and processes, consumer protection, cost-effectiveness, safety, enforcement of regulations, cost-recovery, privatization, and deregulation.

◆ THE ENTERPRISE MISSION

In all this market-driven quality scenario, every enterprise, large or small, service or manufacturing, has some fundamental reason/motive for existence. The four key driving forces are:

- Profitability
- Expanded market share
- Long-term survival
- Service to society

The continued realization of these goals is highly dependent on an enterprise's ability and determination to:

- Improve quality and productivity.
- Reduce costs.
- Meet product/service/regulatory/standards requirements.
- Achieve complete customer confidence/satisfaction/delight.
- Improve reputation and credibility.
- Improve market share.
- Remain competitive.

The strategic focus for improving quality, profitability and competitive position requires:

- Total management commitment
- Development of a mission, vision and continuous improvement strategy
- Constancy of purpose
- Development of a quality culture
- Effective employee participation and empowerment
- Development and implementation of effective quality systems
- Consistency in superior quality output
- Partnering with suppliers and customers

◆ WHY QUALITY

Why do we want quality? Of the many answers to this question, a few key ones are the following:

- Quality is a second nature to us.
- Quality is fundamental to marketability, profitability and survivability.
- Quality is the basic entity that differentiates between a mediocre and an excellent company.
- Quality is the single most powerful entity that provides the winning competitive edge.

Competitiveness is a word much bandied about these days. Still, there is no denying the fact that with shrinking global markets, competition is becoming fiercely intense. Competition comes from two sources: within and between. Firstly, there is competition between the companies within each of the two level of economies: the developed and the developing. Then, there is competition between the developed and developing countries. In each of the two situations, quality plays a paramount role.

The competition between the developed and developing countries is one of capital-intensiveness versus labor-intensiveness. Although, the developed countries have the advantage of being capital intensive, the developing countries, even with the obsolete technology borrowed from developed countries or with the not-so-sophisticated self-developed technology, are able to compete well by producing more volume and variety at a lower cost. Once again, therefore, the only entity that provides the leading edge is "quality".

Following are some of the intrinsic and extrinsic gains that can be realized through improved quality:

Intrinsic Gains
- Reduced costs
- Reduced scrap/waste
- Improved control of operations
- Improved predictability and reliability
- Increased efficiency/productivity
- Increased compliance
- Improved confidence, pride and profitability

Extrinsic Gains

- Improved competitiveness and marketability
- Expanded and continued market share
- Improved credibility, reputation and dependability
- Ability/capability to balance out the differential between labour-intensiveness and capital-intensiveness
- Customer satisfaction/delight
- Service to society

◆ QUALITY CONCERNS

Every enterprise in today's business world strives to achieve success. Translating success into tangibles, it means profitability, credibility and sustainable marketability. All these entities are by-products of quality, excellence and customer satisfaction. Business successes and failures render profound testimony to the fact that the single most crucial element of success is 'Quality'. When everything else is equal in competition, *Quality* provides that additional winning edge. Most companies are cognizant of this fact and they are willing to dedicate their efforts and resources to achieve quality and excellence.

Most companies have basically two fundamental concerns about quality:

- How to achieve sustainable quality? How to make quality a second nature of the business operability? What methods/means should be used to implement, maintain and continuously improve quality?
- Having achieved quality, how to demonstrate the achievement? How to get accreditation and recognition of the achievement? How to let everyone know that this company is operating on and is committed to the highest levels of quality?

Quality improvement does not come in a ready-made package, nor it is a separate planning activity. Everything - quality philosophies, practices, tools, techniques, and training - must be embedded in the business plan. There are layers of activities that needs to be undertaken to address quality improvement concerns.

To start with, a quality thought-revolution and a wave of quality-mindedness and quality-consciousness must be initiated to pave the way for establishing a sustainable quality culture. This is what we are annotating as "Total Quality Business Transformation" (TQBT) - details are appended in Chapter 3. TQBT will assist in permeating quality and productivity improvement fervor at all levels in the organization.

Within the overall framework of TQBT, there are, then, three major activities to be undertaken:

- Implement a structured organization-wide TQM (Total Quality Management) System.
- Institute Process Enhancement TQM System.
- Encourage the development of a Personal TQM driving force.

For implementing a TQM system, a company can indeed exercise many options, some of which are as follows:

- Develop its own program/model based on the fundamental principles of quality.
- Use the approach outlined in the International Standard: "ISO 9004-1: Quality Management and Quality System Elements - Guidelines".
- Follow the philosophies and methodologies propounded by the various quality experts and gurus such as: Deming, Juran, Crosby, Fegenbaum, Ishikawa (Japan), etc.

Detailed descriptions regarding all these important aspects are appended in the proceeding chapters.

Demonstration of the fact that a company has actually achieved a certain level of quality and is operating under well-established quality system principles can be done through the process of accreditation/certification to the criteria stipulated by any of the following:

- ISO 9000 series of Quality System Standards
- Malcolm Baldrige Award
- Deming Prize
- George M. Low Award: NASA's Quality and Excellence Award
- Presidential Award for Quality (U.S.A.)
- Canada Award for Business Excellence
- Any other nationally/internationally recognized accreditation/certification protocol.

◆ IS QUALITY A PASSING FAD

The path to quality is not exactly a bed of roses. To tread on this path requires profound dedication and absolute commitment. Consequently, before a company ventures into and commits itself to this mammoth undertaking, it must completely exuviate any skepticism about quality.

Quality is not a tactical but a strategic issue. Quality does not come through piecemeal efforts or through a single quality improvement program, procedure or process. It is the result of a totally integrated set of actions with a long-term commitment. Quality is not a short-term function but a long-term focus.

Quality cannot be instantly manufactured; it is infused and embedded into a product or service through systematic means. Quality is achieved, piece by piece, process by process, within the overall umbrella of a total quality management system. It must be clearly understood that today when we talk of quality, we mean the quality of all aspects of production such as: the quality of products and services, the quality of work-life, employee involvement and empowerment, productivity improvement, competitive position, customer satisfaction, etc. A total quality system encompasses all the processes that collectively contribute to the achievement of total quality.

Is quality a passing fad? Most certainly not! Pursuit for quality and excellence is not new. We have always wanted good quality products and services, and we always will. This desire for quality is ingrained in us.

It is undoubtedly true that acronyms, connotations or buzz-words around the subject of quality keep changing with time. For instance, today total quality systems are referenced through several different names: TQBT (Total Quality Business Transformation), TQM (Total Quality Management), TQA (Total Quality Assurance), CWQC (Company-Wide Quality Control, used by the Japanese), TQC (Total Quality Control), TQI (Total Quality Improvement), CQA (Corporate Quality Assurance), SQM (Strategic Quality Management), etc. Perhaps we cannot live with one buzz-word for any more than five years. Therefore, while it is possible that the popular acronyms, like TQM, may disappear with time and be replaced by another acronym, the basic instinct, intent and need for quality will always remain unchanged and unchallenged. Quality is neither dead nor dormant. Quality is a vital force that, if nurtured and supported, produces remarkable emotional, intellectual, and tangible benefits for individuals and organizations. Quality has eternal life.

It is, therefore, naturally imperative for companies who are genuinely interested in continuously improving the quality of their products and services, to focus on establishing sustainable quality improvement systems with little or no concern for what acronym the system is addressed under. By doing so, the quality exercise would not seem to be a reactive effort vis-à-vis the fad of the time but a proactive responsiveness to a constancy of purpose - "quality improvement".

◆ BEYOND THE HORIZON

While quality and quality system certification is imperative, there is something more fundamentally important beyond the horizon that all proactive organizations must sensitize themselves to "the competitive survivability". At the moment, our preoccupation is with establishing total quality systems and achieving recognition through certification to international quality assurance standards, such as the ISO 9000 series. This is important as well as imperative. It would help companies achieve a competitive edge against both the labor-intensive markets and the capital-intensive markets. However, crystal-balling is essential for strategic planning for those futuristic situations when most companies would have achieved higher quality status. Then, the competition would be intensely fierce and survival would require additional strategic action. The most fundamental such action that would help keep companies afloat is to "produce more, more cheaply and consistently better".

Excellent companies are those who would not wait to take necessary steps before they are thrown into the competitive pit; they would plan now and ensure that the proper action is integrated and implemented with their operational planning framework and infrastructure. Essentially, companies have to be cognizant of and work towards the following:

- Establish self-correcting and self-rejuvenating quality systems.
- Keep strong emphasis on continuous quality maintenance and improvement.
- Improve productivity and reduce costs.
- Provide competitive pricing.
- Establish long-term partnership with customers.

2

QUALITY: THE DEFINITIONS

◆ **TOWARDS A DEFINITION OF QUALITY**

Before proceeding any further, it would be in order to first understand the meaning of the word "**Quality**". The word *quality* is much like the word "stress" - a profoundly fashionable term that has become an integral part of the popular lexicon. Yet, it has as many meanings and interpretations as there are people who experience it.

Quality is indeed a complex and multifaceted concept. It is not a singular activity or characteristic, nor a system or a department. It is the sum total of all characteristics of a product or service that contributes to its superiority and excellence.

Quality has been defined in a variety of ways. Table 1 lists some of the popularly used definitions of "quality", including the one developed by the International Organization for Standardization (ISO), in the international standard: "ISO-8402: Quality Vocabulary".

As a functional definition, we prefer to define Quality and Excellence as follows:

> **Quality → Variation Reduction + Continuous Enhancement**
> **Excellence → Quality + Ethics**

Table 2: Quality: Definitions

- Quality is customer satisfaction/delight.
- Quality means conformance to specified requirements.
- Quality means fitness for use.
- Quality means value for money.
- Quality means zero defects.
- Quality is efficiency and productivity.
- Quality is an investment for profitability.
- Quality means on-time delivery.
- Quality is a collective attitude of mind.
- Quality is a systematic approach to excellence.
- Quality is the ultimate expression of craftsmanship.
- Quality is excellence in output.
- Quality is never-ending cycle of improvement.
- Quality means pride of ownership.
- Quality means consistently producing conforming product.
- Quality means credibility.
- Quality means guarantee of confidence.
- Quality is thought revolution in management.
- Quality means innate excellence.
- Quality means constancy of purpose.
- Quality means continued and expanded market share.
- Quality is a race without the finish line.
- Quality means value-added products and services.
- Quality means loss imparted to society from the time a product is shipped (Japanese).

ISO-8402: Quality Vocabulary

- Quality: Totality of characteristics of an entity that bear on its ability to satisfy stated and implied needs.

- Quality   → Variation Reduction + Continuous Enhancement

- Quality is all of the above.

Variability is, perhaps the single most profoundly important entity which impacts and governs our lives. Variability means deviation, dispersion, displacement, non-constancy or variation. Variation, however, does not mean variety. Variety is something that we like, but we may not want unwarranted variation in variety.

A large proportion of our time is spent on minimizing or reducing variability - be it in our social, economic, political or personal life exigencies. In terms of products and services, customers prefer constancy, uniformity, consistency and reliability. Customers would like to receive a product that meets their specifications and expectations and they would like to consistently receive the same or better product. They do not appreciate unpredictability, surprises, ups and downs or variability.

Consequently, the first major task for every company is to control the variability of their processes, products and services. Once that is accomplished, then the company would work toward minimizing or eliminating variability through a continuous improvement strategy. Reduction in variability and continuous enhancement yields a superior quality product.

Although quality is imperative for competitive survivability, there is something beyond quality that differentiates between a mediocre and excellent company - "ethics". Superiority and excellence is, therefore, a resultant of quality and ethics. Excellence requires:

- Consistently providing high quality products and services.
- Improving quality of work-life within the company.
- Operating on high ethical standards for external customers as well as internal company employees.

◆ TOTAL QUALITY MANAGEMENT: DEFINITIONS

Total quality systems are referenced through several different names: TQM (Total Quality Management), TQA (Total Quality Assurance), CWQC (Company-Wide Quality Control, used by the Japanese), TQC (Total Quality Control), TQI (Total Quality Improvement), SQM (Strategic Quality Management), CQA (Corporate Quality Assurance), etc.

Total Quality Management (TQM) can, perhaps be defined as follows:

- TQM refers to the totality of functions necessary for the overall management of products and services to achieve the highest levels of quality.
- TQM involves the application of quantitative methods and human resources to improve the materials and services supplied to an organization.
- TQM integrates philosophy, customer focus, guiding principles, fundamental management techniques, and technical tools and systems to provide a disciplined approach to continuous improvement.

The definition of Total Quality Management given in the International Standard, "ISO 8402: Quality Vocabulary", along with "notes " is as follows:

- **Total Quality Management:** Management approach of an organization, centered on quality, based on the participation of all its members and aiming at long-term success through customer satisfaction, and benefits to all members of the organization and to society.

  Notes:

  - The expression "all its members" designates personnel in all departments and all levels of the organizational structure.
  - The strong and persistent leadership of top management and the education and training of all members of the organization are essential for the success of this approach.
  - In total quality management, the concept of quality relates to the achievement of all managerial objectives.
  - The concept "benefits to society" implies, as needed, fulfilment of the requirements of society.
  - Total Quality Management (TQM) or parts of it are sometimes called "Total Quality", "CWQC" (Company Wide Quality Control), "TQC" (Total Quality Control), and so on.

◆ OTHER QUALITY RELATED DEFINITIONS

Some other important quality related definitions included in ISO 8402 and other standards are appended below for reference. Most of the definitions in the standard have accompanying explanatory notes, which are also reproduced here.

- **Customer:** Recipient of a product provided by the supplier.

  Notes:

  - In a contractual situation, the customer is called the purchaser.
  - The customer may be, for example, the ultimate consumer, user, beneficiary or purchaser.
  - The "customer" can be either external or internal to the organization.

- **Purchaser:** Customer in a contractual situation.

  Note:

  - The purchaser is sometimes referred to as the "business second party".

- **Supplier:** Organization that provides a product to the customer.

  Notes:

  - In a contractual situation, the "supplier" may be called the "contractor".
  - The "supplier" may be, for example, the producer, distributor, importer, assembler, or service organization.
  - The "supplier" can be either external or internal to the organization.

- **Subcontractor:** Organization that provides a product to the supplier.

  Notes:

  - In English, the "subcontractor" may also be called "sub-supplier".
  - In French, the "sous-contractant" may also be called, as appropriate, "sous-traitant" or "sous-commandier".

- **Process:** Set of inter-related resources and activities which transform inputs into outputs.

  Note:

  - Resources may include personnel, finance, facilities, equipment, techniques and methods.

- **Procedure:** Specified way to perform an activity.

  Notes:

  - In many cases, procedures are documented (e.g. quality system procedures).
  - When a procedure is documented, the term "written procedure" or "documented procedure" is frequently used.
  - A written or documented procedure usually contains the purposes and scope of an activity; what shall be done and by whom; when, where and how it shall be done; what materials, equipment and documents shall be used; and how it shall be controlled and recorded.

- **Product:** Result of activities or processes.

  Notes:

  - A product may include service, hardware, processed materials, software or combination thereof.
  - A product can be tangible (e.g. assemblies or processed materials) or intangible (e.g. knowledge or concepts), or a combination thereof.
  - A product can be either intended (e.g. offering to customers), or unintended (e.g. pollutant or unwanted effects).

- **Service:** Results generated by activities at the interface between the supplier and the customer and by supplier internal activities to meet the customer needs.

  Notes:

  - The supplier or the customer may be represented at the interface by personnel or equipment.
  - Customer activities at the interface with the supplier may be essential to the service delivery.
  - Delivery or use of tangible products may form part of the service delivery.
  - A service may be linked with the manufacture and supply of tangible product.

- **Quality:** Totality of characteristics of an entity that bear on its ability to satisfy stated and implied needs.

  Notes:

  - In a contractual environment, or in a regulated environment, such as the nuclear safety field, needs are specified, whereas in other environments, implied needs should be identified and defined.
  - In many instances, needs can change with time; this implies a periodic review of requirements for quality.
  - Needs are translated into characteristics with specified criteria. Needs may include, for example, aspects of performance, usability, safety, dependability (availability, reliability, maintainability), environment, economics and aesthetics.
  - The term *quality* should not be used as a single term to express a degree of excellence in a comparative sense, nor should it be used in a quantitative sense for technical evaluations. To express these meanings, a qualifying adjective should be used. For example, use can be made of the following terms: "relative quality" where entities are ranked on a relative basis in the degree of excellence or comparative sense (not to be confused with grade); "quality level" in a quantitative sense (as used in acceptance sampling) and "quality measure" where precise technical evaluations are carried out.
  - The achievement of satisfactory quality involves all stages of the quality loop as a whole. The contributions to quality of these various stages are sometimes identified separately for emphasis; for example, quality due to definition of needs, quality due to conformance, quality due to product support throughout its lifetime.

- In some references, quality is referred to as "fitness for use" or "fitness for purpose" or "customer satisfaction" or "conformance to the requirements". These represent only certain facets of quality, as defined above.

- **Quality Management:** All activities of the overall management function that determine the quality policy, objectives and responsibilities, and implement them by means such as quality planning, quality control, quality assurance and quality improvement within the quality system.

Notes:

- Quality management is the responsibility of all levels of management but must be led by top management. Its implementation involves all members of the organization.
- In quality management, consideration is given to economic aspects.

- **Quality Policy:** Overall intentions and direction of an organization with regard to quality, as formally expressed by top management.

Note:

- The quality policy forms one element of the corporate policy and is authorized by top management.

- **Quality Planning:** Activities that establish the objectives and requirements for quality and for the application of quality system elements.

Note:

- Quality planning covers:
  - Product planning: identifying, classifying and weighting the characteristics for quality as well as establishing the objectives, requirements for quality and constraints.
  - Managerial and operational planning: preparing the application of the quality system including organizing and scheduling.
  - The preparation of quality plans and the making of provisions for quality improvement.

- **Quality Plan:** Document setting out the specific quality practices, resources and sequence of activities relevant to a particular product, project or contract.

Note:

- A quality plan usually makes reference to the parts of the quality manual applicable to specific case.
- Depending on the scope of the plan, a qualifier may be used, for example, "quality assurance plan", "quality management plan".

- **Quality System:** Organization structure, procedures, processes and resources needed to implement quality management.

  Notes:

  - The quality system should be as comprehensive as needed to meet the quality objectives.
  - The quality system of an organization is designed primarily to satisfy the internal managerial needs of the organization. It is broader than the requirements of a particular customer, who evaluates only the relevant part of the quality system.
  - For contractual or mandatory quality assessment purposes, demonstration of the implementation of identified quality system elements may be required.

- **Quality Control:** Operational techniques and activities that are used to fulfill requirements for quality.

  Notes:

  - Quality control involves operational techniques and activities aimed both at monitoring a process and at eliminating causes of unsatisfactory performance at all stages of the quality loop in order to achieve economic effectiveness.
  - Some quality control and quality assurance actions are interrelated.

- **Quality Assurance:** All the planned and systematic activities implemented within the quality system, and demonstrated as needed, to provide adequate confidence that an entity will fulfill requirements for quality.

  Notes:

  - There are both internal and external purposes for quality assurance:
    - Internal quality assurance: within an organization, quality assurance provides confidence to the management.
    - External quality assurance: in contractual or other situations, quality assurance provides confidence to the customers or others.
  - Some quality control and quality assurance actions are interrelated.
  - Unless requirements for quality fully reflect the needs of the user, quality assurance may not provide adequate confidence.

- **Quality Improvement:** Actions taken throughout the organization to increase the effectiveness and efficiency of activities and processes in order to provide added benefits to both the organization and its customers.

- **Management Review:** Formal evaluation by top management of the status and adequacy of the quality system in relation to quality policy and objectives.

Notes:

- Management review may include review of the quality policy.
- Quality audit results are one of the possible inputs to management review.
- The term "top management" refers to the management of the organization whose quality system is being reviewed.

- **Quality Manual:** Document stating the quality policy and describing the quality system of an organization.

  Notes:

  - A quality manual may relate to the totality of an organization's activities or only to a part of it. The title and scope of the manual reflects the field of application.
  - A quality manual will normally contain or refer to, as a minimum:
    - quality policy
    - the responsibilities, authorities and inter-relationships of personnel who manage, perform, verify or review work affecting quality.
    - the quality system procedures and instructions.
    - a statement for reviewing, updating and controlling the manual.
  - A quality manual can vary in depth and format to suit the needs of an organization. It may comprise more than one document. Depending on the scope of the manual, a qualifier may be used, for example, "quality assurance manual", "quality management manual".

- **Quality Audit:** Systematic and independent examination to determine whether quality activities and related results comply with planned arrangements and whether these arrangements are implemented effectively and are suitable to achieve objectives.

  Notes:

  - The quality audit typically applies to, but is not limited, a quality system or elements thereof, to processes, to products, or to services. Such audits are often called "quality system audit", "process quality audit", "product quality audit", or "service quality audit".
  - Quality audits are carried out by staff not having direct responsibility in the areas being audited but, preferably, working in cooperation with the relevant personnel.
  - One purpose of a quality audit is to evaluate the need for improvement or corrective action. An audit should not be confused with quality surveillance or inspection activities performed for the purpose of process control or product acceptance.
  - Quality audits can be conducted for internal or external purposes.

- **Third-Party Certification System:** A certification system managed by a certification body or under its surveillance.

- **Laboratory Accreditation:** A formal recognition that a testing laboratory is competent to carry out specific tests or specific types of tests.

- **Environmental Management:** That aspect of the overall management function that determines and implements the environmental policy.

- **Environmental Management System (EMS):** The organizational structure, responsibilities, practices, procedures, processes, and resources for implementing environmental management.

3

TQBT: TOTAL QUALITY BUSINESS TRANSFORMATION

◆ TQM IMPLEMENTATION: THE BEGINNINGS

It is a normal part of the process that at the commencement of any important program or activity, there is a sense of haziness, confusion, apprehension and a flurry of inquisitive questions. So is the case with implementing a quality improvement system. Managers at all levels, who bear the responsibility of directing the organizations towards a successful path, are generally insistent on being fully cognizant of the pros and cons of any new endeavour before making any serious commitment of financial and human resources. Experience indicates that the most commonly asked questions about TQM system implementation revolve around the following concerns:

- **Reasons for TQM Implementation**
  - Why do we need to implement TQM?
  - How would TQM implementation benefit the organization?

- **TQM vs. Traditional Approaches to Quality**
  - How is TQM different from the current quality activities such as: Quality Control (Q.C.) and Quality Assurance (Q.A.)

- **Selection of TQM Model**
  - Which TQM model is appropriate for our organization?
  - What is the most appropriate approach to implement the model?

- **Resources**
  - What kind of financial and human resources do we need to implement an effective TQM?
  - How and when can we realize gains vis-à-vis the resources expanded?

- **TQM Sustainability**
  - How can we measure the impact of TQM implementation?
  - How can we maintain and sustain the quality gains?

- **Quality Accreditation**
  - What and how can we achieve accreditation/accolade for TQM implementation?

Most of these concerns are genuine and must be proactively addressed. The key to a successful implementation of a sustainable TQM lies in exuviating any skepticism and building-up a strong positive attitude and confidence in the organization's ability to improve quality. Answers to these questions are amply detailed throughout the book; however, as a partial response, the following may be noted:

- Quality is the key to profitability and competitive survivability.
- A good quality improvement program brings forth many tangible and intangible benefits. Some of these can be realized almost instantly while others may take a long time to surface.
- With the right model, right approach and a mind-set for performance, the quality system implementation exercise does not have to be excessively exorbitant or enervating.

◆ QUALITY FOCUS: YESTERDAY vs TODAY

With the maturing of the marketplace and democratization of working milieu, the *Quality* agenda has also undergone colossal transformations. While the traditional focus of quality was product-oriented, today the emphasis is on the whole system approach. Table 3 presents a schematic comparison of the traditional versus modern approach to quality. In the past, quality efforts were centred around "Quality Control" and "Quality Assurance" activities and the final inspection was the only means of assessing the level and extent of quality. Today the focus is on management responsibility, people empowerment, and improvement of quality through on-line process control.

As is evident, quality cannot be inspected-in. Final product inspection can only identify the product as conforming or nonconforming - it cannot infuse any improvement. When the improvement efforts are expended at the process level, the final product, in all probability, would be right the first time. Today's quality system, therefore, alleviates the need for extensive final product inspection, resulting in saving of much needed wasted resources.

Table 3: The Quality Focus

YESTERDAY

Q.C.	Q.A.

• Focus on:
  • Machines
  • Methods
  • Technology
  • Defect Identification
 	
• Emphasis on:
  • Specifications
  • Quality records
  • Corrective action
  • Individual responsibility
  • Verification
  • Compliance
	• Focus on:
	  • Final inspection
	  • End product compliance
	  • Customer needs
	  • Contractual requirements
	
	• Emphasis on:
	  • Prevention
	  • Total Manufacturing Control
	  • Safety, reliability
	  • Good judgement
	  • Interdisciplined responsibility

TODAY

TQM

- Focus on all aspects of product/service quality
  - Management
  - Machines
  - Systems
  - Procedures
  - Processes
  - People
- Total system approach
- Prevention oriented
- Partnership with suppliers and customers
- Focus on customer satisfaction/delight
- Teamwork and employee empowerment
- Disciplined systems and methodologies
- Process management/improvement
- Continuous improvement

Additionally, the emphasis of today's quality systems is on shared-responsibility, operational transparency, worker happiness and pride, customer-supplier partnering and continuous improvement.

◆ THE QUALITY MODEL

A TQM system can be implemented in almost any conceivable situation. However, the magnitude and extent of the TQM exercise would depend upon the nature of the enterprise, its size and complexity, the type of activity, quality requirements, financial and resource base, clientele, etc. Consequently, the TQM model and its implementation has to be commensurate with the overall profile of the organization. Basically there are three distinct organization types with their own specifically unique requirement:

- Manufacturing Organizations
  - Tangible product production/assembly
  - Servicing
  - Customer satisfaction
  - Marketability/profitability

- Service Organizations
  - Provision of services, with or without tangible products
  - Customer satisfaction
  - Profitability

- Government/Public Sector Organizations
  - Provision of services
  - Fulfilment of social/legal mandate

Although there is an underlying commonality of attributes/elements of a quality system for these three organization types, it is still imperative to develop a suitable quality model commensurate with the specific needs of the enterprise.

The question that confronts most managers is: how to select or develop the most appropriate quality model. As we have indicated earlier, a TQM system can be developed and established through a variety of ways. Following are some of the possible options:

- Develop your own system based on the fundamental principles of quality
- Follow the guidelines recommended in the International Standard: ISO 9004-1
- Follow the philosophies/methodologies profounded by quality experts/gurus, such as: Deming, Juran, Crosby, Feigenbaum, Ishikawa, etc.

Although, any approach or model can provide suitable quality system framework, the success will be determined by the organization's own ability to manage and control the system effectively. Experience indicates that the greatest amount of lasting success is achieved by those companies/organizations who develop their own quality model commensurate with their own specific needs and infrastructural profile. Indeed, it is not to say that such an approach could not utilize the enormous wealth of knowledge and innovative ideas outlined in any or all of the existing systems or philosophies/methodologies propounded by the well-known experts.

A self-developed/self-directed model would have a high probability of success because of the following distinct characteristics:

- It would be a system developed by people within the organization.
- It would fit and be compatible with the existing quality framework of the organization.
- It would make optimal use of available resources.
- It would be participative, meaningful, value-adding and understandable to everyone collectively.
- It would be people-developed/people-empowered/people-driven/people-owned model.

◆ TQM IMPLEMENTATION APPROACH

There are basically two approaches to implementing TQM in any organization:

- **Top-Down Approach**
- **Bottom-Up Approach**

In the *Top-Down* approach, the exercise starts from the top - the Chief Executive Officer (CEO). The whole organization makes a decision to implement TQM and, accordingly, the development of strategic directions, decisions and activities permeate throughout the organization top-down with everyone involved in the implementation process. The flow of activities can undergo the following sequence:

- The Executive Management identifies the need for improving quality and outlines their commitment, support and involvement.
- A suitable quality infrastructure is established: TQM coordinator, steering committee, organizational responsibilities, requisite personnel/financial resources, etc.
- A strategic plan and a viable road-map is drawn-up.
- A suitable quality model and implementation plan is developed.
- Organizational policies, objectives and goals are outlined.
- Quality improvement teams are established.
- Projects are initiated and implemented.
- Results are measured and analyzed.
- Quality system effectiveness/performance is evaluated.
- Continuous improvement opportunities are further explored and acted upon.

The *Bottom-Up* approach is applicable when there is no company-wide decision on TQM implementation but there is, however, a silent quality revolution brewing-up and everyone or several components in the organization are desirous of improving the quality of their products, services or processes. The quality improvement initiatives can be started project-by-project or process-by-process and ultimately the collective impact permeates into the organization upwards to bring about a total quality system implementation. The process can start from one or several Divisions in the organization. The sequence of activities can be outlined as follows:

- Identify all the processes within a Division, where quality/process improvement efforts can be expended.
- Establish Process Management Teams (PMTs).
- Follow the process improvement methodology: Plan-Upgrade-Record-Improve (see Figure 2 in this Chapter).
- Interface and extend improvement initiatives to other processes within the Division and across Divisions in the organization.
- Coordinate improvement initiatives and activities.
- Measure results and assess performance.
- Integrate process improvement efforts to bring the activity to the level of company-wide TQM.

It must be clearly understood that TQM, by itself, is a meaningless entity. It is simply a collection of activities and functions which collectively produces a resultant effect of implementing a quality system. TQM is not something that you can tangibly see, like a piece of furniture. It is a system that is superimposed on the company's operability framework to ensure that the products and/or services they produce are of good quality. For example, when you go into a food processing plant which produces sausages and ask someone if they have implemented TQM, they cannot physically show you TQM as a separate tangible entity. It is a system superimposed on what they produce, ie., sausages - the production of sausages being the primary objective indeed. Thus, companies are not in the business of developing quality systems, but they are in the business of making products and a quality system is implemented simply to ensure high quality of their products.

Thus, TQM does not have to be a big ball from Heaven that no one knows what to do about. The big ball has to be broken down into manageable pieces that people can handle, control, understand, implement and improve upon. Quality is achieved piece-by-piece, process-by-process, within the overall umbrella of a TQM system. Therefore, it does not matter which approach is being used, top-down or bottom-up, the idea is to proceed slowly and systematically to achieve the ultimate goal - "excellence in quality".

◆ TQBT: THE GRAND SYSTEM

In searching for a suitable TQM model, the foremost concern of the organization is to ensure that, both, the short-term and longer-term needs are accommodated. Organizations are cognizant of the fact that quality is a long-term perspective and they are willing to make sacrifices to a feasible extent. However, they have to live by the fact that there are short-term day-to-day market pressures and demands which must be fulfilled.

The company's longer-term quality perspective revolves around establishing a sustainable quality culture and a mind-set for excellence. The short-term needs call for the establishment of a quality system, a process improvement strategy, and motivating people to improve quality and productivity. Figure 1 presents a schematic of a layered quality model addressing these needs.

The overall intent of any quality system, vis-à-vis long-term as well as short-term focus, can generally be expressed as follows:

- To establish a sustainable quality culture
- To inculcate a mind-set for performance
- To improve quality of products and services
- To maintain an amicable relationship with suppliers and customers

- To achieve total customer satisfaction
- To improve market share and profitability
- To enhance productivity and reduce costs
- To create a pleasant and enjoyable working milieu for employees

TQBT

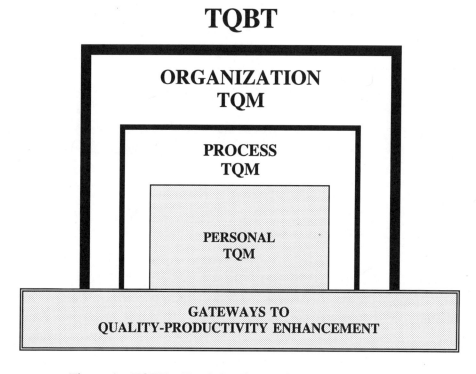

Figure 1: TQBT: Total Quality Business Transformation

The quality paradigm that we are presenting comprises of a whole integrated system approach to quality. The model looks at the quality focus from the viewpoint of "Total Quality Business Transformation (TQBT)". Depending upon the specific long-term and/or short-term needs of an enterprise, this layered quality model can be utilized either in its entirety or in parts. The message and approach inherent in the various components of the model, as schematically presented in Tables 4, 5, and 6 and Figure 2, is almost self-explanatory. The basic premise of the TQBT system can be outlined as follows:

- TQBT: Implementing a quality culture
- Organization TQM: Implementing a total quality system
- Process TQM: Process-by-process enhancement system
- Personal TQM: A self-superimposed personal excellence mandate

We shall now elucidate the TQBT system to provide guidelines for developing a workable quality model.

TQBT: TOTAL QUALITY BUSINESS TRANSFORMATION

The twelve axioms of TQBT (see Table 4) serve as the umbrella for creating a long-term quality mindset and culture. The model requires management ingenuity, commitment and dedication to develop means of permeating the message inherent in these axioms throughout the organization.

Table 4: TOTAL QUALITY BUSINESS TRANSFORMATION
Vision 2000+

TQBT Axioms

Axiom #1:	Dynamic Customer Orientation
Axiom #2:	Participative Management
Axiom #3:	Infrastructural Stability
Axiom #4:	Self-Directed Organization
Axiom #5:	Operational Framework Flexibility
Axiom #6:	Integrated Systems Approach
Axiom #7:	System Effectiveness Measurability
Axiom #8:	Process Enhancement Focus
Axiom #9:	Genuine Employee Emphasis
Axiom #10:	Continuous Reengineering
Axiom #11:	Proactive Change Management
Axiom #12:	Total Excellence Mindset

Guidelines: TQBT Axioms

- **Dynamic Customer Orientation**

  Develop a mechanism through which a continuous linkage can be established with the customer, for example:

  - Consultative process/meetings
  - Feedback questionnaire/survey
  - Customer hotline
  - Personal visits

Pursue a proactive and dynamic customer satisfaction policy and perspective. Assure the customer, through some tangible means, that the organization has a business mandate, dedication and commitment to customer satisfaction. Make known to all employees the extent of seriousness the organization attaches to the issue of customer satisfaction.

- **Participative Management**

Management commitment alone is not enough: management must actively participate and involve itself in the process of building and maintaining the quality system. Some of the aspects of involvement may include: self-directed work teams, steering group meetings, system review meetings, strategic planning, system auditing, etc.

- **Infrastructural Stability**

Organizational and/or infrastructural stability and maturity elevates morale and confidence. A stable and mature environment provides a pleasant working milieu. A perpetually changing infrastructure creates unpredictability and insecurity. It is, therefore, imperative to establish a sense of operational stability in the functional units. Even when an infrastructural change is necessary and unavoidable, make sure that the change is neither demeaning nor dehumanizing. People must fully participate in the change process.

- **Self-Directed Organization**

In as much as possible, the organization should be self-dependent and self-sufficient. Develop your own quality system/model, if possible, commensurate with your own needs and operating principles. A people-developed/people-driven/people-empowered/people-owned model would have the greatest chance of lasting success. Even if a model is adopted from external sources, make sure that the process ownership is in the hands of the employees. People must have the authority, empowerment and responsibility to institute any necessary changes in the system to make it more efficient. Let not systems drive people; let people drive the systems.

- **Operational Framework Flexibility**

Systems cannot afford to be inflexible in a volatile environment. Rigid systems which have little alignment with the changing needs and priorities would soon become outmoded and obsolete. Continuous environmental scanning is required to acquire an up-to-date understanding of changing marketplace needs, demands, paradigm shifts and customer requirements. Your internal systems must be flexible enough to admit and accommodate these changing and evolving demands.

- **Integrated Systems Approach**

  The functional framework of today's business world is complex and intricate. Its management calls for establishing an integrated cross-functional network in the organization. A coordinated whole system approach ensures operational consistency and uniformity. An effective cross-functional interface can be developed through self-directed work teams. Effective information system and operational transparency generates a feeling of self-confidence in employees and as a result there is high level of motivation that becomes instrumental in productivity improvement.

- **System Effectiveness Measurability**

  Subjective assessment of system effectiveness or the extent of accomplishments is valuable only to some extent. It is fundamentally important to establish viable measurement systems to provide valuable data and information that can be properly analyzed through analytical means. No organization can afford to continue building a system without appraising its viability and usefulness. A step-by-step measuring and monitoring system should be an integral part of the quality system.

- **Genuine Employee Emphasis**

  An organization is merely a sum total of individuals. The success of any undertaking in the organization is dependent on its people. Today's workplace is highly democratized and we are back to the realization that human endeavour and commitment is singularly the most indispensable driving force for the success of any system. It is, therefore, imperative to focus our attention to creating the most conducive working environment for our people. People are at their best when they are given responsibility, they are empowered to make decisions, they are well informed, and the organization demonstrates a genuine concern and appreciation for their contribution. Employee participation and productivity can be significantly enhanced through the establishment of process management teams.

- **Continuous Re-engineering**

  Dormancy breeds decay. To succeed, the organization must constantly reengineer, evolve and adapt its strategies and systems to the demands of marketplace. This TQBT axiom emphasizes the need for continuous:

  - Environmental scanning
  - Customer needs analysis
  - Organizational capability assessment
  - System evaluation
  - Employee emphasis
  - Improvement focus

- **Proactive Change Management**

  Change is inevitable. It is indispensable for avoiding stagnation and remaining viable in the marketplace. However, change cannot be bought about by dictate. Change is a people-dependent phenomenon and for change to be accepted wholeheartedly, people must perceive a congruence between the nature of change and their beliefs. Managers must act as change agents. The management must provide appropriate support systems to make the process of change as smooth as possible.

- **Total Excellence Mindset**

  The final TQBT axiom accentuates the fact that *Quality* is a thought revolution in management - a collective attitude of mind. Quality means innate excellence. Quality does not come through implementing just a few programs or projects; it requires a vision, a dedication to a cause one truly believes in, a total excellence mindset.

- **ORGANIZATION TQM**
  - Under the overall umbrella of TQBT, this ten-step plan (Table 5) presents the second level, ie, the working level, for implementing the fundamental TQM elements.
  - A strategic plan should be developed outlining a systematic set of initiatives and activities for each of the element.
  - With these "Ten TQM Absolutes" forming the basis of the quality system, a detailed framework for developing a self-developed/self-directed model is outlined in Chapter 5.

Table 5: ORGANIZATION TQM
The Ten Absolutes
1.   *Management Readiness*
2.   *Customer-Supplier Partnering*
3.   *Environmental Scanning*
4.   *Current System Evaluation*
5.   *Strategic Planning*
6.   *TQM Training*
7.   *Disciplined System Implementation*
8.   *Process Enhancement*
9.   *Performance Evaluation*
10.   *Continuous Improvement*

- **PROCESS TQM**
  - A simple and highly effective step-by-step process enhancement/improvement model is presented in Figure 2. Further details about the application of this method are appended in Chapter 23.
  - This method can be used for making improvements in all projects, processes and activities initiated under the TQM plan.
  - The wheel (Fig. 2) can also be used as a stand-alone guide for process improvement/ management in bottom-up approach to implementing quality improvement system as identified earlier.

- **PERSONAL TQM**
  - The ten-commandments appended in Table 6 present a fresh new look at the whole process of implementing a TQM system.
  - The model accentuates the comparative roles and responsibilities, of both the organization and the individuals, in making the system successful.
  - Organizations are merely a sum total of people. Everything in the organization would remain inert and static unless moved, driven and directed by the only live and dynamic force and energy - "the people".
  - The emphasis is on the organization is to provide suitable motivational impetus and on the individual to tap their own psyche to create excellence.
  - The model is expounded in greater details in Chapter 6.

Table 6: PERSONAL TQM
The Ten Commandments

1.	*Create a vision*
2.	*Understand personal role*
3.	*Determine personal potential*
4.	*Respond to challenge*
5.	*Practice participative involvement*
6.	*Cultivate proactive attitude*
7.	*Instill creative mindedness*
8.	*Impose self-directed performance appraisal*
9.	*Assess personal fulfilment*
10.	*Exercise continuous introspective analysis*

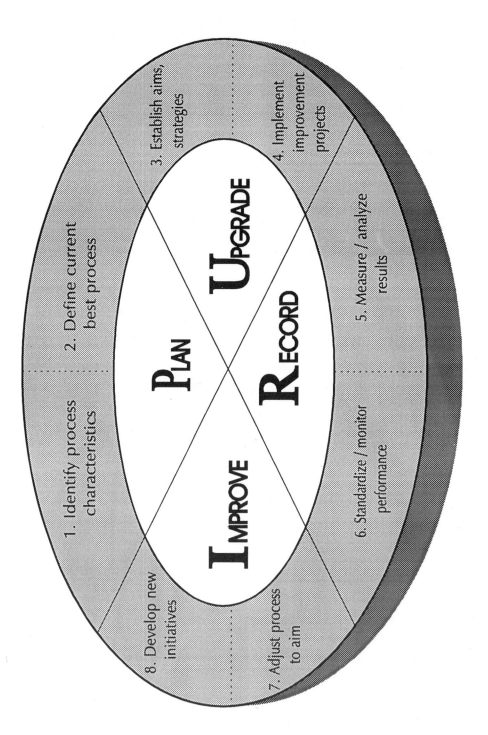

Figure 2 : "PURI" Process Enhancement Wheel

◆ TQM: FAIL-PROOFING THE SYSTEM

The success or failure of a system indeed depends on many diverse factors and circumstances. Many a times, though, it may be extremely valuable to be cognizant of the reasons why systems fail before initiating its implementation. This may help avoid the pitfalls and assist in developing a strategy that would ensure more than a passing chance of success. Experience has indicated that lack of attention in some or all of the following areas have generally been instrumental in either a total failure of the quality system or in achieving only a partial success. These key factors described below would in themselves serve as guidelines and action items to control the system and minimize its demise.

- **Key Factors Linked to System Failure:**

  - Insufficient management commitment, participation, direction and leadership.
  - Lack of dynamic and conscientious customer orientation by the organization.
  - TQM/ISO 9000 exercise considered to be a separate planning activity with little or inadequate link with the main-frame strategic business plan.
  - TQM envisaged as a project or program with limited shelf-life rather than a quality improvement, undertaking on a continuum.
  - Company does not generate a self-developed/self-directed TQM model that is commensurate with their specific needs and operability framework, but instead imports an inappropriate model that is foreign to its current systems and culture.
  - TQM/ISO 9000 exercise becomes so ludicrously magnanimous that it overwhelms people and most people either lose personal touch and interest with the system or get disoriented and dissipated into the TQM jungle.
  - When most employees consider TQM/ISO 9000 responsibility/ownership to be the exclusive domain of TQM/ISO 9000 Coordinator, this general lack of collective ownership reduces the system effectiveness to minuscule proportions.
  - TQM activity framework is not adequately transformed into a workable action plan.
  - Implementation framework is generally deficient in customized planning and tailored guidelines.
  - TQM exercise does not adequately take into account appropriate prioritization of the company's short-term demands and pressures and longer-term focus and perspective.
  - TQM/ISO 9000 implementation is left totally in the hands of an external consultant; internal personnel resources are not appropriately/adequately utilized and there is a lack of process ownership by the employees.
  - Insufficient awareness and hands-on training provided to the employees.

- Managers are insufficiently prepared for change management.
- Very little emphasis is placed on measuring the effectiveness and impact of TQM/ISO 9000 implementation.

In addition to the above generic key elements relating to the manufacturing/services sector, another set of postulates, specifically germane to the application of TQM in the public sector, are appended below.

- **Key Factors Linked to System Failure in the Public Sector:**

  - Lack of genuine and honest management commitment and hands-on exemplary leadership.
  - Managers apprehensive about loss of power and controls via people empowerment; decision-making overly centralized.
  - Hierarchical working relationship is fuzzy - everyone seems to be working for a "Greater God", yet no one knows who that God is - perhaps the taxpayer; consequently, there is a lack of personalized accountability and empathy for resource utilization.
  - A perpetual state of infrastructural instability and political dependency and intervention accentuates ineffectiveness.
  - Service operability burdened with excessive bureaucratic red-tape and regulatory overkill.
  - Service output without tangibles; input-output-profitability relationship being non-existent.
  - Absence of competition and consequent lack of impetus for higher productivity.
  - Service operates in a reactive/delivery mode rather than proactive/result-oriented mode.
  - Service portrays the perception of a gesture of favour to the customer rather than a mandated requirement and responsibility.
  - Nature of service being repetitive and error-prone.
  - Customer's perception - nature of services are "customer-hostile".
  - Insufficient contact and projection of day-to-day activities on to an identifiable customer.
  - Lack of continuous reengineering vis-à-vis environmental scanning.
  - System inflexible - follows rigid rules rather than guiding principles.
  - Too much focus on system rather than people; emphasis on driving the system rather than improving and motivating people.
  - TQM approach being piecemeal and unintegrated.
  - Lack of empathy for teamwork.
  - Fear of reprisal and performance appraisals limits personal innovativeness, gusto, motivation and self-confidence.

ISO 9000 (1994)
QUALITY STANDARDS

◆ QUALITY AND STANDARDIZATION

Throughout the process of planning, achieving and improving quality, it becomes absolutely necessary to know:

- How much quality is better quality?
- How much more to improve?
- Is there a yardstick to measure the level and extent of quality achieved?
- Is everyone else using the same measuring gage to assess quality?
- How can a comparative evaluation of the quality status of various suppliers be made?
- Can a "common quality denominator" be established?

For an enterprise, this information is vital to strategic planning for continuous improvement, marketability and profitability. For the customer, it affords a measure of assurance, reliability and comparative evaluation. For the regulators, it provides assurance about compliance, consumer protection, market transparency and fair competition.

Standardization provides the most basic and effective means of addressing these questions. *Standardization* is defined as: "a process of formulating and applying rules for an orderly approach to a scientific activity." Standardization of quality activities, therefore, helps to:

- Establish a "common denominator" of business quality accepted by everyone.
- Create simplicity out of complexity.
- Harmonize diverse practices.

- Generate compatibility and uniformity in the application of industrial practices.
- Act as a medium of communication of ideas and information between the buyer and the seller.
- Assist in reducing trade barriers.
- Encourage market transparency and fair competition.

◆ QUALITY SYSTEM STANDARDS

Quality system standards are developed by accredited standard-writing organizations at the national as well as the international level. Standards can be developed for specific industry applications or can be generic in nature, having applications across industry lines. There are many international bodies which are engaged in developing standards for specific industry applications, but the activity on the development of quality assurance standards has generally been limited to the national level.

National standards on quality are normally developed under the umbrella of the National Standards System of the country. Most of the industrialized infrastructures have well-established quality standards. For example, some of the well-known national Quality System Standards include:

Canada:	Z-299 series
France:	AFNOR X 50-110
Germany:	DIN 55-355
Netherlands:	NEN 2646
U.K.:	BS-5750 series
U.S.A.:	ANSI/ASQC Z-1.15, C-1; MIL-Q-9858A, etc.
NATO:	AQAP series

Despite the existence of these national standards, there has always been a desire and a need to have a universally accepted, harmonized set of generic quality assurance standards applicable across all industry lines. This gap has been filled by the International Organization for Standardization (ISO) through one of its technical committees, ISO/TC 176: Quality Management and Quality Assurance. This committee, through its deliberations, provided in 1987 a series (known as the ISO 9000 series) of quality system standards. The ISO 9000 series was derived, through the consensus principle, from a number of national standards to provide the industry with guidelines on how to establish a system for managing product quality in a manufacturing situation. Its objective is to promote the development of standards world-wide to improve operating efficiency, productivity and quality.

◆ INTERNATIONAL ORGANIZATION FOR STANDARDIZATION (ISO)

ISO (International Organization for Standardization), founded in 1946 and headquartered in Geneva, Switzerland, is a worldwide federation of National Standards bodies comprising 92 countries. The object of ISO is to promote the development of standardization and related activities in the world with a view to facilitiating international exchange of goods and services, and to developing coorperation in the sphere of intellectual, scientific, technological and economic activity. The results of ISO technical work are published as *International Standards*.

The organization's short name, ISO, was borrowed from the Greek word, *ISOS*, meaning "equal", which fits well with the conceptual framework of uniformity in standardization. The scope of ISO covers standardization in all fields except electrical and electronic engineering standards, which are the responsibility of another Geneva-based organization - the International Electrontechnical Commission (IEC).

ISO brings together the interests of producers, consumers, governments and the scientific community, in the preparation of International Standards. The standards developed by ISO, however, are voluntary consensus standards. They do not carry any legal mandate, unless bilaterally agreed upon by two parties or countries for a specific purpose.

◆ THE ISO 9000 SERIES

The basic ISO 9000 series of generic quality system standards originally developed by ISO/TC176 in 1987 are appended in Table 7. The series comprises of two types of standards:

- Guidance Standards: ISO 8402, ISO 9000, ISO 9004
- Conformance Standards: ISO 9001, ISO 9002, ISO 9003

Table 7: 1987 Series: Quality System Standards
Guidance Standards
ISO 9000: Quality Management and Quality Assurance Standards - Guidelines for Selection and Use
ISO 9004: Quality Management and Quality System Elements - Guidelines
ISO 8402 (1986): Quality - Vocabulary
Conformance Standards
ISO 9001: Quality Systems - Model for Quality Assurance in Design/Development, Production, Installation and Servicing
ISO 9002: Quality Systems - Model for Quality Assurance in Production and Installation
ISO 9003: Quality Systems - Model for Quality Assurance in Final Inspection and Test

Guidance Standards

They are descriptive documents that are only advisory in nature, providing guidelines. They do not contain perscriptive requirements and companies do not register to these documents.

- ISO 8402: Quality-Vocabulary

  This document was the first in the series developed in 1986 to provide a uniform set of definitions and terms commonly used in the area of quality assurance and quality management.

- ISO 9000: "Quality Management and Quality Assurance Standards-Guidelines for Selection and Use".

  ISO 9000 provides guidelines and a road-map for the selection and use of the appropriate quality system, namely, ISO 9001, 9002, or 9003. It also provides guidance on using ISO 9004 for internal quality management purposes.

- ISO 9004: "Quality Management and Quality System Elements - Guidelines.

ISO 9004 provides quality management and quality system element guidelines for any producer organization to develop and implement a quality system and to determine the extent to which each quality system element is applicable. A detailed discussion on the approach taken by ISO 9004 to implement a TQM System is outlined in chapter 7.

Conformance Standards

The three-tier model, ISO 9001, ISO 9002 and ISO 9003, represents three distinct forms of functional or organizational capability suitable for external quality assurance purposes. They constitute the actual three-level series of conformance standards for use in a two-party or three-party contractual situation. Each standard contains a set of quality system elements. ISO 9001 is the most comprehensive while ISO 9003 is the least comprehensive. Each model is a complete, independent document. It is for each company to select the appropriate model vis-à-vis their quality system needs. A comparative schematic of the necessary quality system elements of the three levels is shown in Table 8.

As orginally intended, these conformance standards were developed to be used as a second-party contractual document between the buyer and seller to assure the buyer that the seller could furnish an acceptable product or service at the stipulated level of quality. However, due to their commanding potentiality and world-wide acceptance, the role and application of the series have gone beyond its original mandate. Today, most organizations are seeking third-party accreditation and certification to one of the three quality levels (ISO 9001, 9002, 9003) as a means of demonstrating and assuring, at large, that the company is operating on and committed to meeting the standards of quality commanded by these international standards. A third-party certification/registration to ISO 9000 means that a company's total quality system has been assessed by a third party independent registrar and has been found to meet the applicable requirements of the chosen level of the standards.

Table 8: ISO 9000 Series (1987): International Quality System Standards

Clause #	ISO 9001	ISO 9002	ISO 9003
4.1	Management Responsibility	Management Responsibility	Management Responsibility
4.2	Quality System	Quality System	Quality System
4.3	Contract Review	Contract Review	↓
4.4	Design Control	↓	↓
4.5	Document Control	Document Control	Document Control
4.6	Purchasing	Purchasing	↓
4.7	Purchaser Supplied Product	Purchaser Supplied Product	↓
4.8	Product Identification and Traceability	Product Identification and Traceability	Product Identification
4.9	Process Control	Process Control	↓
4.10	Inspection and Testing	Inspection and Testing	Inspection and Testing
4.11	Inspection, Measuring and Test Equipment	Inspection, Measuring and Test Equipment	Inspection, Measuring and Test Equipment
4.12	Inspection and Test Status	Inspection and Test Status	Inspection and Test Status
4.13	Control of Nonconforming Product	Control of Nonconforming Product	Control of Nonconforming Product
4.14	Corrective Action	Corrective Action	↓
4.15	Handling, Storage, Packaging and Delivery	Handling, Storage, Packaging and Delivery	Handling, Storage, Packaging and Delivery
4.16	Quality Records	Quality Records	Quality Records
4.17	Internal Quality Audits	Internal Quality Audits	↓
4.18	Training	Training	Training
4.19	Servicing	↓	↓
4.20	Statistical Techniques	Statistical Techniques	Statistical Techniques

◆ REVISION (1994): ISO 9000 SERIES

All ISO standards are subject to a review approximately every five year, including the ISO 9000 series,. The five-yearly review of the 1987 series (known as Revision 1 within the Technical Committee ISO/TC 176) has been completed and the revised standards are available for use. Table 9 presents the revised ISO 9000 Series.

Table 9: 1994 Series: Quality System Standards	
Guidance Standards	
ISO 9000-1:	Quality Management and Quality Assurance Standards - Part I: Guidelines for Selection and Use
ISO 9004-1:	Quality Management and Quality System Elements - Part I: Guidelines
ISO 8402:	Quality Management and Quality Assurance - Vocabulary
Conformance Standards	
ISO 9001:	Quality Systems - Model for Quality Assurance in Design/Development, Production, Installation and Servicing
ISO 9002:	Quality Systems - Model for Quality Assurance in Production, Installation and Servicing
ISO 9003:	Quality Systems - Model for Quality Assurance in Final Inspection and Test

Only minor changes have been incorporated into the 1994 revision; more significant changes are anticipated for the next revision (Revision 2) that is likely to be available by 1997. ISO/TC 176 has also developed a long-range plan, called *Vision 2000*, which discusses the future use of the ISO 9000 series through the year 2000.

Note: Throughout the remainder of this book, we have utilized the 1994 version of the ISO 9000 series.

Highlight of changes

- The revised ISO 9000 is now designated as ISO 9000-1, because more documents have been developed under this number in the series. Also the revised version has been expanded substantially to provide better understanding of the application of the ISO 9000 family for the development, implementation, selection and use of a quality system.

- The revised ISO 9001, ISO 9002, ISO 9003 are still designated as such. Essentially, the changes are editorial in nature, however, there is more emphasis on management involvement and maintenance of the systems.

  ISO 9001 still has twenty system elements, though some elements have been realigned to reflect consistency with the guidelines presented in ISO 9004-1.

  ISO 9002 has been augmented from eighteen elements to nineteen elements. "Servicing" is now an integral part of ISO 9002. Thus, the only difference between ISO 9001 and ISO 9002 is that ISO 9001 has the additional requirement of the "Design Control" clause; otherwise ISO 9001 and ISO 9002 are identical in content and extent of requirements.

  The level of requirements in ISO 9003 have been slightly upgraded as can be seen by comparing the requirements in Tables 8 and 10. The committee is still considering to further upgrade the requirement in ISO 9003 because there is a general feeling that the present level of ISO 9003 does not involve much value-added benefits to quality of products and services.

  Table 10 presents a comparative schematic of the 1994 version of ISO 9001, 9002 and 9003 conformance standards.

◆ PREMISE OF ISO 9000 SERIES

The ISO 9000 series provides a harmonzied set of generic quality assurance standards applicable to any manufacturing or service situation, with or without some requisite modifications. The series can be conveniently used in conjunction with any existing

Table 10: ISO 9000 Series (1994): International Quality System Standards

Clause #	ISO 9001	ISO 9002	ISO 9003
4.1	Management Responsibility	Management Responsibility	Management Responsibility
4.2	Quality System	Quality System	Quality System
4.3	Contract Review	Contract Review	Contract Review
4.4	Design Control	↓	↓
4.5	Document and Data Control	Document and Data Control	Document and Data Control
4.6	Purchasing	Purchasing	↓
4.7	Control of Customer Supplied Product	Control of Customer Supplied Product	Control of Customer Supplied Product
4.8	Product Identification and Traceability	Product Identification and Traceability	Product Identification and Traceability
4.9	Process Control	Process Control	↓
4.10	Inspection and Testing	Inspection and Testing	Inspection and Testing
4.11	Control of Inspection, Measuring and Test Equipment	Control of Inspection, Measuring and Test Equipment	Control and Inspection, Measuring and Test Equipment
4.12	Inspection and Test Status	Inspection and Test Status	Inspection and Test Status
4.13	Control of Nonconforming Product	Control of Nonconforming Product	Control of Nonconforming Product
4.14	Corrective and Preventive Action	Corrective and Preventive Action	Corrective Action
4.15	Handling, Storage, Packaging, Preservation and Delivery	Handling, Storage, Packaging, Preservation and Delivery	Handling, Storage, Packaging, Preservation and Delivery
4.16	Control of Quality Records	Control of Quality Records	Control of Quality Records
4.17	Internal Quality Audits	Internal Quality Audits	Internal Quality Audits
4.18	Training	Training	Training
4.19	Servicing	Servicing	↓
4.20	Statistical Techniques	Statistical Techniques	Statistical Techniques

quality assurance or industry specific standards. It is not the purpose of these standards to enforce uniformity of quality systems. Needs of organizations vary. The design and implementation of a quality system must necessarily be influenced by the particular organization objectives, products and processes, and specific practices.

The ISO 9000 series provides excellent guidelines on how to commence structuring and implementing an effective quality management system. It provides the foundation on which to build a suitable quality improvement system. The standards are not product specification standards but quality system standards. The emphasis is not on the quality of the product/service per sè but on the system that produces a quality product. It is concerned with how organizations provide quality in their products and services to customers consistantly all the time.

Most companies have quality control in some shape or form, and they are generally very happy with their system. Although quality control has its virtues and a place in the total quality management system, its scope is limited. The basic purpose of quality control is to verify, after the job is done, that it's been done correctly. This after-the-fact police force action has little proactive emphasis on the elimination of the causes of nonconformity. Also, quality control actions are generally not formally recorded or anlayzed to identify why things went wrong and to make sure the same thing does not reoccur.

The ISO 9000 series attempts to address the overall quality management system to improve and maintain the quality of products and services. It recognizes that the total quality process involves all the departments and functions of the organization. Everyone has a role to play in assuring quality. Consequently, it emphasizes a documented disciplined approach in:

- Clearly identifying management policies and commitment
- Identifying roles, responsibilities and authority
- Establishing clear set of instructions to all personnel affecting quality
- Developing precise procedures and instructions in all areas of operational activity to ensure consistency and uniformity

Thus, by shifting the focus of quality from the traditional approaches of quality control and quality assurance to management control and process improvement, the standard ensures the production of the right quality, the first time. However, by doing so, the standard indeed does not profess to deal with only the highest possible level of product quality. It is quite sensitive to commercial reality in the market place and does not seek to impose levels of quality which are unrealistic, unnecessary or commercially non-viable. It equates "quality" to "fitness for purpose" and the quality system standards as the basic framework for the application of common sense principles to achieve operational consistency. Notwithstanding however, the series should still be looked upon as a set of minimum quality system requirements - as the lowest common denominator of quality system elements applicable across all industries, technologies and services.

◆ THREE-TIER MODEL: ISO 9001, 9002, 9003

The type of information contained in these three models is as follows:

Model 1: ISO 9001

This model is for use when conformance to specified requirements is to be assured by the supplier throughout the whole cycle from design, production, installation to servicing. It covers organizations such as, engineering and construction firms and manufacturers that design, develop, produce, install, and service products.

ISO 9001 consists of twenty required quality system elements (see Table 11). It represents the fullest and most stringent requirements for system elements outlined in ISO 9004-1.

Model 2: ISO 9002

A slightly less stringent than ISO 9001 level, this model is for use when conformance to specified requirements are to be assured during production, installation and servicing. This level is particularly suited to the process industries (food, chemical, pharmaceutical, etc.) where the specific requirements for the product are stated in terms of an already established design or specification.

ISO 9002 also accommodates nearly all the quality system elements listed in ISO 9004-1. This model involves nineteen of the twenty system elements of ISO 9001. The one element that is not part of ISO 9002 is: "Design Control".

Table 11: ISO 9001 (1994): Quality System Elements

1. Management Responsibility

   - Quality policy
   - Organization
     - Responsibility and authority
     - Resources
     - Management representative
   - Management review

2. Quality System

   - General
   - Quality system procedures
   - Quality planning

3. Contract Review

   - General
   - Review
   - Amendment to a contract
   - Records

4. Design Control

   - General
   - Design and development planning
   - Organizational and technical interfaces
   - Design input
   - Design output
   - Design review
   - Design verification
   - Design validation
   - Design changes

5. Document and Data Control

   - General
   - Document and data approval and issue
   - Document and data changes

6. Purchasing

   - General
   - Evaluation of subcontractors
   - Purchasing data
   - Verification of purchased product
     - Supplier verification at sub-contractor's premises
     - Customer verfication of sub-contracted product

7. Control of Customer-Supplied Product

8. Product Identification and Traceability

9. Process Control

10. Inspection and Testing

    - General
    - Receiving inspection and testing
    - In-process inspection and testing
    - Final inspection and testing
    - Inspection and test records

11. Control of Inspection, Measuring and Test Equipment

    - General
    - Control procedure

12. Inspection and Test Status

13. Control of Nonconforming Product

    - General
    - Review and disposition of nonconforming product

14. Corrective and Preventive Action

    - General
    - Corrective action
    - Preventive action

15. Handling, Storage, Packaging, Preservation and Delivery

    - General
    - Handling
    - Storage
    - Packaging
    - Preservation
    - Delivery

16. Control of Quality Records

17. Internal Quality Audits

18. Training

19. Servicing

20. Statistical Techniques
    - Identification of Need
    - Procedures

Model 3: ISO 9003

This model applies to situations where the supplier's capabilities are to be assured only for final inspection and tests. It is suitable for small shops, divisions within an organization, laboratories, or equipment distributors that inspect and test supplied products.

Since ISO 9003 relates only to those elements concerning final inspection and test, it has the least number of requirements of the three models.

◆ ADOPTION OF ISO 9000 SERIES

Since the inception of the ISO 9000 series of Quality System Standards, a number of significant developments have been set into motion:

- A base line agreement about a quality system's minimum requirements has been established.
- Conformance to ISO 9000 is becoming a business mandate of the 1990's.
- Companies are implementing the ISO 9000 series to keep up with registered competitors and to distinguish themselves from non-registered competitors.
- Companies who have not been previously involved in any serious quality improvement effort are being forced, by increasing competition in both local and international markets, to implement quality management systems and conform to ISO 9000 standards.
- For some companies, registration may be a legal requirement to enter the regulated EC (European Common) market. Registration may also help a company to meet a domestic regulatory mandate, if any.
- Customers are getting the opportunity to evaluate the quality performance of suppliers regardless of the product type or location of production.
- When the series was first released in 1987, its acceptance as national standards by the memeber bodies was a bit slow. However, the popularity and acceptance of the ISO 9000 series grew very quickly and most industrialized contries either adopted these standards under their own national numbering system or realigned them with their existing national standards.

Some examples of the adoption of the 1987 series of ISO 9000 was as follows:

- U.S.A.: The equivalent standards in the U.S.A. were known as the Q90 series. Except for some cosmetic changes, the Q90 series was identical to the ISO 9000 series.
- U.K.: The BS 5750 series of the U.K. was equivalent to the ISO 9000 series.

- European Community (EC) Standards Organizations (CEN/CENELEC): The EN 29000 to EN 29004 series of the EC corresponded to the ISO 9000 to ISO 9004 standards.
- Canada: The original Canadian national standards on quality assurance were a four-tier model: Z-299.1 to Z-299.4. To align these with the 3-tier ISO 9000 standards, Canada developed the Q 9000 series, accommodating both the Z-299 series and the ISO 9000 series. Thus, for example, CAN/CSA: Q 9001 was made up of ISO 9001 plus a supplementary set of requirements which were originally a part of Z-299.1 but were not accomodated by ISO 9001.

Now, when the ISO 9000 series has been revised, the international community has been urged to adopt the 1994 version of the standards as their national standards in its entirety without making any alterations, realignments or changes. Many countries are attempting to comply with this requirement. The revised ISO 9000 series would now appear, without any changes, as follows:

- U.S.A.: ANSI/ISO Q 9000 Series
- Canada: CAN/CSA/ISO 9000 Series
- U.K.: BS/ISO 9000 Series
- Europe: EN/ISO 9000 Series

◆ QUALITY STANDARDS - FURTHER DEVELOPMENTS

As part of their mandate, ISO/TC 176 has the continual responsibility to:

- Develop other relevant and supporting quality system standards.
- Undertake the requisite review/revision of standards.

As of this writing, the additional quality related standards that have either been completed or are in the process of being completed, are appended in Table 12.

◆ OTHER QUALITY RELATED STANDARDS/GUIDES

It is almost imperative for every company implementing a TQM system or preparing for ISO 9000 certification, to understand that process management and improvement is fundamental to an effective TQM or ISO 9000 implementation and maintenance. Process improvement is accomplished through the use of Statistical Process Control (SPC)

Table 12: ISO/TC 176: Quality System Standards

ISO 9000: Quality Management and Quality Assurance Standards:

ISO 9000-1 : Part 1: Guidelines for Selection and Use
ISO 9000-2 : Part 2: Generic Guidelines for Application of ISO 9001, ISO 9002, and ISO 9003
ISO 9000-3 : Part 3: Guidelines for the Application of ISO 9001 to the Development, Supply and Maintenance of Software
ISO 9000-4 : Part 4: Application for Dependability Management

ISO 9004: Quality Management and Quality System Elements:

ISO 9004-1 : Part 1: Guidelines
ISO 9004-2 : Part 2: Guidelines for Services
ISO 9004-3 : Part 3: Guidelines for Processed Materials
ISO 9004-4 : Part 4: Guidelines for Quality Improvement
ISO 9004-5 : Part 5: Guidelines for Quality Plans
ISO 9004-6 : Part 6: Guide to Quality Assurance for Project Management
ISO 9004-7 : Part 7: Guidelines for Configuration Management
ISO 9004-8 : Part 8: Guidelines on Quality Principles and their Application to Management Practices

ISO 10011: Guidelines for Auditing Quality Systems:

ISO-10011-1: Part 1: Auditing
ISO-10011-2: Part 2: Qualification Criteria for Quality System Auditors
ISO-10011-3: Part 3: Management of Audit Programmes

ISO 10012: Quality Assurance Requirements for Measuring Equipment:

ISO-10012-1: Part 1: Metrological Qualification System for Measuring Equipment
ISO-10012-2: Part 2: Measurement Assurance

ISO 10013: Preparation of Quality Manual

ISO 10014: Economics of Quality

ISO 10015: Continuing Education and Training Guidelines

ISO 10016: Records of Product Inspection and Test-Guidelines for Preparation of the Results and their Conformance

methods, such as Pareto diagrams, Cause-Effect diagrams, control charts, sampling methods, Quality Function Deployment, etc.

The ISO Technical Committee, ISO/TC 69: "Applications of Statistical Methods", carries out this task of developing standards and guides on tools and methodologies that provide process control and analytical support to quality system standards such as the ISO 9000 series. Some of the important contributions of this committee are appended in Table 13.

In addition, the ISO (International Organization for Standardization) and its sister organization, the IEC (International Electrotechnical Commission), both headquartered in Geneva, have produced some other useful guides pertinent to quality system accreditation and certification. A selected list is appended in Table 14. A majority of these guides relate to either laboratory accreditation work or accredited registration bodies. These guides do not provide any direct information for ISO 9000 certification; they are listed here only as a useful secondary source of information.

◆ AVAILABILITY OF STANDARDS

Copies of the standards can be purchased either from a national standards body within the country or directly from the central secretariat of the ISO. Some of the corresponding addresses are as follows:

- CANADA

  Standards Council of Canada
  45 O'Connor Street
  Ottawa, Ontario   K1P 6N7
  Telephone: 613-238-3222
  Telefax: 613-995-4564

- U.K.

  British Standards Institution
  2 Park Street
  London, England   W1A 2BS
  Telephone: +44 1629 90 00
  Telefax: +44 1629 05 06

Table 13: ISO/TC 69: Quality Related Standards

ISO-3534: Statistics-Vocabulary and Symbols

  Part 1: Probability and General Statistical Terms
  Part 2: Statistical Quality Control
  Part 3: Design of Experiments

ISO-2859: Sampling Inspection Procedures for Inspection by Attributes

  Part 0: Introduction to ISO-2859
  Part 1: Sampling Plans Indexed by Acceptable Quality Level (AQL) for Lot-by-Lot Inspection
  Part 2: Sampling Plans Indexed by Limiting Quality (LQ) for Isolated Lot Inspection
  Part 3: Skip Lot Sampling Plan

ISO-3951: Sampling Procedures and Charts for Inspection by Variables for Percent Nonconforming

ISO-7870: Control Charts-General Guide and Introduction

ISO-8258: Shewhart Control Charts

ISO-7966: Acceptance Control Charts

ISO-5725: Accuracy (Trueness and Precision) of Measurement Methods and Results (six parts)

ISO-8550: Guide for Selection of an Acceptance Sampling System Scheme or Plan

ISO-8422: Sequential Sampling Plans for Inspection by Attributes

ISO-8423: Sequential Sampling Plans for Inspection by Variables for Percent Nonconforming (Known Standard Deviation)

Under Preparation

- Process Capability and Performance Measures
- Introduction to Cumulative Sum Charts
- Guidelines for Implementation of Statistical Process Control
- Process Potential Studies
- Machine Capability Studies
- Statistical Aspects of Sampling from Bulk Material
- Acceptance Sampling Plans for Bulk Material
- Applications of Statistical Methods in Standardization and Specifications
- Linear Calibrations using Reference Materials
- Tests for Departure from the Normal Distribution
- Acceptance Sampling Plans for Continuous Production

Table 14: ISO/IEC Guides Relating to Quality System Accreditation/Certification/Registration

Guide 2: General terms and their definitions concerning standardization and related activities

Guide 7: Requirement for standards suitable for product certification

Guide 16: Code of principles on third-party certification systems and related standards

Guide 22: Information on manufacturer's declaration of conformity with standards or other technical specifications

Guide 23: Methods of indicating conformity with standards for third-party certification systems

Guide 25: General requirements for the technical competence of testing laboratories

Guide 27: Guidelines for corrective action to be taken by a certification body in the event of misuse of its mark of conformity

Guide 28: General rules for a model third-party certification system for products

Guide 30: Terms and definitions used in connection with reference materials

Guide 33: Uses of certified reference materials

Guide 39: General requirements for the acceptance of inspection bodies

Guide 40: General requirements for the acceptance of certification bodies

Guide 42: Guidelines for a step-by-step approach to an international certification system

Guide 43: Development and operation of laboratory proficiency testing

Guide 44: General rules for ISO or IEC international third-party certification schemes for products

Guide 45: Guidelines for the presentation of test results

Guide 48: Guidelines for third-party assessment and registration of a supplier's Quality System

Guide 49: Guidelines for development of a Quality Manual for a testing laboratory

Guide 53: An approach to the utilization of a supplier's quality system in third-party product certification

Guide 56: An approach to the review by a certification body of its own internal quality system

Guide 57: Guidelines for the presentation of inspection results

Guide 58: Calibration and testing laboratory accreditation system-general requirements for operation and recognition (Replaces ISO/IEC Guidelines 38, 54 and 55)

- U.S.A.

  American National Standards Institute
  1430 Broadway
  New York, N.Y. 10018
  Telephone: 212-354-3300
  Telefax: 212-302-1286

  American Society for Quality Control
  611 East Wisconsin Avenue
  P.O. Box 3005
  Milwaukee, WI 53202-3005
  Telephone: 414-272-8575
  Telefax: 414-272-1734

- ISO Office

  International Organization for Standardization
  Central Secretariat
  1, rue de varembé
  Case Postale 56
  CH-1211 Genève 20, Switzerland
  Telephone: +41 22 749 01 11
  Telefax: +41 22 733 34 30

◆ ISO 9000 CERTIFICATION/REGISTRATION

ISO 9000 quality system certification involves the assessment and audit of a company's (supplier's) quality system by a third party, known as a Quality System Registrar. The process of certification involves the following:

- Company identifies the level of standard (ISO 9001 or 9002 or 9003) to which compliance is required.
- Quality system documentation is prepared:
  - Quality Manual
  - Quality System Procedures Manuals
  - Standard Operating Procedures or Manufacturing Procedures
  - Work Instructions
  - Forms, proformas, books, records, etc.
- Quality system elements are implemented in such a way as to permeate the requirements all the way down to the working level documents and procedures employed by the company.

- Quality system is internally audited to ensure that it is effectively implemented and meets the requisite system requirements of the chosen level of standard.
- Company selects a registrar and makes an application for certification.
- The registrar conducts a comprehensive on-site audit of the company's system to ensure full conformance to the requirements of the chosen level of standard.
- Registrar confirms the company's system conformance to the standard and a certificate of registration is awarded.
- Certification status is listed in a register that is available to the public.
- Company is allowed to display the registrar's mark on advertsing, stationary, etc., as evidence of having achieved registration. Note that the registration mark cannot be identified on the product itself, because the certification is for the quality system and not for the quality of the product per sé.

A detailed description of the process of certification, its documentation and preparation is outlined in the proceeding chapters.

PART TWO

THE

QUALITY

MANAGEMENT

DEVELOPING A TQM MODEL

◆ INTRODUCTION

The world of business typically revolves around two entities: the vendor and the vendee. The seller has to know what the buyer wants and provide it in a manner which satisfies the buyer while competing against a host of competitors. The success in this competitive environment will belong to those producers who can consistently provide products and services that have:

- Technological Superiority
- Quality Excellence
- Competitive Pricing
- Customer Satisfaction

Customers buy products because:

- They need them
- The products would provide them value-added benefits in terms of:
  - Operability
  - Economic affordability
  - Ego satisfaction and pride in ownership

When customers go out to buy a manufactured product, their evaluation/perception of quality involves the following two aspects of quality:

- **Visible Quality Factors**

  These are the ones that they can examine right there and then at the time of purchase:

  - Looks and Appearance
  - Technological Innovativeness
  - Operability Features
  - Competitive Pricing
  - Credibility of the Manufacturer
  - Warranties
  - After Sales Service

- **Invisible Quality Factors**

  These are the ones that they can examine only after having used the product:

  - Ease of Operability
  - Functional Reliability and Dependability
  - Performance
  - Satisfaction
  - Pride in Ownership

A dynamic organization seeking to gain competitive edge via quality must, therefore, take into consideration all of these quality aspects in their strategic planning framework for the design, development, display and marketability of their products.

As indicated earlier, different organizations react differently to quality improvement pressures. Those in the reactive mode have generally a short-term focus and, consequently, their efforts are limited to quality control and quality assurance activities to improve the quality of their products and services. Proactive organizations operate on longer-term goals. Their efforts are expended on improving the quality of all aspects of work-life. While ensuring continuous quality improvement of their products and services, these companies are also concerned about the welfare of their employees, total customer satisfaction, partnership with their suppliers/subcontractors, and service to society in general. By doing so, they virtually guarantee for themselves an expanded marketability, continuous growth, high productivity, profitability and long-term survivability.

Quality, indeed, is a long-term perspective - it takes time to build quality in. Quality is not an entity you can buy and bring it in to implement - if requires patience, dedication and proper planning. Neither Rome was built in a day nor Japanese quality superiority sprung-up overnight. Most corporate boardrooms understand and agree that quality improvement will take time; yet, they would still rush into implementing quick-fix programs and start expecting profound improvements overnight. Instead, they encounter profound failures and frustrations.

Despite the understanding that short-term actions will only produce short-term success, why do most companies jump into this morbid chasm? Because, as the argument goes, if we don't produce quality overnight, we won't survive the next morning and the long-term focus, therefore, becomes redundant. But the incongruence is, that there is no survival even with the short-term initiatives. Remember! having achieved quality and then loosing it would be more profoundly perilous than having never achieved in the first place. Regretfully, the quality dilemma is much like politics. If the government and politicians of the day do not produce quick results within the short period of their tenure, they don't get re-elected. If they do operate on short-term visions, the country is doomed.

The solution to this dilemma is not as complicated as most organizations may think. What is required is an optimal mix of both, the long-term as well as the short-term focus embedded into the planning framework. A simple strategic plan should involve, as a minimum, the following elements:

- Set your priorities right. Develop a "**Must-List**" and a "**Wish-List**" of the deliverables vis-à-vis the short-term and long-term perspectives and needs.
- Appropriately manoeuvre and allocate resources to both lists.
- Measure/analyze performance.
- Review/revise/reset priorities.
- Continuously maintain focus on prioritized short-term as well as long-term goals.

◆ SELF-DEVELOPED/SELF-DIRECTED TQM SYSTEM

We shall now direct our attention to developing a self-directed Organization TQM model on the lines of the TQBT approach outlined in Chapter 3. Typically, a TQM System, irrespective of any approach or philosophy, would have at least the following components:

- Management structures and processes
- Quality system procedures and processes
- Disciplined methodologies and tools

- **Management Structures and Processes**
  - Sets the stage for establishing a quality culture and high performance mindset
  - Identifies management commitment and leadership
  - Formalizes quality policies, objectives, responsibilities and authority
  - Provides structure and regimentation to all requisite systems

- **Quality System Procedures and Processes**
  - Establishes all requisite quality system procedures
  - Provides a disciplined and structured systems approach to quality improvement
  - Helps to establish formal standard operating procedures
  - Facilitates proper documentation of procedures

- **Disciplined Methodologies and Tools**
  - Helps to measure and analyze process improvement and system effectiveness
  - Assists in standardizing the processes and monitoring their continued viability
  - Assists in continuous evaluation and improvement of the quality system

Some of the essential elements in these three components of a TQM system would include the following:

Management Responsibilities

- Vision
- Mission
- Commitment
- Responsibility
- Cultural Change
- Leadership

- Employee Involvement
- Teamwork
- Support Systems
- Disciplined Methodology
- Knowledge and Skills
- Customer Focus

Support Systems

- Procurement Control
- Design Control
- Production Control
- Process Control
- Inspection/Testing
- Nonconformity
- Corrective/Preventive Action
- Cost Control
- Documentation

- Evaluation
- Quality Audits
- Verification Control
- Quality Records
- Training
- Servicing
- Marketing Control
- Post-Production Control
- Customer Feedback

Tools and Methodologies

- Brainstorming
- Flow Chart
- Checksheet
- The Visual Factory
- Cause-Effect Diagram
- Pareto Chart
- Just-in-Time
- 'PURI' Process Enhancement Wheel
- Control Charts
- Statistical Process Control (SPC)
- Design of Experiments
- Systematic/Tree Diagram
- Arrow Diagram

- Quality Function Deployment (QFD)
- Force Field Analysis
- Shewhart - Deming Cycle
- Nominal Group Technique
- Benchmarking
- Block Diagram
- Relations Diagram
- Affinity Diagram/KJ Method
- Matrix Diagram
- Matrix Data - Analysis
- Process Decision Program Chart (PDPC)
- Concurrent Engineering

In order to develop a customized self-directed, sustainable TQM model from the system elements listed above, the company first needs to clarify and delineate an overall road map by identifying the requisite elements appropriate to each of the following components:

- The Mission
- The Vision
- The Customer
- The Supplier
- The Company

The Mission

- Clearly define the company's business.
- Identify the company's needs, interests and mission.
- Who are the current customers?
- Who are the potential customers?
- Identify the customer requirements.
- Assess the company's current capabilities vis-à-vis the customer requirements.
- Identify the company's strengths and weaknesses.
- Determine what needs to be done to meet the customer's needs and expectations.
- Identify the changes, modifications, or improvements required in the company's operations to accomplish the mission.
- Determine the company's competitors as well as their strengths and weaknesses.
- Identify how and by what means the company can gain a competitive edge.

The Vision

- For long-term strategic planning, establish the company's vision.
- Develop long-term goals and objectives.
- Identify the potential customers and their requirements.
- Identify how the company's capabilities need to be realigned or augmented to meet the requirements of the potential customers.
- Who are likely to be the company's potential competitors? Identify their strengths and weaknesses.
- Plan, strategize and act to gain a competitive edge.

The Customer

- Customer satisfaction is the primary goal. Establish a long-term relationship with the customer and identify how this will be achieved.
- Identify the customer's total needs and expectations.
- Establish the infrastructure necessary for continuous dialogue with the customer to clearly understand his requirements.
- Translate the customer's needs into operational actions.

The Supplier

- Identify the materials, supplies, equipment and subcontracted tasks needed to provide products and services as per the customer's requirements.
- Select appropriate suppliers and subcontractors.
- Establish a partnership with your suppliers to ensure a continuous supply of high quality materials.
- Liaise with the suppliers and establish suitable material control procedures.
- Establish effective communication with the suppliers to clarify your requirements.
- Develop an appropriate material verification system.

The Company

- Plan and generate a global framework for a total quality management system commensurate with the strategic requirements identified in the mission, vision, and customer/supplier interface.
- Establish the quality policy and objectives.
- Identify management commitment.
- Define and establish the quality infrastructure and responsibilities.
- Develop quality plans and appropriate systems.
- Identify quality procedures, processes and methodologies.
- Implement quality improvement projects and initiatives.

- Involve everyone in the company through process improvement teams.
- Implement process improvement strategies.
- Establish a quality audit/verification system.
- Measure, analyze and assess performance.
- Institute an effective corrective/preventive action mechanism.
- Establish a continuous cycle of improvement.
- Maintain focus on customer satisfaction.

Once a complete road map has been outlined, the basic framework of a TQM System can be easily established. The system has to be well structured and documented so that everyone in the company can follow it consistently and uniformly. A typical TQM program would have the following basic elements:

- **Management:** vision, mission, commitment, leadership, quality policy and objectives

- **Strategic Planning:** quality plans, procedures, processes, activities; quality infrastructure

- **Human Resource Management:** employee involvement and empowerment; process improvement teams; education and training

- **Input Controls:** market analysis; customer needs; incoming quality assurance; supplier-customer partnering

- **In-Process Controls:** control of design, specifications, material, equipment; process control; documentation control; production control; process/product audit and verification

- **Measurement / Analysis:** data collection and analysis; statistical process control

- **Output Controls:** output audit and verification; conformance to contractual and regulatory requirements

- **Customer Satisfaction:** customer requirements and expectations, services standards, commitment, complaint resolution, satisfaction determination, satisfaction results

These key elements of the TQM System can be summarized through the "Ten Absolutes" as appended in Table 5 in Chapter 3 and now reproduced here in Table 15. The guidelines for implementing an Organization TQM were elucidated in Chapter 3.

Table 15: ORGANIZATION TQM

The Ten Absolutes

1. Management Readiness
2. Customer-Supplier Partnering
3. Environmental Scanning
4. Current System Evaluation
5. Strategic Planning
6. TQM Training
7. Disciplined System Implementation
8. Process Enhancement
9. Performance Evaluation
10. Continuous Improvement

◆ THE 7-STEP TQM MODEL

From the above discussion, we can now draw up a workable TQM model as schematically illustrated in Table 16. To implement the system, the company must develop a corporate TQM guidebook describing, step-by-step, all its operational functions, procedures, and processes, commensurate with the model. The following factors describe the major areas of consideration to be included in this documentation:

Step 1: Management

- Develop a mission statement.
- Identify the company's vision.
- Identify management commitment and a long-term perspective.
- Involve people in the quality process through a steering committee and process management teams.
- Identify the process by which customer needs and expectations are communicated, understood and fulfilled.
- Specify the cross-functional support systems utilized for the quality system.
- Identify the precise and structured methods, procedures and techniques used to improve quality.
- Delineate how education and training needs are met.

Step 2: Mission

- First determine the customer's needs and requirements.
- Next identify the company's mission with respect to the suppliers and sub-contractors.
- Finally define and establish the company's own infrastructure, responsibilities and requirements needed to interface with the suppliers and to satisfy the customers.

Step 3: Processes

- Identify all the processes impacting quality.
- Describe process requirements.
- Establish improvement goals and priorities.

Step 4: Projects

- Establish and implement improvement projects.
- Develop a measurement system to assess performance.

Step 5: Continuous Improvement

- Collect data to analyze the processes and projects.
- Institute appropriate corrective/preventive measures.
- Identify improvement opportunities.
- Develop strategic initiatives.
- Implement additional improvement projects.

Step 6: Evaluation

- Establish audit/evaluation procedures.
- Identify the system's strengths and weaknesses.
- Take appropriate management decisions.

Step 7: Review/Revision

- Repeat the continuous improvement cycle.

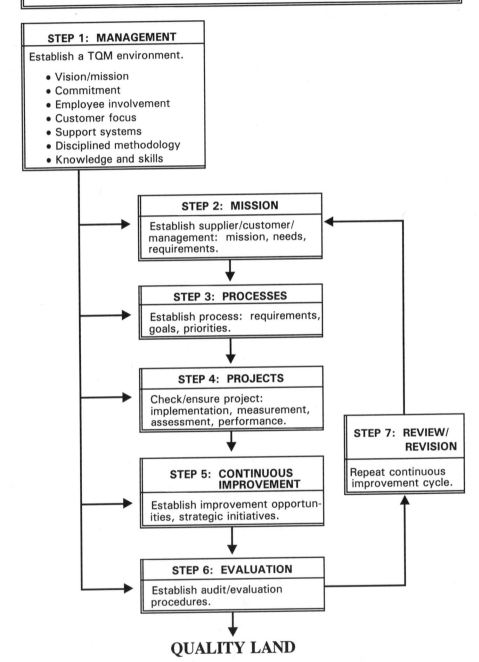

Table 16: The 7-Step TQM Model

STEP 1: MANAGEMENT

Establish a TQM environment.

- Vision/mission
- Commitment
- Employee involvement
- Customer focus
- Support systems
- Disciplined methodology
- Knowledge and skills

STEP 2: MISSION

Establish supplier/customer/management: mission, needs, requirements.

STEP 3: PROCESSES

Establish process: requirements, goals, priorities.

STEP 4: PROJECTS

Check/ensure project: implementation, measurement, assessment, performance.

STEP 7: REVIEW/REVISION

Repeat continuous improvement cycle.

STEP 5: CONTINUOUS IMPROVEMENT

Establish improvement opportunities, strategic initiatives.

STEP 6: EVALUATION

Establish audit/evaluation procedures.

QUALITY LAND

◆ PHASES OF TQM IMPLEMENTATION

Consider the following systematic sequence of steps for the design, implementation, and maintenance of the 7-Step TQM model outlined in Table 16.

Phase One

- Ensure management commitment.
- Foster management awareness/education/discussion.
- Establish a TQM Steering Committee.
- Appoint a TQM Coordinator.
- Develop a TQM mission statement.
- Identify/document a quality policy.
- Develop quality objectives.
- Provide employee orientation/awareness/education.

Phase Two

- Partner with suppliers and identify needs/requirements/mission.
- Partner with customers and identify needs/requirements/mission.
- Develop constancy/trust with suppliers and customers.
- Identify management responsibilities/mission commensurate with supplier-customer partnering.

Phase Three

- Identify all processes in the total production cycle, from the procurement of raw material to the supply of finished product.
- Establish Process Management Teams (PMT'S).
- Define process boundaries and requirements for each process.
- Define the current best process.
- Establish goals and priorities.
- Identify process control/improvement requirements and requisite resources.

Phase Four

- Implement control/improvement projects.
- Establish measures of performance.
- Assess conformance to specified requirements.
- Eliminate process variability; control the processes.
- Bring process under statistical control.

- Assess process capability.
- Take corrective/preventive action.

Phase Five

- Identify improvement opportunities.
- Establish strategic initiatives.
- Identify/allocate requisite resources.
- Continue process improvement.

Phase Six

- Establish audit/evaluation procedures.
- Review each process and take corrective/preventive action.

Phase Seven

- Repeat the entire cycle of activities, initiatives and actions to continuously improve the system.

◆ PROCESS IMPROVEMENT PLAN

The overall quality system is generally a sum total of many processes. To improve the overall system, therefore, it is imperative to concentrate efforts on improving the processes. The "PURI" - Process Enhancement Wheel (see Figure 2, Chapter 3) provides a simple and effective method for process improvement. Some of the key considerations for process improvement involve the following:

- Identify all the processes that impact quality.
- Define the current capability of the process.
- Specify the expected/required capability.
- Identify and implement improvement initiatives.
- Bring the process under statistical control.
- Analyze the process.
- Measure its performance and assess its process capability.
- Identify improvement actions and strategies.
- Repeat the continuous improvement cycle.

Consider the following four-step plan for process improvement:

Step One

- Select/define the process of interest.
- Organize PIT's (Process Improvement Teams)
- Define process boundaries/requirements.
- Establish process flow charts.
- Assess/define the present status of the process.

Step Two

- Define the process output quality.
- Identify the supplier/customer capabilities, requirements and mission.
- List the key quality characteristics.
- Set goals/priorities on the quality characteristics.

Step Three

- Identify/establish a process measurement system for the key quality characteristics.
- Obtain data/information on the process operations.
- Analyze the data with statistical process control methods.
- Identify/eliminate the causes of variability.
- Bring the process under statistical control.
- Assess the process capability.

Step Four

- Adjust the process to aim.
- Identify the key process variables.
- Evaluate cause-effect relationships for the process characteristics and the process variables.
- Reduce/eliminate variability in the process variables and consequently in the process characteristics.
- Identify improvement initiatives.
- Innovate and continuously improve the process.

◆ TQM: THE PRODUCT PROFILE

Consider now an overall application of the TQM system elements defined in the precedings sections, as they apply to the total product profile. We outline the life cycle of a product and identify its corresponding requisite TQM system elements.

Product

- Customer needs
- Market analysis
- Total product profile
- Profit-cost ratio

Design

- Design development
- Design qualification, requalification
- Design verification
- Design review/change control
- Market readiness

Procurement

- Qualified suppliers
- Receiving inspection
- Verification methods
- Quality records

Production

- Supplies, utilities, environment
- Production control
- Process control
- Process capability

Inspection

- Product identification, disposition
- Documentation
- Problem analysis

- Corrective action
- Preventive action

Marketing

- Handling, packaging and delivery
- Identification and traceability

Servicing

- Warranties, complaints
- Corrective action
- Continued post-sales service

Market Analysis

- Customer satisfaction
- Market changes
- Competition

◆ TQM: THE FINALE

Summarizing the above discussion on TQM, the following order of events is recommended for the implementation of a TQM System:

- Top management undergoes TQM orientation.
- Top management and senior executives become involved and lead the way.
- Management identifies commitment, makes quality the top priority and establishes a strategic quality plan.
- The company seeks customer involvement and input.
- Employees at all levels are trained in appropriate aspects of TQM.
- Employee involvement is sought through the establishment of a TQM Steering Committee and Process Management Teams (PMT's).
- Qualified suppliers are identified and a quality partnership is established.
- Management develops a quality policy and corresponding objectives.
- A cross-functional quality infrastructure is established with appropriate delineation of responsibilities.
- TQM elements, procedures, and processes are developed and adopted on a consistent basis.
- Quality improvement projects and initiatives are implemented.

- Data and information are collected and analyzed to study the effectiveness of the TQM System.
- System deficiencies are corrected and preventive measures are implemented.
- Quality improvement and the results are demonstrated.
- A continuous cycle of improvement is followed.

For a hands-on implementation of a TQM System, a simplified ten-phase road map is appended in Table 17.

In order to ensure effective TQM implementation and sustained quality improvement levels, a complete cultural transformation is essential. Following are some of the key factors to be considered:

- Ensure that management is truly committed and demonstrates its commitment across the entire organization.
- Develop open, responsive, group-driven quality leadership.
- Continuously reassert that quality is everyone's responsibility and not just that of a few key people. There is a need to be obsessed with quality and excellence.
- Strike out a balance between long-term goals and successive short-term objectives. Establish a sense of constancy of purpose and a focus on long-term continuous improvement.
- Use a systematic approach and disciplined methodology to clearly understand the external and internal customer requirements. Make the organization customer-satisfaction driven.
- Establish a mutually supportive control and improvement partnership with the suppliers.
- Use process management teams to involve everyone and seek improvement ideas and opportunities.
- Recognize employee achievement and establish an effective incentive program.
- Institute a continuous process of education, training, learning and self-improvement.
- Ensure that the emphasis on customer focus and continuous improvement permeates the whole organization.

Finally it must be emphasized that maintainability and sustainability of the system is of paramount importance. A TQM exercise is not an entity with a limited shelf-life; it is an exercise on a continuum, one which has no beginnings or endings. It is a race without the start or finish line. One cannot simply and abruptly start a full scale TQM program in a day and end the program at a pre-determined stipulated date. The system requires time and patience to establish and it must be sustainable. A word of advice - it would be better for an enterprise not to venture into implementing a quality system in the first place if it cannot maintain it. For, it may be possible to survive without a

Table 17: TQM Implementation: Road-Map

Phase 1: **Management Readiness**
- Management orientation/awareness
- Management blessing/commitment
- Establish a steering committee/council
- Identify TQM coordinator
- Develop vision/mission statements
- Formulate quality policy/objectives

Phase 2: **Customer-Supplier Partnering**
- Highlight and commit to customer focus
- Partner with customers to identify needs, requirements and expectations
- Partner with suppliers and specify needs, requirements and mission
- Develop constancy/trust with suppliers and customers

Phase 3: **Strategic Planning: Needs Analysis**
- Select appropriate TQM model
- Develop a master TQM implementation plan
- Identify goals/time schedules
- Identify resources

Phase 4: **Current Systems: Evaluation**
- Outline current infrastructure, responsibilities, systems, procedures, processes and methodologies
- Evaluate strengths and weaknesses of current systems vis-à-vis customer requirements and supplier capabilities
- Identify current documentation: Quality Manual, Procedures Manuals, Work Instructions

Phase 5: **Implementation Framework**
- Identify all operating processes
- Establish Process Management Teams (PMT's)
- Delineate responsibilities
- Involve/empower people

Table 17: TQM Implementation: Road-Map
(Continued)

Phase 6:   **TQM: Training**

- TQM awareness sessions for all employees
- TQM implementation: Process management sessions for key personnel
- Process improvement sessions for coordinators and key personnel responsible for developing procedures
- Provide lead-auditor/auditor training for Quality Manager, TQM coordinator and key internal auditors

Phase 7:   **System Implementation**

- Develop improvement projects
- Implement all requisite systems
- Document systems, procedures, processes

Phase 8:   **Process Improvement**

- Define the current best process
- Establish goals/strategies
- Use process improvement tools/methodologies
- Monitor/improve process

Phase 9:   **Performance Evaluation**

- Measure and statistically analyze results
- Identify/quantify improvements made
- Continuously evaluate/audit system effectiveness

Phase 10:   **Continuous Improvement**

- Continuously partner with suppliers and customers
- Identify improvement opportunities
- Establish strategic initiatives
- Allocate requisite resources
- Focus on never-ending cycle of continuous improvement

system, but having established one and lost it would be dangerously perilous. The justification for not having a quality system may be plausibly acceptable, but the loss of credibility upon failure of the system would be unrecoverable. Table 18 presents an overview of some of the salient features regarding the sustainability of a quality system.

Table 18: TQM Sustainability	
Sustainable ...if	*Not Sustainable ...if*
• Quality is a strategic issue. • Resources are used in continuous cycle. • Reliable sources of suppliers are used continuously. • Changing customer needs are accommodated. • Focus is on delighting the customer. • Systems are manageable and cost-effective. • Emphasis is on on-line process control/management. • Systems are mutually supportive. • Emphasis is on teamwork, consultative decision-making, employee empowerment and appreciation. • Change is systematic, meaningful and participatory.	• Quality is a tactical issue. • Inputs of new resources is continuously required. • Suppliers are determined on the basis of price-tag alone. • Operability is unaccomodatingly rigid. • Focus is on meeting specifications. • Systems and infrastructures becomes larger than life-size. • Emphasis is on inspecting-in quality. • Newer systems lead to the extinction of existing reliable systems. • Rigidity about quotas, deadlines, rank-order and authority is rampant. • Change is abrupt, de-humanizing and authoritative.

The key characteristics of a sustainable TQM, therefore, are:

• It is a system that keeps on going and no one thinks that TQM came and went.
• The quality system becomes a second nature to everyone.
• The system has a built-in self-correcting, self-rejuvenating and self-reenergizing mechanism.
• The system is people-driven/people empowered.
• The system ownership belongs to everyone and not just a few people in the organization.

- The management continuously supports the system and commits adequate resources.
- The system does not get overburdened by unnecessary documentation and procedural stringency, complexity or inflexibility.
- The system is flexible and controllable.
- The system is simple and user-friendly.
- The system is adequately linked to new and innovative ideas and continous improvement initiatives.
- The system makes everyone a winner.

6

THE PERSONAL TQM

◆ THE PARADIGM SHIFT

There is a new world order today. Tremendous changes have transpired in the societal infrastructure within the past few decades. Of these changes, the most predominant is the democratization of the workplace. We are back to the realization that human endeavour and commitment is singularly the most indispensable driving force for the success of any undertaking. The same holds true for the successful development of a TQM system. TQM success is virtually people-dependent.

An organization is merely a sum total of individuals. The success of any activity/ undertaking in the organization, therefore, is in direct proportion to the nature and extent of the contributions made by its members, collectively as well as individually. To make the continuous quality improvement exercise a total success, diligence of action is, therefore, required from both ends: organizational thrust and individual impetus.

In this chapter, we wish to address a rather new and unique concept - the *Personal TQM*. It is my belief that, in as much as, it is the responsibility of the organization to provide suitable operational environment, it is truly an individual's own dedication and commitment that is imperative for the success of any undertaking. The organization, indeed, bears profound responsibility for rejuvenating and reenergizing the workplace. The extent to which an individual can exploit and utilize his potential depends heavily on the receptiveness of the working environment. The organization has to endeavour to re-engineer the environment so that it is conducive to the optimal utilization of an individual's capabilities. Notwithstanding however, no amount of organizational momentum can generate sustainable quality improvement impetus unless it is genuinely supported and shared by the enthusiasm of the individual workers.

The organization can play its role in a variety of ways by proactively providing the requisite support. Some of the critical areas requiring special attention are as follows:

- Identification of individual's strengths and weaknesses
- Identification of worker's needs: operational, functional, personal
- Identification of appropriate opportunities
- Development of suitable initiatives
- Provision of adequate resources
- Provision of effective leadership and direction
- Development of team approach
- Empowerment of people
- Effective change management

A more detailed description of some of these essential entities is appended in later sections.

◆ PERSONAL TQM

Personal TQM refers to the individual's own desires and efforts to improve his performance and contributions to himself, the organization and to the society at large. It is a sense of self-imposed accountability, regimentation and genuine desire to improve quality and performance, the resultant effect of which would entail into:

- Self fulfilment, embellishment and satisfaction
- Organizational growth and enhancement
- Societal enrichment

The role of an organization can go as far as establishing viable systems and creating a suitable working environment to encourage people to achieve lasting success. The focus, of course, must be on the people rather than the system. You don't drive the systems - you have to drive the people who would then drive the system. But the irony is, that if people are not self-motivated and self-driven, no amount of organizational effort can bring fruit. As the saying goes - " you can take a horse to water, but you can't make him drink".

In this section, we are striving to make a bold attempt to appeal to the psyche of every individual worker to rise above the ordinary, to set goals for themselves, and to give their personal best, individually and collectively, towards a shared vision of excellence. Table 19 sets out the basic ten commandments of Personal TQM.

Table 19: Personal TQM
The Ten Commandments

1. Create a vision
2. Understand personal role
3. Determine personal potential
4. Respond to challenge
5. Practice participative involvement
6. Cultivate proactive attitude
7. Instill creative mindedness
8. Impose self-directed performance appraisal
9. Assess personal fulfilment
10. Exercise continuous introspective analysis

Personal TQM has very little to do with any organizational performance appraisal or rating system. It is a proactive approach to self-awakening and self-fulfilment. To generate a framework for self-super-imposing Personal TQM, the following sequence of actions is suggested:

- Introspective Analysis: identify your current state of functional performance
- Gap-Analysis: identify your strengths and weaknesses
- Needs-Analysis: identify what needs to be done to enhance your performance
- Action Plan: develop a systematic approach to implement the planned set of activities
- Performance Analysis: evaluate the extent of improvements made

As a first step to " Personal TQM", every individual should undergo an introspective analysis and identify his strengths and weaknesses, needs and requirements, personal and organizational contributions, and suitable framework for improvement. Following are some of the critical factors that needs to be probed via an introspective analysis.

Personal TQM: Introspective Analysis

- What is my role in the organization?
- In what processes am I involved?
- Do I know how/where my role/work fits in the overall organizational framework?
- Do I have the requisite resources to do my job?
- Do I have proper education/training/experience to do my job?

- Who is my inter/intra cross-functional interface?
- How helpful am I to others?
- Do I have a long-term plan to improve the quality of my work?
- Am I managing my time well?
- Am I doing my job productively?
- At the end of the day, can I tangibly identify my accomplishments?
- Have I ever analytically measured and evaluated my performance/productivity/effectiveness?
- Am I limited to doing what someone tells me or am I a self-motivated innovator?
- Am I empowered?
- Do I take control/ownership of processes in my own hands?
- Do I operate in a active or proactive mode?
- How do I work in a team environment?
- Do I actively and effectively participate in a team effort?
- Do I willingly accept responsibility?
- How do I handle change?
- What is my overall contribution to the organization?
- What is my contribution to myself?
- What is my contribution to society?

An introspective analysis such as this should provide sufficient information to proceed further to identify:

- Personal strengths and weaknesses
- Personal needs and requirements
- The nature and extent of organizational support required
- Basic framework for improvement

From here onwards, it is a joint responsibility of the management and the individual: the management to provide effective support systems for the individual's development, and the individual to work towards self-improvement and genuine concern for the welfare of the organization.

◆ QUALITY LEADERSHIP

Total quality management requires a total management transformation. To achieve sustained quality, the traditional roles of supervisors and managers have to be replaced by proactive quality leaders. Table 20 presents some of the fundamental areas where a shift in quality approach is necessary.

Table 20: Management Transformation	
Traditional Managers ⟶	**Proactive Leaders**
• Short-range view	• Long-range perspective
• Focus on mission	• Focus on mission and vision
• Focus on system structure	• Focus on people
• Controlling people	• Inspiring people
• Administering people	• Innovating people
• Blaming workers	• Sharing responsibility
• Accepting status quo	• Challenging status quo
• Focus on maintenance	• Focus on development
• Focus on fixing, correcting	• Focus on prevention
• Focus on imitation	• Focus on originality
• Doing things right	• Doing right things

Today's quality environment requires dedicated and committed leaders. The success of any TQM System is highly dependent on the people who manage, lead, drive and reenergize the system. Following are some of the typical attributes and deeds displayed by a good leader:

- Focuses on the customer
- Possesses an absolute clarity of direction, goals, mission and vision
- Has a complete determination, dedication and commitment to quality and constancy of purpose
- Functions through teamwork and helps to create more leaders
- Motivates and encourages employees, models the way and inspires a shared vision
- Provides judgement, direction as well as coaching
- Listens, forgives and generates trust
- Understands system/process variability and works towards achieving constancy and predictability
- Continually improves through training and education

Typically, the most essential elements that a leader must be cognizant of, are:

- Motivating people
- Directing/leading people
- Empowering people

Each of these elements are quite complex in nature and the leader/manager must develop a well planned and structured approach to addressing these issues. Firstly, people must be motivated to accept process ownership and responsibility and they must imbibe a sense of inner desire to proactively seek excellence in quality and a performance mindset. Experience indicates that there are two basic prerequisites to any task or undertaking that people must be informed about before motivation sets-in: "what" and "why". We would like to annotate these as the 11th and 12th commandments as appended in Table 21.

Table 21: Motivational Commandments
11TH COMMANDMENT   *People are willing to perform any task*   *once*   • They know why they are doing it   • They know what they will get out of it
12TH COMMANDMENT   *People can solve any problem*   *once*   • They can find the problem   • They have the tools to solve it

Once the motivation sets-in, the next thing people are looking for is a sense of clear direction, a road map and a facilitator/team leader to get things started. This is where the ability of the leader comes in, to engage people/teams to operate in a self-directed mode, to encourage them to talk/discuss, to direct/lead them, to make them feel valuable, and to set high exemplary standards of operability and performance. Lastly, people need to be empowered to plan strategies, make decisions, implement initiatives and take full control of the undertaking.

◆ TEAM APPROACH TO QUALITY

One of the major components of any TQM program is employee involvement and empowerment. Quality does not come through isolated and disjointed efforts; it is the result of the collective effort of all the employees at every level within the organization. As identified elsewhere, the two essential team structures required for TQM implementation are the following:

* TQM Steering Committee
* Process Management Team (PMT)

TQM Steering Committee

At the top of the quality hierarchy pyramid, the Steering Committee comprises the management representatives and the process improvement team leaders. It establishes quality strategies and improvement initiatives and oversees the effective implementation of the total quality management system. Some of the basic roles and functions of the committee are as follows:

* Developing effective quality strategies
* Identifying and initiating quality improvement projects that have the best chance of success
* Identifying requisite resources
* Monitoring progress
* Addressing/solving problems identified through Process Management Teams (PMT's) and initiating preventive actions
* Providing guidance and technical assistance
* Providing leadership
* Identifying and providing suitable education and training opportunities
* Maintaining effective communication lines and employee involvement
* Ensuring a strong customer focus in the TQM System

Process Management Team (PMT)

For each process that collectively contributes to the overall quality system structure, a process management team must be established, comprising a team leader and some key personnel responsible for the process quality improvement. A PMT provides a platform for problem identification/resolution, process improvement and employee involvement/ empowerment. The basic operational framework of a PMT involves the following components:

- Enhanced communication and involvement
- Exchange of ideas and learning from the opinions of others
- Collection and analysis of meaningful data and information
- Identification of the root causes of problems
- Developing appropriate and optimal solutions
- Planning and implementing suitable changes
- Recommending quality improvement initiatives, opportunities and strategies
- Helping to achieve teamwork and establish a quality culture

◆ PEOPLE EMPOWERMENT

When a society becomes highly democratized and there is a prevailing sense of realization and trust in human strength and commitment, the only way to tap this enormous wealth of energy is through empowerment. Born out of a fairly natural and realistic progression of events, the concept of empowerment is still, perhaps, the most widely misunderstood entity of our times. Since people are the back bone of any organization, empowerment simply means trusting people and giving them the pride and the pleasure to utilize their potential to the fullest extent to create excellence. The following description should assist in dispelling any mystery or myth as to what empowerment means or does not mean.

Empowerment does not mean:

- That anyone can function/operate independently in isolation as he/she pleases
- Chaos/anarchy/end of monarchy/abdication of throne/coup d'etat
- That the manager is stripped of all his powers, authority and responsibility
- That there is no hierarchical infrastructure operating in the organization

Empowerment means:

- Sharing a common vision
- Achieving collective benefit from individual expertise
- Creating excellence through teamwork
- Creating an integrated cross-functional interface for goal accomplishment

- Enabling people to work freely and innovatively
- Letting people have the pride in workmanship
- Allowing people to accept process ownership and responsibility
- Enabling people to focus on strategic priorities
- Focusing on standardized and disciplined approach to solving problems
- Allowing people to focus on long-term strategic responsibilities while executing short-term actions

The spectrum of empowerment is very wide - it can range from a nominal involvement to a total self-directed working environment. Empowerment is a disciplined way of working in a partnering relationship - a give and take relationship. The management puts their trust in the workers' abilities, allows them to function freely and hopes to achieve excellence in all aspects of business operability. The worker, having been given the freedom, pride and privileged to function under the umbrella of shared responsibility, without hierarchical hang-ups, feels elevated and in turn attempts to provide his personal best for the welfare and success of the organization. In all simplicity, empowerment is a win-win approach to doing business. Summarizing, empowerment typically means:

- Responsibility
- Authority
- Process ownership
- Information
- Resources
- Accountability

7

TQM MODEL VIA ISO 9004-1

◆ INTRODUCTION

There are many companies who either do not have any systematic framework and infrastructure for quality control and management or have a rudimentary and fragmented set of activities around quality. These companies have a desperate need for a simple, effective and user-friendly TQM System that can be moulded vis-à-vis the company's current resources and operability. The system has to be credible, cost-effective and easily implementable.

The quality system standard in the ISO 9000 series, "ISO 9004-1: Quality Management and Quality System Elements - Guidelines", provides just such an alternative approach for companies to establish a TQM System. The model is well-structured and easy to understand and implement. Companies who intend on seeking quality system certification to the ISO 9000 series would find it especially beneficial to utilize the approach outlined in ISO 9004-1 in developing and implementing a TQM System.

◆ PREMISE OF ISO 9004-1 (1994)

The document addresses the aspects of quality management system in relation to company's needs and interests as well as to a customer's needs and expectations. For a company, there is a business need to achieve quality at optimum cost and to ensure profitability, expanded market share and survivability. The enterprise, however, must understand that there are risks and costs associated with the production of deficient products and services, such as, loss of reputation/credibility, loss of markets, complaints, liability, waste of resources, and costs associated with repair, rework, replacement, reprocessing and warranties.

The customer, on the other hand, needs confidence in the ability of the enterprise to consistently provide high quality products and services. If the enterprise fails to provide the stipulated quality, the customer also suffers risks and associated costs such as those pertaining to loss of confidence, health and safety, availability, marketing claims, and costs associated with safety, acquisition, downtime, maintenance, repair and disposal.

It is, therefore, fundamentally important for a company to implement an effective quality management system to protect its own interests as well as to satisfy the customer's needs and expectations. To accomplish this, the system must be developed and implemented with great tenacity and must accommodate at least the following characteristics:

- It must be appropriate for the type of activity and for the product or service being offered.
- It must be commensurate with the company's quality policy and objectives.
- The system should include an effective control mechanism to prevent the recurrence of quality deficiencies.

The ISO 9004-1 has been developed with such a premise in mind. It provides guidelines for systematically implementing all aspects of total quality management. The model stresses the role of planning and preventative actions to improve quality.

◆ ISO 9004-1: TQM MODEL

ISO 9004-1 describes the quality system principles in the form of a "Quality Loop" which encompasses all the activities and phases, from the initial identification through to the final satisfaction of customer requirements and expectations. The major components of the loop are those set of elements/activities that exercise most influence and impact on quality, such as:

- Marketing and market research
- Product design and development
- Process planning and development

- Purchasing
- Production, or provision of services
- Verification
- Packaging and storage
- Sales and distribution
- Installation and commissioning
- Technical assistance and servicing
- Post market surveillance
- Disposal or recycling at the end of useful life

Having identified the key elements, the document sets out to provide detailed guidelines for developing a structured quality system. Each element of the system and its requisite framework is laid out systematically. For an easy and quick reference, a summary checklist of the ISO 9004-1 system elements is appended in Table 22. A more detailed discussion of the system elements and a TQM implementation plan is provided in the next section.

The overall approach adopted by the standard is basically the same and is compatible with any other quality management approach based on the fundamental principles of quality. The major focus of the system revolves around the following five components that comprise the TQM framework:

- **Quality Management System:** includes all the quality management aspects such as management responsibility, policy, management systems, control systems, cost systems, evaluation systems, improvement systems, market analysis, resource allocation, etc.

- **Quality Control:** comprises all the critical control points and the operational and technical aspects of controlling quality during production.

- **Procurement Quality Assurance:** includes the quality assurance procedures required to ensure a supply of high quality input.

- **Internal Quality Assurance:** contains the in-house assessment procedures to ensure on-line process control and off-line product quality.

- **External Quality Assurance:** provides a contractual quality assurance protocol to ensure to the regulatory authority, the purchaser, or ultimately the consumer, that the delivered product is of high quality.

Table 22: ISO 9004-1: TQM System Elements - Master Checklist

- **Management responsibility:** quality policy and objectivies, planning, management system, organizational structure and responsibilities.

- **Structure of the quality system:** quality responsibility and authority, organizational structure, resources and personnel, operational procedures, configuration management.

- **Documentation of the quality system:** quality policies and procedures, quality manual, procedures manuals, work instructions, quality plans, quality records.

- **Auditing the quality system:** audit program, extent of audits, audit reporting, follow-up action.

- **Review and evaluation of the quality system:** management reviews, independent evaluation, internal audits.

- **Quality improvement:** management commitment/support, quality values/ attitudes, improvement goals, teamwork, recognition/incentive programs, education/training.

- **Financial considerations of quality systems:** selection of appropriate methods of financial reporting of quality system activities/methods: quality costing method, gain/cost ratio method, quality loss method, quality cost categories (detection, appraisal, prevention, internal failure, external failure), cost reporting to management.

- **Quality in marketing:** analysis of market requirements, defining product specifications, customer feedback information.

- **Quality in specification and design:** design planning and objectives, product testing and measurement, design review, design verification, design qualification/validation, final design review and production release, market readiness review, design change control, design requalification, configuration management in design.

- **Quality in purchasing:** definitions of purchasing requirements (specifications, drawings, purchase orders), selection of acceptable sub-contractors, agreement with sub-contractors on quality assurance requirements and verification methods, methods of dispute settlement, planning and control of receiving inspection, maintenance of quality records related to purchasing.

- **Quality of processes:** planning for process control, process capability studies, control of supplies/utilities/environment, control in handling of product-incoming, in-process and final.

Table 22: ISO.9004-1: TQM System Elements - Master Checklist (continued)

- **Control of processes:** material control, traceability and identification of product, equipment control and maintenance, process control management, documentation control, process change control, control of verification status, control of nonconforming product.

- **Product verification:** verification of incoming material's and parts, in-process verification, finished product verification.

- **Control of inspection, measuring and test equipment:** measurement control, all requisite calibration control elements, sub-contractor measurement control, corrective action, control of outside testing/calibration.

- **Control of nonconforming product:** identification, segregation, review, disposition, action on nonconformities, avoidance of recurrence of nonconformities.

- **Corrective action:** identification of nonconformities for corrective action from sources such as: audits, process nonconformity reports, management reviews, market feedback, customer complaints; assignment of responsibility for corrective action; evaluation of importance of activity on quality; investigation of possible causes; analysis of problem, elimination of causes; process controls, permanent changes.

- **Post-production activities:** storage, delivery, installation, servicing, post marketing surveillance, market feedback.

- **Quality records:** documented procedures for identification collection, indexing, access, filing, storage, maintenance, retrieval and disposition of quality records; quality records: inspection reports, test data, qualification and validation reports, survey and audit reports, etc.; control of quality records.

- **Personnel:** training: general, executive and management personnel, technical personnel, process supervisors and operating personnel; qualifications; motivation: quality awareness, measurement of quality.

- **Product safety:** safety standards, designing for safety, analyzing information for safety, traceability to facilitate product recall, development of emergency plans.

- **Use of statistical methods:** application of statistical methods to: market analysis, product design, reliability specifications, capability studies, process improvement, safety evaluation and risk analysis, etc.; use of statistical techniques such as: design of experiments, tests of significance, control charts, statistical sampling, etc.

A TQM model based on ISO 9004-1 can be conveniently developed by appropriately rearranging the identified system elements commensurate with the type of activity and the nature of products and services offered by the organization. A detailed TQM document or quality manual must be prepared, addressing these system elements and describing the management responsibilities, systems, procedures, processes and methodologies operating in the company.

◆ TQM: THE MANAGEMENT PROFILE

The guidelines presented in ISO 9004-1 can be utilized in a variety of ways to develop a TQM System. For example, a company can structure its TQM plan on the framework of the following elements. For each of the elements itemized below, a clear set of instructions must be outlined in the Quality Manual and Procedures Manuals so as to facilitate an effective implementation of the quality system.

Management Responsibility

- Quality policy
- Quality objectives
- Organizational responsibilities
- Organizational infrastructure
- Resources and personnel

Management Systems

- Operational framework
- Quality plans
- Quality manual
- Quality procedures
- Quality records
- Reporting system
- Communication system
- Management reviews

Control Systems

- Design/specification control
- Material/equipment control
- Process control
- Change/verification control
- Nonconformance control
- Documentation control
- Post-production/servicing control

Cost System

- Operating quality costs: appraisal, failure, prevention
- External quality costs
- Cost reporting system

Evaluation System

- Incoming inspection
- In-process inspection
- Final inspection
- Measurement system
- Performance evaluation
- Problem analysis
- Corrective/preventive action

Quality Improvement System

- Quality awareness program
- Education/training
- Productivity improvement programs
- Employee motivation
- Merit award system

◆ TQM IMPLEMENTATION VIA ISO 9004-1

As indicated earlier, ISO 9004-1 provides a suitable alternative for implementing a TQM System. By using this model, a company can minimize or eliminate the aggravation and need to search for an appropriate TQM model, approach or philosophy. However, it is also imperative for an enterprise to understand clearly the strengths and weaknesses of the ISO 9004-1 approach before venturing into its full application.

Strengths of ISO 9004-1

- The Standard does not attempt to enforce uniformity of quality systems across varying organizations and functions, but only provides basic guidelines for implementing a quality system. The model, therefore, can be easily moulded to suit any company's operations.
- The Standard provides an easy, systematic, well-structured and regimented approach.
- The model can be implemented with a minimal of external assistance.
- Implementing TQM via this model will facilitate the process of ISO 9000 certification, if a company wishes to achieve one.

Weaknesses of ISO 9004-1

- The system is slightly lacking on the humanistic, motivational, leadership and cultural aspects of quality. Therefore, an enterprise would have to augment the system with additional activities to ensure that quality is permeated to all levels in the organization and everyone is involved in the exercise.
- The system does not have enough emphasis on the maintenance and continuous improvement aspects of quality. Consequently, additional measures are required to ensure a long-term focus on quality.

Structure of ISO 9004-1

The primary intent of the standard is to emphasize the need for focusing attention on the quality of products and services. The success of an organization is dependent on offering products/services that, as a minimum, have the following attributes:

- Meets a well defined specific need, use or purpose.
- Meets or exceeds customer's expectations.
- Is competitively priced and economically affordable.
- Complies with all regulatory, environmental and societal requirements, needs, specifications, and expectations.

The standard compartmentalizes the quality system elements into the following categories and provides detailed guidelines on the implementation activities associated with each element.

- Management responsibility
- Quality system elements
- Financial considerations of quality systems
- Quality in marketing
- Quality in specification and design
- Quality in purchasing
- Quality in processes
- Control of processes
- Control of inspection, measuring and test equipment
- Control of nonconforming product
- Corrective action
- Post production activities
- Quality records
- Personnel
- Product safety
- Use of statistical methods

ISO 9004-1: TQM Implementation Guidelines

- **Management Responsibility**
  - Identify management readiness; awareness; commitment and involvement.
  - Formulate a steering group/committee.
  - Develop and document quality policy commensurate with company's needs; goals and expectations, as well as customer's expectations.
  - Document quality objectives and goals.
  - Formulate a strategic plan to develop a quality system implementation road map.

- **Quality System Elements**
  - Identify all phases of life cycle of the product.
  - Develop a structure of the quality system, defining all interfaces.
  - Delineate appropriate quality responsibilities and authority.
  - Establish requisite organizational functions related to the quality system.
  - Identify and procure all requisite resources and personnel to implement and maintain the quality system.
  - Define and organize all operational procedures and establish methods of control of quality.
  - Establish procedures for configuration management to assist in the operation and control of design/development/production/use of product. Configuration management may include: configuration identification, control and audit.
  - Document the system properly via several tiers of requisite documents such as: Quality Manual, Procedures Manual and/or Work Instructions.
  - Develop effective quality plans for the system activities.
  - Develop and establish procedures for maintaining quality records.
  - Establish and maintain comprehensive procedures for auditing the quality system implementation/effectiveness.
  - Establish procedures and an environment for continuous quality improvement activities.

- **Financial Considerations of Quality System**
  - Cost-effectiveness of the quality system is a critical factor for almost all companies. Procedures should, therefore, be established to collect, analyze and report all financial aspects of quality system implementation/maintenance/improvement to ensure effective functioning of the system.

- **Quality in Marketing**
  - Develop a framework for market needs-analysis and total product profile:
    - Type/nature of product needed
    - Design/specification of product
    - Customer's requirements/expectations
    - Nature/extent of competition

- **Quality in Specification and Design**
  - Establish a plan for each design/development activity. The activities would include:
    - Delegation of responsibilities
    - Organizational and technical interfaces
    - Design specification/requirements
    - Customer needs
    - Safety/regulatory requirements
    - Acceptance criteria
    - Testing/measurement methods
    - Design output approval criteria

- Establish procedures for:
  - Design review with respect to customer needs, product/process specification requirements
  - Design verification
  - Design qualification/validation
  - Final design review and production release
  - Market readiness review
  - Design change control
  - Design requalification
  - Configuration management in design

- **Quality in Purchasing**
  - The purchasing quality program should include the following elements as a minimum:
    - Applicable issues of specifications/drawings/technical data/purchase orders
    - Selection of qualified subcontractors
    - Agreement on quality assurance
    - Agreement on verification methods
    - Provision for settlement of disputes
    - Receiving inspection procedures
    - Receiving controls
    - Receiving quality records

- **Quality of Processes**
  - All processes that impact quality must be operated under controlled conditions, including: controls for materials; approved production, installation, and servicing equipment; documented procedures or quality plans; computer software; reference standards; handling of materials/products; approval of processes/personnel/supplies/utilities/environments.
  - Establish documented procedures and/or work instruction for control of processes.
  - Establish statistical process control methods and quality improvement tools/ techniques to control and improve processes.
  - Establish monitoring/verification procedures.
  - Conduct process capability studies.

- **Control of Processes**
  - Establish documented control procedures for:
    - Material control, traceability and identification
    - Equipment control and maintenance
    - Process control management

- Control of verification status
- Control of nonconforming product

- **Product Verification**
  - Establish documented procedures for:
    - Incoming materials and parts verification
    - In-process verification
    - Finished product verification

- **Control of Inspection, Measuring and Test Equipment**
  - Establish control procedures over all measuring systems used in the production/ development/installation/servicing of product.
  - Establish procedures to monitor the measuring process itself.
  - Establish calibration procedures for all inspection, measuring and test equipment, including test software and hardware.
  - Extend the control procedures and test methods for the measuring, test equipment to all subcontractors also.

- **Control of Nonconforming Product**
  - Establish control procedures for the identification/segregation/review/disposition of nonconforming materials and products.
  - Prompt corrective/preventative action must be taken on nonconformities.

- **Corrective Action**
  - Establish procedures for taking corrective action on nonconforming product. Specific actions may include:
    - Delineation of responsibility
    - Evaluation of importance of impact on quality
    - Investigation of possible causes
    - Analysis of problem
    - Elimination of causes
    - Process controls
    - Implementation of changes resulting from corrective action

- **Post Production Activities**
  - Appropriate procedures are required to be established for post-production activities, such as:
    - Storage
    - Delivery
    - Installation

- Servicing
- Post marketing surveillance
- Market feedback

- **Quality Records**
  - Establish a system to maintain and control all quality records on: test/ calibration data; reports from inspection, qualification, validation, survey and audits, material review, and quality related costs.
  - Documents requiring control may include: drawings; specifications; inspection procedures and instructions; test procedures; work instructions; operation sheets; quality manual; quality plans; operational procedures; and quality system procedures.

- **Personnel**
  - Establish procedures to control activities related to personnel, such as:
    - Training of personnel: executive, management, technical, process supervisors and operators
    - Qualification of personnel
    - Motivational aspects of personnel

- **Product Safety**
  - The TQM system should also take into consideration the safety aspects of product, such as:
    - Meeting requisite safety standards and regulations
    - Testing of designs and prototypes
    - Developing/maintaining requisite safety instruction manuals and procedures
    - Developing means of product traceability and recall
    - Developing an emergency plan

- **Use of Statistical Methods**
  - Establish documented procedures for the application of statistical methods to all processes, including: market analysis; product design; reliability specification, longevity and durability predictions; process control and process capability studies; determination of quality levels in sampling inspection plans; data analysis; process improvement; safety evaluation and risk analysis.
  - Specific statistical techniques may include: design of experiments, sampling methods, statistical process control, Pareto analysis, etc.

8

SERVICE QUALITY
MANAGEMENT/CERTIFICATION

◆ SERVICE QUALITY

A large proportion of our industrial infrastructure comprises service organizations, yet very little is done towards managing the quality of services. This incongruity may perhaps be due to our:

- Excessive preoccupation with quality of manufactured products.
- Assumptions that service quality is of secondary importance.
- Difficulty in defining roles and functions of a service.
- Inability to define service quality characteristics.
- Lack of knowledge and expertise for developing a service TQM model.

The trends and activities in the domain of quality have undergone tremendous changes during the past two decades. There is a market-driven quality revolution and its impact is now being felt equally in the manufacturing and the service sectors. While demanding high quality products at competitive prices, the customers are also expecting excellence in services. Service quality management has taken on a new perspective and there is an ever increasing interest in service quality improvement.

What is a service? Basically, a service can be defined as an activity that does not produce a product. The international standard ISO 8402 defines a service as:

> "**Service**: Results generated by activities at the interface between the supplier and the customer and by supplier's internal activities to meet the customer needs."

The following "notes" also accompany this definition in the standard:

- The supplier or the customer may be represented at the interface by personnel or equipment.
- Customer activities at the interface with the supplier may be essential to the service delivery.
- Delivery or use of tangible products may form part of the service delivery.
- A service may be linked with the manufacture and supply of a tangible product.

Service quality implies the quality of the internal as well as external processes that lead to providing services that meet the customer's needs and requirements. Generally, service quality is referenced with respect to the following two situations:

- Service that is directly related to a tangible entity or product, ie., the after-sales servicing function associated with the sale of a manufactured product
- Service that is solely an intangible service entity with little or no product involved

The quality aspects of product-related servicing function, being an integral part of any product-oriented TQM System, has been adequately covered in the preceding chapters. In this chapter, we shall outline the development and implementation of a TQM System as applicable to organizations that are involved solely in the provision of intangible services. Some examples of such services are: banks, department stores, large scale retailers, hotels, restaurants, taxis, airlines, amusement clubs, communications, health, education, financial, legal and consulting services, etc.

◆ SERVICE QUALITY CHARACTERISTICS

Although the basic principles of quality management are universally applicable to manufacturing as well as service operations, services have some unique and special characteristics that must be carefully taken into consideration when developing a service TQM model. Some of these special features may include the following:

- Services are intangible even when they may involve tangible products.
- Services are personalized.
- Services also involve the customer to whom service is being delivered.
- Services are produced on demand.
- Services cannot be manufactured prior to delivery.
- Services are produced and consumed at the same time.

- Services cannot be shown or exhibited prior to delivery.
- Services are perishable; they cannot be stored or stocked.
- Services cannot be inspected or tested.
- Services do not produce defects, scrap or rejects.
- Service quality deficiencies cannot be eliminated before delivery.
- Services cannot be substituted or sold as second choice.
- Services are labour-intensive; they may involve complex cross-functional integration of several support systems.

◆ SERVICE QUALITY DIMENSIONS

Measuring and evaluating the quality of manufactured products is not so difficult. Standards of conformance can be set, products can be inspected and tested, defective rates can be identified, deficiencies can be corrected, and performance levels can be established.

In comparison, service quality performance is hard to measure because services are intangible, perishable and subjective in nature. It is the customer who decides what constitutes a quality service. The customer generally bases his evaluation process on such characteristics as: his image, expectations, and perceptions about quality; the way the service is delivered; the end result of the service; and the extent of his satisfaction. Most of these characteristics are hard to quantify. Measuring service quality, therefore, poses a phenomenal challenge -anticipating customer's wants, needs and expectations for something that is intangible, involves the customer himself, cannot be seen or tested, and may be judged on purely subjective idiosyncratic basis.

Another difficulty with evaluating service quality is that there are no standards against which to measure performance. Service quality standards are difficult to establish because service is subjectively measurable and every customer has his or her own set of expectations and perspectives about what constitutes a quality service.

Despite the obvious difficulties in measuring, evaluating or standardizing quality service performance, however, the following attributes are considered essential to service operations:

- Efficiency, accuracy
- Consistency, constancy

- Responsiveness, approachability
- Dependability, reliability
- Competence, capability
- Safety, security
- Courtesy, care, understanding
- Price, affordability
- Satisfaction, delight

Commensurate with these quality dimensions, we can outline some of the key factors in a customer's expectations of a quality treatment:

- Prompt attention
- Understanding of what the customer wants
- Complete and undivided attention
- Courteous and polite treatment
- Expression of interest in the customer
- Responsiveness to a query
- Expression of proactive helpfulness
- Efficiency in the delivery of service
- Accuracy in the end result of service
- Explanation of procedures
- Expression of pleasure in serving the customer
- Expression of thanks
- Attention to complaints
- Resolution of complaints to the customer's satisfaction
- Acceptance of responsibility for personal or company errors

◆ DEVELOPING A SERVICE TQM MODEL

Like any manufacturing situation, continuous service quality improvement also requires the implementation of an integrated total quality system. The basic framework of a service TQM model is no different from that for the manufactured products. Therefore, any of the methods and approaches outlined in earlier chapters can be applied, with appropriate modifications, to develop the system.

Notwithstanding, it is essential to clearly understand the distinct differences and similarities that exist between the manufacturing and service situations.

Quality system implementation is relatively easier in the manufacturing situations because all the processes involved in the production of the product are clearly identifiable. All that remains to be done is to delineate responsibilities, allocate resources and establish appropriate systems, procedures and processes. The sequence of steps in the production cycle are systematic and everyone has a clearly well-defined and distinct role to play.

The situation with service industries is, however, not as simple. The process steps may be identifiable, but the collective cross-functional integration and understanding of each other's roles and functions may not be evident. The customer, for example, does not buy from the CEO, the manager or the owner. The customer's contact is limited to the front desk, the salesperson who is actually delivering the service. These and only these persons typically determine the quality of the service rendered. The management may not even be aware of the actual service quality level. Thus, in the case of service operations, a well coordinated process improvement system has to be established and the entire infrastructure of the organization has to be involved.

The basic similarities and differences between manufacturing and service operations can be summarized as follows:

Manufacturing vs Services: Similarities

- Creating the Quality environment/culture
- Management commitment/involvement
- Team approach to problem-solving and decision-making
- Employee involvement/empowerment
- Education and training
- Customer focus
- Continuous improvement emphasis

Manufacturing vs Services: Differences

- Developing a strong proactive customer feedback/feed-forward system
- Needs analysis vis-à-vis customer's specifications
- Definition/concept of a process
- Measurement/qualification/analysis of information
- Creating effective personnel motivational programs
- General nature of business and business delivery

In view of the above discussion, a typical service TQM model is suggested here in Table 23. The main elements of the model almost follow the same sequence as the generic TQM model described earlier in Chapter 5.

Table 23: Service TQM Model

Step 1: Customer Needs
Step 2: Management Responsibility
Step 3: Service Processes
Step 4: Improvement Projects
Step 5: Continuous Improvement
Step 6: Evaluation
Step 7: Review/Revision

Step 1: Customer Needs

- Define and identify customer needs and requirements.
- Develop a system to identify customer's expectations.
- Identify customer's perspective relating to:
  - Service quality characteristics/attributes
  - Service delivery attributes
  - Service end result expectations
  - Satisfaction criteria
- Use all possible means to obtain customer's input: surveys, questionnaires, observations, mail/personal/telephone interviews, complaints, etc.

Step 2: Management Responsibility

- Define your mission.
- Establish policies, objectives, goals.
- Identify the nature of your service.
- Establish improvement infrastructure: process management teams, steering committee.
- Identify all the processes that collectively make up the service.
- Identify the service competency vis-à-vis customer's needs.
- Develop a quality improvement plan.
- Identify service deficiencies.
- Identify the activities and actions needed to eliminate deficiencies to satisfy customer requirements.
- Identify your suppliers and subcontractors.
- Identify the supplier's strengths and weaknesses.
- Establish a partnership with the suppliers.

Step 3: Service Processes

- Identify all the processes involved in the service.
- Define process goals and priorities.
- Define process requirements and boundaries.
- Flow chart the processes.
- Evaluate process capability.
- Identify improvement opportunities.

Step 4: Improvement Projects

- Establish and implement improvement projects.
- Establish a measurement system to assess performance.
- Report the quality and service information data.

Step 5: Continuous Improvement

- Collect data to analyze the processes and projects.
- Review reports and performance levels.
- Analyze the nature and extent of errors, trends and quality costs.
- Institute appropriate corrective/preventive measures.
- Monitor implementation.
- Assess improvements made.
- Identify further improvement opportunities.
- Develop strategic initiatives.
- Implement additional improvement projects.

Step 6: Evaluation

- Establish audit/evaluation procedures.
- Identify the system's strengths and weaknesses.
- Audit the procedural compliance.
- Monitor the data integrity.
- Take appropriate management decisions.

Step 7: Review/Revision

- Repeat the continuous improvement cycle.

◆ THE CUSTOMER FOCUS

As is evidenced, one aspect that clearly deserves special attention in a service quality operation is the role of the customer. A customer is the most important person in a service business. In fact, service business is totally customer-dependent.

The following quotation aptly and succinctly defines the role and importance of a customer:

> *"A customer is the most important visitor on our premises. He is not dependent on us. We are dependent on him. He is not an interruption on our work. He is the purpose of it. He is not an outsider on our business. He is part of it. We are not doing him a favor by serving him. He is doing us a favor by giving us an opportunity to do so."*
>
> **Mahatma Gandhi**

Service organizations must be cognizant of this fact and they should ensure that customer remains the focal point of all planning activities. Every process, procedure or initiative that is put into place for improving service quality must, therefore, viably address and accom-modate the customer's needs and expectations.

In a sense we are all customers. When we walk into an organization to receive a service, we have a set of expectations about the service delivery mode (see Figure 3). The first thing that we are looking for is: responsiveness, courtesy and helpfulness. Then we are looking for competency, efficiency and dependability of service. Lastly, we expect the service to be of high quality, competitively affordable and satisfying.

A continuous evaluation of the customer's needs, requirements and perceptions about service quality is fundamentally important for profitability and competitive survival. All possible means should be utilized to obtain customer's input. It is absolutely essential to know what characteristics of the service pleases or displeases a customer. This information is vitally important to institute any measure of process improvement. Customer feedback can be obtained by any of the well-established available methods of data/information collection, such as:

- Questionnaires: on-site or by mail
- Interviews: personal or by telephone
- Surveys

The structure and format of the technique for obtaining customer feedback must be commensurate with the nature of business operations and the needs and expectations of the customer vis-à-vis the service.

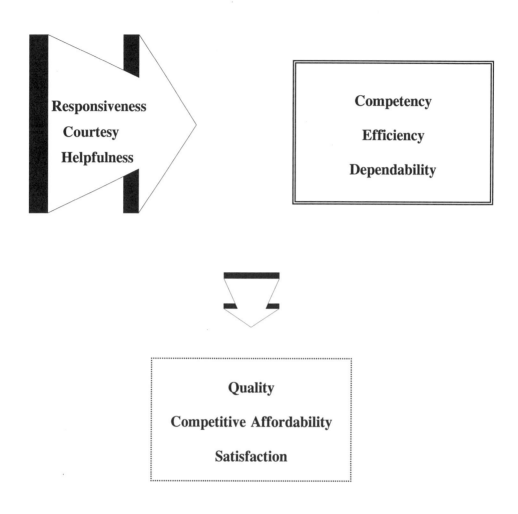

Figure 3: Customer's Basic Expectations

◆ THE *UPSIDE-DOWN* SERVICE MODEL

Another important aspect to discuss is the role of the "front-desk" - the persons at the front end who are responsible for the actual delivery of service. As indicated earlier, customers do not buy from the CEOs. They buy or are serviced by individuals who do the work: salespersons, repair persons, telephone clerks, bank tellers, waiters, etc. These are the people who impact the quality of the service rendered.

A large majority of service organizations fail to improve quality and consequently fail to remain competitive because they utilize what we have termed here "The *Upside-Down Service Model*" (see Table 24). It is a model in which the quality management activities run from top to bottom rather than bottom-up.

Companies fail to realize that the most important entity in a service operation is the "front-desk", the personnel who actually physically comes into direct contact with the customers during the process of service delivery. Companies spend phenomenal amounts of time and resources in implementing a service TQM model throughout the organization from top to bottom but fail to put greater emphasis where it is due - the "front-desk".

Our actual life experiences are replete with examples which testify to the fact that for each situation where we have received the service, with or without quality, our contact has been mainly with one or two specific persons providing the service on behalf of the organization. The span of such organizations range from restaurants, hotels, financial institutions, airline travels, department stores, government offices, etc.

Whenever the quality of service received is good, we would repetitively like to seek the same service, entity or organization. On the other hand, if we have experienced aggravation and dissatisfaction with the service, we would tend to take any one or more of the following actions, depending on our personal mode of operability:

- Walk out quietly with what we get, knowing well that we are not coming back there again and that we would be going to another competitor.
- Make a scene and/or report to the manager.
- Recite the "dissatisfaction story" over and over again to friends; intuitively in the hope that no one will ever go to that organization for services.

The points to be pondered by service organizations from this scenario of "poor quality service delivery" are the following:

- How often would a dissatisfied customer go right up to the Chief Executive Officer (CEO) to make a complaint - almost never?
- How often would a CEO come to know that the quality of service provided to the customer by his employees was not good and the customer was dissatisfied - almost never?

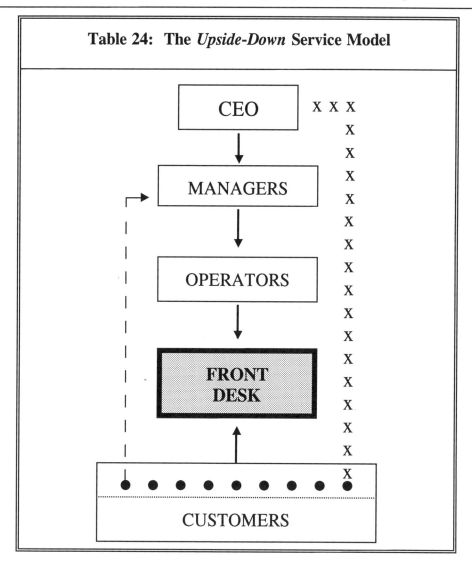

Table 24: The *Upside-Down* Service Model

It is no wonder, then, that many organizations fail to understand why despite their best efforts and high-powered quality programs, they are losing customers and markets. The basic reason of failures is that the quality improvement efforts are not targeted appropriately. The answer to this dilemma is simple:

- Improve your "front-desk - the missing link".
- Select personnel on the basis of their ability and willingness to deal with people.
- Motivate people. Establish and implement effective programs to improve communication skills.
- Establish means for measuring performance.

- Continuously seek customer feedback through any one of the many well-established methods of data/information collection.
- Analyze the information and utilize the results to augment/improve the systems.
- Go out of your way to extend your hand to reach the customer.

◆ ISO 9004-2: SERVICE TQM MODEL

Another excellent source of information for developing a service TQM model is the International Standard: "ISO 9004-2 (1991): Quality Management and Quality System Elements - Part 2: Guidelines for Services." This standard is a useful addition to the ISO-9000 series and has been prepared on the same basic quality management principles as given in the ISO-9000 to ISO-9004 series of international standards. Table 25 provides a list of elements covered in ISO 9004-2. The model presented in ISO 9004-2 can be suitably applied to many types of services, such as: Administration, Communications, Financial Services, Health Services, Hospitality Services, Maintenance, Professional Services, Purchasing, Scientific Services, Trading, and Utilities. In this section, we shall present a basic framework of the systems elements as outlined in ISO 9004-2 for implementing a TQM system for service organizations.

In this chapter, we are also presenting a road map for preparing for ISO 9000 certification. For more extensive and in-depth details of systems elements, the reader is advised to consult the standard.

The approach outlined in ISO 9004-2 for developing a total quality system for services recommends the following sequence of activities:

- Defining and identifying service quality characteristics and a service delivery mechanism.
- Establishing management responsibilities and infrastructure.
- Identifying, developing and improving personnel and material resources.
- Establishing a quality system structure.
- Interfacing with customers.
- Planning and developing operational procedures.

Table 25: ISO 9004-2: System Elements

5. Quality system principles
5.1 Key aspects of a quality system
5.2 Management responsibility
  5.2.1 General
  5.2.2 Quality policy
  5.2.3 Quality objectives
  5.2.4 Quality responsibility and authority
  5.2.5 Management review
5.3 Personnel and material resources
  5.3.1 General
  5.3.2 Personnel
    5.3.2.1 Motivation
    5.3.2.2 Training and development
    5.3.2.3 Communication
  5.3.3 Material resources
5.4 Quality system structure
  5.4.1 General
  5.4.2 Service quality loop
  5.4.3 Quality documentation and records
    5.4.3.1 Documentation system
    5.4.3.2 Documentation control
  5.4.4 Internal quality audits
5.5 Interface with customers
  5.5.1 General
  5.5.2 Communication with customers
6. Quality system operational elements
6.1 Marketing process
  6.1.1 Quality in market research and analysis
  6.1.2 Supplier obligations
  6.1.3 Service brief
  6.1.4 Service management
  6.1.5 Quality in advertising
6.2 Design process
  6.2.1 General
  6.2.2 Design responsibilities
  6.2.3 Service specification
  6.2.4 Service delivery specification
    6.2.4.1 General

    6.2.4.2 Service delivery procedures
    6.2.4.3 Quality in procurement
    6.2.4.4 Supplier-provided equipment to customers for service and service delivery
    6.2.4.5 Service identification and traceability
    6.2.4.6 Handling, storage, packaging, delivery and protection of customers' possessions
  6.2.5 Quality control specification
  6.2.6 Design review
  6.2.7 Validation of service, service delivery and quality control specifications
  6.2.8 Design change control
6.3 Service delivery process
  6.3.1 General
  6.3.2 Supplier's assessment of service quality
  6.3.3 Customer's assessment of service quality
  6.3.4 Service status
  6.3.5 Corrective action for nonconforming service
    6.3.5.1 Responsibilities
    6.3.5.2 Identification of nonconformity and corrective action
  6.3.6 Measurement system control
6.4 Service performance analysis and improvement
  6.4.1 General
  6.4.2 Data collection and analysis
  6.4.3 Statistical Methods
  6.4.4 Service quality improvement

Service Quality Characteristics

- Identify service requirements in terms of the customer's perspectives, expectations or characteristics by which the customer evaluates the service quality.
- Identify the service delivery characteristics.
- Establish an effective service delivery system.
- Monitor, control and evaluate the delivery process.

Management Responsibilities

- Define the company's mission/vision.
- Identify and document quality policies, goals and objectives.
- Develop appropriate service quality infrastructure.
- Assign quality responsibilities and authority.
- Establish quality steering committee and process improvement teams.
- Establish a management review process for the quality system.

Personnel Resources

- Select personnel on the basis of capability to satisfy a defined job specification.
- Provide a work environment that fosters excellence.
- Develop innovative motivational programs for employees.
- Involve everyone through PMTs (Process Management Teams) in quality improvement activities.
- Foster an atmosphere of trust, respect, recognition and empowerment.
- Identify requisite training needs and establish appropriate training and development programs.
- Continuously conduct quality awareness sessions.
- Encourage people to continuously expand their knowledge base.
- Carry out extensive training for personnel in the art of effective communication.
- Establish an effective internal communication network.
- Foster team approach to problem solving and decision making.

Material Resources

- Identify, develop and acquire requisite material resources, such as:
  - Service provisioning equipment and stores
  - Operational needs such as accommodation provisions, transport and information systems
  - Quality assessment facilities, instrumentation and computer software
  - Operational and technical documentation.

Quality System Structure

- Develop, establish, document, implement and maintain a quality system identifying the means by which stated quality policies and objectives are to be accomplished.

- Document the quality system in:
  - Quality manual
  - Procedures manual
  - Quality plan
  - Quality records
- Establish quality system procedures, such as:
  - Document control
  - Internal quality audits
- Establish quality system operational elements:
  - Marketing process
  - Design process
  - Service delivery process
  - Service performance analysis and improvement

Interface with Customers

- Effective interaction and communication between the customers and the service organization's personnel must be established. Communication with customers involves identification of such service characteristics as:
  - Scope and availability of service
  - Cost of service
  - Interrelationship between service, delivery and cost
  - Mechanism for resolution of complaints
  - Customer feedback mechanism

Quality System Operational Elements

The operational elements consist of the three main service provisioning processes: marketing, design and service delivery. Also part of the operational aspect of quality system is the element of "service performance analysis and improvement". These processes operate in a "service quality loop" that can be described as follows:

- Service needs-analysis is formulated between the supplier and the customer.
- Service brief is prepared.
- Service design process is initiated. Service design is vis-à-vis service specifications as well as service delivery specifications.
- Service delivery process is established.
- Service results are assessed by the supplier as well as the customer.
- The supplier conducts service performance analysis and improvement.
- The customer provides feedback on:
  - The way service is delivered
  - The end result of the service
  - The extent of customer satisfaction

- The loop is closed by utilizing the results of overall analysis and feedback to re-evaluate or redesign the service marketing and design process.

Let us now consider some further details of the key elements involved in these quality system operational processes.

Marketing Process

- Carry out a needs-analysis to determine and promote the need and demand for the service.
- Prepare a profile of customer needs and expectations.
- Develop a framework of the requisite service.
- Identify the need for any additional complimentary services for supplementing the basic service framework.
- Develop a profile of competitor activities and performances.
- Identify the requisite legislative/regulatory requirements, if any.
- Carry out ongoing market evaluation to determine changing market trends.
- Document, explicitly or implicitly expressed, company's obligations towards guarantees/warranties.
- Prepare a service brief.
- Establish procedures for planning, organizing and implementing the launch of the service.
- Delineate appropriate functional responsibilities for service operability.
- Acquire requisite resources to provide effective service.
- Establish well-planned advertising strategy to gain competitive advantages.

Design Process

- Process of designing a service involves converting the service brief into service specifications and service delivery specifications vis-à-vis customer's needs and company's policies and capabilities. Service specification defines the service to be provided; service delivery specification defines the means and methods of service delivery.
- Establish strategic plans to meet variations in the service demand.
- Establish procedures for identifying nonconformities and taking corrective/preventive action.
- Establish appropriate design responsibilities for:
  - Planning, preparing, maintaining and controlling service specifications and service delivery specifications
  - Procurement of products/services for service delivery process
  - Designing and establishing quality control and process control procedures as an integral part of service operations
  - Implementing design review process
  - Verifying/validating/reviewing service delivery process
  - Updating/augmenting/improving system effectiveness

- Service specifications should include:
  - Complete and precise statement of the service to be provided
  - Service characteristics and its standards of acceptability
  - Protocol for customer evaluation of service characteristics
- Service delivery specifications should include:
  - Service delivery procedures
  - Standards of acceptability
  - Service delivery resource requirements
  - Procedures for control of purchasing
  - Procedures for handling of supplier provided equipment to customers for service delivery
  - Service identification and traceability procedures
  - Procedures for handling, storage, packaging, preservation and delivery
  - Quality/process control procedures
  - Design review mechanism
  - Validation/verification procedures
  - Design change control procedures

Service Delivery Process

- Assign appropriate responsibilities for service delivery.
- Comply with service delivery specifications.
- Monitor to ensure that service specifications are met.
- Adjust process when deviations occur.
- Establish service quality measurement system.
- Assess service quality at regular intervals.
- Establish mechanism for customer's assessment of service quality.
- Identify and record service quality status.
- Establish corrective/preventive action procedures for nonconforming services.

Service Performance Analysis and Improvement

- Establish evaluation framework.
- Collect and analyze data.
- Use statistical methods.
- Identify problems.
- Develop solutions.
- Develop service quality improvement strategy and initiatives.
- Focus on never-ending cycle of improvement.

◆ SERVICE TQM: STRATEGIC ROAD-MAP

To summarize our discussion on implementing a TQM system for service organizations, a ten-phase road-map is appended in Table 26 to help simplify the implementation process.

Table 26: Service TQM: Strategic Road-Map

Phase 1:   **Business Brief**

- Identify nature, type and extent of service
- Identify service quality attributes and dimensions
- Develop customer profile
- Identify other external activities associated with service
- Develop a profile of your competitors

Phase 2:   **Customer-Supplier Profile**

- Identify customers' needs and expectations
- Develop a profile of customers' preferences
- Identify suppliers, if any

Phase 3:   **Company Profile**

- Identify company's mission, vision, policy and objectives
- Identify service infrastructure and resource base
- Identify company's process management system
- Identify company's modus operandi for service operations

Phase 4:   **Current System: Evaluation**

- Outline current infrastructure, responsibilities, system, procedures, processes and methodologies
- Evaluate strengths and weaknesses of current system vis-à-vis customer requirements
- Identify current documentation: Quality Manual, Standard Operating Procedures, Work Instructions

Phase 5:   **Strategic Planning: Needs Analysis**

- Select an appropriate service quality model
- Develop a master implementation plan
- Identify goals/time schedules, resources
- Identify personnel and responsibilities

Phase 6:   **Implementation Framework: Service Processes**

- Identify and compartmentalize all operating processes
- Establish a steering committee
- Establish Process Management Teams (PMT's)
- Develop a training plan
- Delineate responsibilities

Table 26: Service TQM: Strategic Road-Map (Continued)
Phase 7: **System Implementation** • Develop improvement projects • Implement all requisite systems • Document systems, procedures, processes
Phase 8: **Process Enhancement** • Identify the current best process • Define process goals and priorities • Establish aims and strategies • Implement improvement projects
Phase 9: **Performance Evaluation** • Measure, collect and analyze results • Monitor performance • Assess improvements made • Standardize performance
Phase 10: **Continuous Improvement** • Adjust process to aim • Develop new initiatives and improvement opportunities • Allocate requisite resources • Continuously partner with customers and suppliers • Focus on never-ending cycle of improvement

◆ ISO 9001 CERTIFICATION: SERVICES

Like manufacturing, services organizations can also seek ISO 9000 certification. Most service organizations would probably choose the ISO 9002 model, except the ones who have the "design" function for which ISO 9001 model would be appropriate. ISO 9003 is a much weaker model and is suitable for companies whose functional framework only involves final inspection and testing.

The basic premise for certification starts with the establishment of an effective service TQM System. Such a system can be implemented using any approach or methodology that the enterprise finds appropriate - a self-directed model, the Deming approach or guidelines appended in ISO 9004-2. When referring to ISO 9004-2, it must be clearly understood that the certification is only to either ISO 9001 or 9002 or 9003 and not to ISO 9004-2. ISO 9004-2 is simply a document that provides guidelines for establishing a service TQM system; it has no one-to-one correspondence to ISO 9001 or 9002 or 9003. One can indeed derive useful information out of ISO 9004-2 to prepare for ISO 9001. For this reason, we are presenting, in Table 27, a cross-reference of elements between ISO 9001 and ISO 9004-2 to assist in the preparation for certification. It is by no means obligatory on the companies, however, to follow ISO 9004-2 in order to seek certification to ISO 9001.

In this section, we shall consider certification to ISO 9001 model as an example. The process of certification is indeed the same whether it is a service or manufacturing organization; the differences arise only in the implementation of the quality system elements. A detailed description of the certification process has been outlined in several other Chapters; here we shall elucidate the requirements of the twenty system elements of ISO 9001 as they pertain to services.

4.1 Management Responsibility

- Identify the organization's mission for services.
- Develop the quality policy and objectives for the service delivery.
- Delineate appropriate quality responsibilities and authority
- Appoint a service Quality Manager
- Ensure that management reviews the quality system at defined intervals.

4.2 Quality System

- What constitutes the overall quality system? Describe the elements of the system.

4.3 Contract Review

- How does the company establish interface and communication with the customer?
- Are formal service contracts signed with customers?
- Develop procedures for the review and amendment of contracts.

4.4 Design Control

- Describe and document: design responsibilities, service specifications, service delivery specification, service delivery process, design review, design change control, and service brief.

Table 27: Cross-Reference Between ISO 9001 and ISO 9004-2

Clause in ISO 9001	Clause in ISO 9004-2 (note: see Table 25)
4.1 Management Responsibility	5.2, 5.3.1, 5.3.3
4.2 Quality System	5.4.1, 5.4.2
4.3 Contract Review	5.5, 6.1.2, 6.2.7
4.4 Design Control	6.2.1, 6.2.2, 6.2.3, 6.2.4 6.2.6, 6.2.8
4.5 Document and Data Control	5.4.3
4.6 Purchasing	6.2.4.3, 6.3.2, 6.3.3
4.7 Control of Customer Supplied Product	-
4.8 Product Identification and Traceability	6.2, 4.5
4.9 Process Control	5.3.2.1, 5.3.2.3, 6.1.3, 6.1.4, 6.2.5, 6.4.4
4.10 Inspection and Testing	6.2.7, 6.3.2, 6.3.3
4.11 Control of Inspection, Measuring and Test Equipment	6.3.6
4.12 Inspection and Test Status	6.3.4
4.13 Control of Nonconforming Product	6.3.5.1, 6.3.5.2
4.14 Corrective and Preventive Action	6.3.5.2, 6.4.4
4.15 Handling, Storage, Packaging, Preservation and Delivery	6.2.4, 6.2.4.2, 6.2.4.6 6.2.7, 6.3
4.16 Control of Quality Records	6.1.1, 6.1.5, 6.3.4, 6.4.2
4.17 Internal Quality Audits	5.4.4
4.18 Training	5.3.2.2
4.19 Servicing	5.5, 6.3, 6.4
4.20 Statistical Techniques	6.4.3

4.5 Document and Data Control

- Develop a quality documentation control system.
- Establish a master file of all documents and a procedure for document changes and approvals.

4.6 Purchasing

- Establish procedures for controlling the quality of purchased materials and goods.
- Identify acceptable subcontractors.
- Establish procedures for verification of purchased products.

4.7 Control of Customer Supplied Product

- If there is any material or entity that is provided by the customer to be utilized by the supplier in the service delivery process, this should be controlled properly.

4.8 Product Identification and Traceability

- Record the source of any product or service that forms part of the service provided to ensure traceability in cases of nonconformity, customer complaint or liability.

4.9 Process Control

- Identify how processes are controlled.
- Establish process control procedures.
- Ensure that documented quality system procedures are followed.

4.10 Inspection and Testing

- Identify procedures for inspection and testing of:
  - Incoming goods and services, if any
  - Service specifications
  - Service delivery specification
  - Service delivery procedures

- Identify procedures for:
  - Supplier's assessment of service quality
  - Customer's assessment of service quality

4.11 Control of Inspection, Measuring and Test Equipment

- All equipment used in the service delivery process must be quality controlled and calibrated.

4.12 Inspection and Test Status

- Every item that is utilized in the service delivery process should be identified by a suitable indicator to signify its acceptability status.

4.13 Control of Nonconforming Product

- All nonconformances in the service delivery process should be identified and documented.

4.14 Corrective and Preventive Action

- Establish procedures for talking corrective and preventive action on the nonconformities identified through routine evaluation, internal quality audits or system reviews.

4.15 Handling, Storage, Packaging, Preservation and Delivery

- Establish effective controls for the handling, storage, packaging, delivery and protection of either the customer's possessions which the service organization is responsible for or its own entities.

4.16 Control of Quality Records

- Quality records and data should be effectively controlled and analyzed for service delivery improvement.

4.17 Internal Quality Audits

- Establish a systematic procedure for conducting routine audits of the service delivery function.

4.18 Training

- Ensure that the personnel receive adequate training in all aspects of service delivery function.

4.19 Servicing

- Prepare a service brief.
- Identify procedures for post delivery servicing, if any.

4.20 Statistical Techniques

- Statistical methods can assist in various aspects of data collection and application, whether it is used to gain a better understanding of customer needs, in process control, capability study, or system performance.

Once the intent and requirements of the system elements of ISO 9001 are clearly understood as they apply to services, the process of certification, as appended in Chapter 12, can be easily followed. A recapitulation of the sequence of activities is as follows:

- Prepare a Quality Manual describing the company's operations, systems, procedures and processes in the light of all the clauses of ISO 9001.
- Prepare the Quality System Procedure manuals for each system element of ISO 9001 to identify how the system is implemented and operated.
- Prepare or update the company's Standard Operating Procedures and/or Work Instructions utilized for the physical operation of the service business.
- Document and implement the system properly ensuring the following:
  - Establishment of quality policy and objectives
  - Proper documentation of quality plans and procedures
  - Effective document control system
  - Appropriate delineation of quality responsibilities and authority
  - Quality control of incoming goods and services, if any
  - Capability and training of workers for the effective delivery of services
  - Suitable process control and verification procedures
  - Procedures for identifying nonconformities and taking of corrective/preventive actions
  - Carrying out of scheduled quality audits
  - Maintenance of quality records
- The certification process involves the following steps:
  - Select a suitable registrar and work closely with the registrar
  - Prepare all requisite documents effectively
  - Comply with the audit requirements/findings of the registrar
  - Achieve certification and maintain systems continuously

9

RE-ENGINEERING GOVERNMENT

◆ NEED FOR TQM

The need to enhance productivity and improve quality of services is not limited to any specific group of enterprises. This concern is rampant throughout all types of organizations - manufacturing as well as services. The public service is no exception to it. In fact, it is all the more important to improve the quality of services in the government sector because of the following reasons:

- Government must establish exemplary precedence and lead the way in doing business efficiently vis-à-vis the private sector.
- Government is expected or perhaps mandated by the taxpayer to function efficiently and provide satisfactory service.
- Government must endeavour to establish credibility and trust of the public at large.

The public service has, typically, three target areas of improvement via the application of quality management principles:

- **Productivity enhanced of internal functions**
- **Quality improvement of internal functions**
- **Quality improvement of external service delivery functions**

◆ NATURE OF PUBLIC SECTOR SERVICES

Of the many diverse factors that bear profound influence on the success or failure of any TQM System, the most important one is its commensurability and compatibility with the nature of business and the existing processes, procedures, systems, infrastructure and culture of the organization. The functional nature of public sector services is distinctly different from the private sector services. These differences must be clearly understood and adequately reflected and accommodated in any intended TQM implementation framework in order to achieve sustainable improvements. Some of the noticeable characteristics of the government services, at all levels in the public sector, are as follows:

- They are routinely repetitive and intangible in nature.
- They are institutionalized, regimented and standardized.
- They are perceived by the customer as unfriendly and hostile.
- The functional operability of services is generally susceptible and predisposed to errors.
- They are inflexible and reactive in nature.
- They are bureaucratic, legalistic and regulatory in nature.

◆ TQM: FUNCTIONAL DIFFICULTIES/DILEMMAS

There is an increasing demand for the public sector to improve quality of services. The continued health of an agency directly depends on its credibility. That credibility indeed depends on the taxpayer's perception to whom the agency is accountable for. The executive leaders in the public sector face an enormously difficult challenge. They have to improve quality and productivity with shrinking resources and the programs have to accommodate a host of conflicting needs, requirements and expectations. Since the public agencies are expected to be accountable to every group equally, any quality improvement exercise must take into account the following dilemmas:

- Balancing conflicting and changing political priorities
- Balancing conflicting customer expectations and requirements
- Balancing changing domestic and international markets
- Balancing international pressures and priorities

No wonder, therefore, that reinventing the government is a mammoth undertaking. What type of TQM model would be able to accommodate these functional difficulties? It has to be a system that is sustainable, measurable, and producing quality service that is acceptable to all. The essential ingredients of a successful/sustainable TQM can be typically underlined as follows:

Build a TQM Model That is:

- Politics-proof
- Mission-compatible
- Customer-friendly
- Perceptually-credible
- Management-driven
- Self-managed
- Need/operability-oriented
- Potentially-proactive
- Continuously-enhanceable

- Flexibly-prioritizable
- Magnituditionally-implementable
- Budget-sensitive
- Current system-compatible
- Employee-owned
- Non-threateningly rejuvenating
- Morale-elevating
- Analytically-measurable
- Result-oriented

◆ WHY DO SYSTEMS FAIL

Since the public agencies operate under such complicated and diverse set of circumstances, the rate of failure of quality/productivity improvement systems is undoubtedly high. Systems after systems have come and gone without much sustainability. What assurance do we have that TQM System will survive? How do we develop a fail-proof TQM System? These are some of the questions that are on everybody's mind - especially the public sector executive who bear enormous responsibility on behalf of the taxpayer and the country, to run the systems efficiently.

Before going any further, let us look at some positives of the past. True, that many systems have come and gone, but they weren't a total failure. They made tremendous contribution for the time they were in and their legacy still abounds in many circles. The fact is that the times are changing very fast and along with it the prevailing constraints and circumstances. Although, it is not possible to guarantee that a totally fail-proof TQM System can be developed, we can still make an attempt to design one that would have a high probability of lasting success. To do so, it may be worthwhile to first comprehend the basic reasons as to why systems fail. Many a times, to be cognizant of why systems fail before one attempts to design a system is the most conducive way of making the system fail-proof.

In Chapter 3, we have outlined some key attributes responsible for the failure of the system. The set of elements specifically applicable to the application of TQM in the public sector are once again considered here. These should provide sufficient material to develop a fail-proof implementation framework and a viable road map for ensuring that the quality system is established on a sound footing.

Key factors Linked to System Failure in the Public Sector:

- Lack of genuine and honest management commitment and hands-on exemplary leadership.
- Managers apprehensive about loss of power and controls via people empowerment; decision-making overly centralized.
- Hierarchical working relationship is fuzzy - everyone seems to be working for a "Greater God", yet no one knows who that God is - perhaps the taxpayer; consequently, there is a lack of personalized accountability and empathy for resource utilization.
- A perpetual state of infrastructural instability and political dependency/ intervention accentuates ineffectiveness.
- Service operability burdened with excessive bureaucratic red-tape and regulatory overkill.
- Service output without tangibles; input-output-profitability relationship being non-existent.
- Absence of competition and consequent lack of impetus for higher productivity.
- Service operates in a reactive/delivery mode rather than proactive/result-oriented mode.
- Service portrays the perception of a gesture of favour to the customer rather than a mandated requirement and responsibility.
- Nature of service being repetitive and error-prone.
- Customer's perception - nature of services are customer-hostile.
- Insufficient contact and projection of day-to-day activities on to identifiable customers.
- Lack of continuous re-engineering vis-à-vis environmental scanning.
- System inflexible - follows rigid rules rather than guiding principles.
- Too much focus on system rather than people.
- TQM approach being piecemeal and unintegrated.
- Lack of empathy for teamwork.
- Fear of reprisal and performance appraisals limits personal innovativeness, gusto, motivation and self-confidence.

◆ TQM MODEL: PUBLIC SECTOR

Before outlining a viable TQM implementation approach, a reiteration of some basic essential elements would be in order.

- Develop a clear set of objectives to delineate what would be accomplished via TQM implementation. As indicated earlier, the basic premise of a public agency is to:
  - Improve quality/productivity of functional operability
  - Improve quality/efficiency of service delivery function
- If possible, try to dub the TQM initiatives as "Continuous Improvement Process" rather than a specific project or program; because projects and programs in the public sector are prone to political interference, budgetary cuts and are perceived to have a limited shelf-life. Quality improvement exercise is an ongoing activity with no beginnings or endings.
- Instead of importing an unbefitting regimented model from external sources, try to build an in-house model of your own. Most often, failures occur because organizations bring in programs, models or systems that are foreign to their existing culture, operability framework and infrastructure. High-powered consultant are, sometimes, brought in to implement, or perhaps force-fit these unbefitting systems. Organizations should encourage and empower their own people to develop simple, hands-on systems that are conducive to their current functional framework and requirements. Such systems can be easily evolved from the collective available subject-matter knowledge and expertise in the field. The help of an outside consultant is, sometimes, not only necessary and valuable but mandatory to achieve a high degree of efficiency and precision. However, the role of a consultant ought to be as a catalyst only, and the actual ownership and responsibility of the processes must be collectively assumed by the employees.
- The Chosen TQM approach must:
  - Provide tailored guidelines
  - Be simple, systematic and user-friendly
  - Involve everyone in the organization
  - Address both the short-term and long-term goals of the organization

Detailed guidelines for developing and implementing a TQM system are provided in Chapters 3 and 5 and they can be suitably modified and utilized to develop a TQM model for the public sector. As indicated in Chapter 3, there are two approaches to implementing a TQM System:

- **Top-Down Approach**
- **Bottom-up Approach**

We shall now outline the key features of each approach as applicable to the public sector organizations. As a case study, we shall consider a large Government Department with headquarters consisting of several Branches and Directorates/Divisions/Sections within the Branches, and some regional offices. Suppose the functions of the Department involves providing direction/assistance/service to the producers and consumers, carrying out regulatory/compliance verifications, carrying out research and development, protecting the country's infrastructure, etc.

Top-Down TQM Model: Road Map

Executive Management Readiness

- The executive management commits to implementing a total quality system for continuous improvement of functional operability and quality of services.
- A departmental level steering committee is struck to oversee the process.
- A departmental level mission statement is developed/established either through the steering committee and/or with the help of employees at various levels in the organization.
- The steering committee develops a strategic business plan.
- Requisite resources are identified.
- Appropriate responsibilities are delineated.
- Guidelines are provided to the next levels of the organizations ie., Branches and they are mandated to undertake the process of TQM implementation.

Strategic Planning

- Each unit, ie., Branch, identifies a Process Management Steering Group.
- The unit develops a strategic plan on the lines of the umbrella departmental plan.
- A TQM coordinator is identified.
- If the unit is large in size, these activities can be further disbursed down to the next level, ie., the Directorate or Division.

Environmental Scanning

- Each unit (Branch or Directorate) undergoes the process of identifying external customer needs, requirements and the current state of business constraints and circumstances.
- Issues to identify include:
  - Total customer profile
  - Type of service required
  - Extent of service quality expectation
  - Customer complaints and feedback
  - Regulatory requirements/constraints
  - Political mandate
  - Social and economic considerations
  - Impact of technological changes

Introspective Analysis

- Each unit, section-by-section, embarks upon identifying the total span of their functional responsibilities and nature/type of work performed.
- A section-by-section checklist is developed to identify exactly what business the unit is in. First, major job functions or work areas are identified. Then, each function is further expanded with secondary sub-headings to annotate the nature of the function. Lastly, for each entity, the nature of inputs and outputs is outlined.
- A profile of the total activities/undertakings of the unit is imperative for pinpointing areas needing improvement.

Need/Gap Analysis

- From the results of environmental scanning and introspective analysis, a comparative evaluation is made of the differential between what is required by the customer and what the organization is presently providing.
- The gap analysis would direct the organization to identify needs and actions required to accomplish the mission.
- For each functional area requiring improvement, Process Management Teams (PMT's) can be assigned to implement improvement initiative and monitor progress.
- Training is required for employees in the following areas:
  - TQM principles
  - Process management
  - Change management

TQM Framework

- Hands-on management involvement
- Training at all levels of the organization: TQM elements, process management, team management
- Development of quality policy, objectives, goals
- Development of strategic business plan
- Identification of customer needs
- Evaluation of current systems for their suitability to address customer needs
- Identification of gaps and deficiencies
- Implementation of improvement initiatives
- Process management teams to manage improvement projects/initiatives
- Measurement of performance
- Review/reevaluation of current systems vis-à-vis the accomplishments
- Continuation of improvement cycle

Process Management

- Each designated area requiring improvement, identified through needs analysis, is managed by the PMT.

- To improve any process, one must know:
  - What needs to be improved?
  - What is the current best of the function?
  - What is the goal?
  - How would improvement be measured?
  - How to initiate continuous cycle of improvement?
- The Process Management Teams must follow a disciplined approach to process improvement. A simple process enhancement method is outlined in the "PURI" Wheel in Chapter 3 (Figure 2), and Chapter 23. The basic elements of the method are as follows:

P-U-R-I: Plan - Upgrade - Record - Improve

Plan

- Identify process characteristics
- Define current best process

Upgrade

- Establish aims, strategies
- Implement improvement projects

Record

- Measure/analyze results
- Standardize/monitor performance

Improve

- Adjust process to aim
- Develop new initiatives

Performance Monitoring

- Every process improvement initiative/activity must be monitored and evaluated for performance.
- Improvement opportunities are identified.
- Strategic initiatives are established.
- Continuous cycle of improvement is emulated.

Bottom-Up TQM Model

- This approach is applicable to situations where there is no undertaking at the Departmental level to implement a TQM System; however, at the unit level (Branch or Directorate or Regional), there is desire to employ TQM principles to improve quality of services.
- The sequence of steps for this approach are almost identical to the ones appended above for the Top-Down model.

- **Road Map for Bottom-Up model:**
  - The management of the unit commits to implementing a quality system.
  - A steering group is established.
  - A TQM coordinator is identified.
  - A strategic plan is developed.
  - The steering group undertakes the process of environmental scanning to identify the total profile of customer requirements and business environment.
  - An introspective analysis is carried out to develop a detailed checklist of the total functional work profile of the unit.
  - A gap analysis is conducted to identify the deficiencies or areas needing improvement in the present system vis-à-vis the customer's requirements.
  - For addressing improvement needs of each identifiable area, a Process Management Team is established.
  - Education and training is provided to employees in all requisite areas of TQM implementation.
  - TQM initiatives are put into place.
  - A disciplined approach is followed for process improvement.
  - A system is established to monitor, measure and analyze performance.
  - Strategies are reviewed/revised as per the progress made.
  - A cycle of continuous improvement is set in motion.

In this bottom-up scenario, when the quality improvement activities permeate throughout the organization unit-by-unit, the end result can be envisaged as an organization-wide top-down TQM implementation.

◆ TQM VIA PRESIDENTIAL AWARD FOR QUALITY

The marketplace is replete with countless variety of programs, approaches, methodologies, philosophies and documents providing ways and means to implement a quality system. All one has to do is to extract the most suitable set of elements conducive to an organization's operability framework and come-up with a self-developed/

/self-directed TQM model. A people-developed, people-owned, people-driven, people-empowered model such as this would have the highest probability of lasting success. In this section, we are summarizing the salient features of the TQM approach as outlined in the "Presidential Award for Quality (U.S.A.)" which can provide a wealth of ideas to carve out a suitable quality management system. Further details regarding this award can be obtained from the Federal Quality Institute (see Chapter 11).

Introduction

The President's Quality Award Program, created in 1988, is administered by the Federal Quality Institute and includes two awards:

- The Presidential Award for Quality - designed for organizations that have mature quality management efforts.
- The Quality Improvement Prototype Award - designed for organizations that have recently begun the quality transformation process.

The award is based on Malcolm Baldrige National Quality Award criteria, but reflects the unique federal environment and culture.

Award criteria: Presidential Award for Quality

The criteria embodies certain Core Values and concept of quality management, such as:

- Quality is defined by the customer.
- A focus on continuous improvement is part of all operations and activities.
- Prevention of problems and waste is achieved through building quality into products, services, and processes.
- Success in meeting quality performance goals depends on workforce quality and involvement.
- Senior management creates a customer orientation, clean and visible quality values, and high expectations. Reinforcement of values and expectations requires substantial personal commitment and involvement.
- Employees are valued and recognized for their involvement and accomplishments.
- Management decisions are made based upon reliable information, data, and analysis.
- Long-term commitments are made to customers, employees, suppliers and the community.
- Public responsibilities are fulfilled.
- Partnerships are built with other agencies and the private sector, to better accomplish overall goals.

Award Criteria Elements

- Leadership
- Information and Analysis
- Strategic Quality Planning
- Human Resource Development and Management
- Management of Process Quality
- Quality and Operational Results
- Customer Focus and Satisfaction

The main focus of the award criteria elements is appended below:

- **Leadership**
  - Executive Leadership
  - Managing for Quality
  - Public Responsibility and community citizenship

Leadership examines executives' personal commitment and involvement in creating and sustaining an organization vision and customer focus orientation, as well as clean and visible quality values. It also examines how the vision, values, and customer focus orientation are integrated into the management system, labour relations and external partnerhip, and are reflected in the way public responsibilities are addressed.

- **Information and Analysis**
  - Scope and Management of Quality and Performance Data and Information
  - Similar Provider Comparisons and Benchmarking
  - Analysis and Uses of Organization-Level Data

This element examines the scope, management, and use of data, information and measures, and how they are used to drive quality and operational performance improvement. It also examines the adequacy of the organization's data, information, and analysis system to support improvement of customer satisfaction, products, services, and processes.

- **Strategic Quality Planning**
  - Quality and Operational Performance Planning Process
  - Quality and Operational Performance Plans

This element examines the organization's planning process, and how key quality requirements are integrated into overall planning. Both the organization's short and longer-term plans are examined, as well as how quality and operational performance improvement goals are deployed to all work units.

- **Human Resources Development and Management**
  - Human Resource Planning and Management
  - Employee Involvement
  - Employee Education and Training
  - Employee Performance and Recognition
  - Employee Well-Being and Satisfaction

This element examines how the entire workforce is enabled to develop its full potential, and to pursue quality and operational performance improvement goals. It also examines efforts to build and maintain an environment for workforce excellence, which is conducive to increased involvement, personal and organizational development.

- **Management of Process Quality**
  - Design and Introduction of Quality Products and Services
  - Process Management: Product and Service Production and Delivery Processes
  - Process Management: Business Processes and Support Services
  - Supplier and Intermediary Quality
  - Quality Assessment

Managing of Process Quality examines the systematic process used by the organization for continuous improvement of quality and operational performance improvement. It also examines design and management of process quality for all work units, the management of internal customer-supplier relationships, supplier and intermediary quality, and quality assessment.

- **Quality and Operational Results**
  - Product and Service Quality Results
  - Operational Performance Results
  - Business Process and Support Service Results
  - Supplier and Intermediary Quality Results

The criteria elements examines the organization's trends and quality levels for products and services, operational performance, business process and support services, supplier and intermediary quality, and comparison/benchmark data.

- **Customer Focus and Satisfaction**
  - Customer Expectations: current and future
  - Customer Relationship Management
  - Commitment to Customers
  - Determination of Customer Satisfaction
  - Customer Satisfaction Results
  - Customer Satisfaction Comparison

This element examines the organization's knowledge of external customer requirements, and how relationships with customers are established and mainframed. It also examines the methods used to determine customer satisfaction, and the trends and current levels of customers satisfaction.

The President's Quality Award is open only to the Federal agencies in the United States of America. The award was created to:

- Recognize organizations that have implemented quality management in an exemplary manner, resulting in high quality products and services, the effective use of taxpayer dollars.
- Promote quality management awareness and implementation throughout the Federal Government.

In this section, we are emphasizing the fact that irrespective of the intent and applicability of the award, the guidelines appended in the award criteria can be gainfully used by any public sector organization to develop an effective TQM model.

◆ GOVERNMENT TQM: SYNOPSIS

We shall now summarize our discussion on the basic action-oriented sequence of steps required to implement a quality system at any level of the organization.

- Prepare a strategic business plan. This would include what is required by the customer and what the organization has decided to do to meet the business mandate.
- Prepare a unit-by-unit detailed checklist of the work profile and the functions of each unit.
- Check to ensure that the existing functions address and accommodate the requisite elements of the business plan.
- Conduct a detailed analysis of each function to assess its effectiveness vis-à-vis the deliverables.

- Identify the gaps.
- When the overall profile of functional deficiencies are identified through the gap analysis, develop a list of processes where improvement initiatives can be implemented.
- For each process, identify the characteristics/variables/attributes that impact the process.
- Identify the current best of the process.
- Develop Process Management Teams (PMTs) to manage process improvement.
- Institute improvement initiatives.
- Provide requisite training to teams.
- Monitor, measure, analyze processes to identify the extent of improvements made.
- Match the improvements with the requirements of the strategic plan.
- Repeat the sequence of steps by:
  - Continuously identifying the customer requirements through environmental scanning
  - Reviewing/revising the strategic business plan
  - Monitoring and controlling service delivery processes
  - Implementing new improvement initiatives
  - Monitoring the continuous cycle of improvement

10

TQM MODEL: ADDITIONAL APPROACHES

◆ INTRODUCTION

In addition to the approaches outlined in the preceding chapters, a TQM model can also be developed based on the philosophies and methodologies set forth by various quality experts. The following are considered in this chapter as methods for deriving a TQM System:

- Deming Approach
- Juran Approach
- Crosby Approach

It should be noted that only a basic framework of these approaches is described here. For serious application of any approach selected from these, the reader is advised to consult other useful sources and references.

◆ TQM SYSTEM: DEMING APPROACH

It was in Japan, in 1950, where Dr. W. Edwards Deming first introduced and emphasized the use of statistical quality control methods to improve quality. Later, he developed his 14-point philosophy (see Table 28) for establishing a total quality system. The 14 points do not offer any exotic theory of behaviour, nor any structured set of system elements for establishing a TQM system. They are derived from first-hand observations and, therefore, reflect Deming's insight and experience for improving quality.

Table 28. Dr. Deming's 14 Points

1. Create constancy of purpose for improvement of product and service.

2. Adopt the new philosophy.

3. Cease dependence on inspection to achieve quality.

4. End the practice of awarding business on the basis of price tag alone. Instead, minimize total cost by working with a single supplier.

5. Improve constantly and forever every process for planning, production, and service.

6. Institute training on the job.

7. Adopt and institute leadership.

8. Drive out fear.

9. Break down barriers between staff areas.

10. Eliminate slogans, exhortations, and targets for the work force.

11. Eliminate numerical quotas for the work force and numerical goals for management.

12. Remove barriers that rob people of pride of workmanship. Eliminate the annual rating or merit system.

13. Institute a vigorous program of education and self-improvement for everyone.

14. Put everybody in the company to work to accomplish the transformation.

Deming's 14 points provide a thought-provoking framework for management to come to grips with the realities of the competitive quality revolution and to institute changes and transformations to improve and maintain quality. The most befitting analogy to Deming's concept is the statement made by the late Kaora Ishikawa of Japan, "Quality control is a thought revolution in management". Good quality, according to Deming, means a predictable degree of uniformity and dependability at low cost, with the quality suited to the market. This emphasis is portrayed in Deming's famous chain reaction, given as follows:

Improve Quality → Improve Productivity →
Decrease Costs → Lower Prices → Capture Markets →
Stay in Business → Provide Jobs → Return on Investment

The essence of Deming's 14-point philosophy can be stated as follows:

- Commitment to quality, constancy of purpose
- Effective leadership
- Continuous improvement of products/services
- Reduction/elimination of variability
- Process improvement with statistical methods
- Continuous training/retraining
- Teamwork, effective communication
- Pride in workmanship
- Quality - everyone's business

Although it is not easy to develop a structured TQM System using Deming's philosophy, the following provides a list of essential activities and actions that the management must undertake to develop and implement an effective quality improvement system.

Deming Point #1

- Define the quality mission and vision.
- Define the quality policy, objectives and standards.
- Develop long-range plans.
- Identify management commitment and continued responsibility to quality.
- Develop quality leadership.
- Institute continuous training.
- Put resources into research, education and the maintenance of equipment.
- Innovate and constantly improve the design of the product.
- Command constancy of purpose and dedication.

Deming Point #2

- Bring about management transformation and accept the challenge of doing things right the first time.
- Constantly review and analyze the systems and related quality procedures.

- Replace inadequate supervision with leadership.
- Teach, develop skills and abandon the mentality that permits an acceptable level of deficiency.

Deming Point #3

- Quality cannot be inspected in; it has to be manufactured in.
- Reduce dependence on mass inspection to achieve quality.
- Achieve quality through process control.
- Produce right in the first place.

Deming Point #4

- Select suppliers based on their ability to provide quality material and services rather than on the price tag.
- Establish a long-term partnership with the suppliers.
- Establish a process control and improvement system with the suppliers.

Deming Point #5

- Continuously hunt for areas to be improved: procurement, design, production, data collection, measurement system, customer satisfaction, employee involvement, etc.
- Constantly improve the system of production and services. Use Deming's continuous quality improvement cycle, PDSA - Plan, Do, Study, Act.
- Understand variation and its causes. Use statistical process control methods to eliminate deficiencies and improve processes.

Deming Point #6

- Institute modern methods of training on the job.
- Train workers in the concepts of Statistical Process Control (SPC) to improve processes.
- Provide employee training opportunities in new and effective techniques.
- Set standards for new recruits.
- Establish a schedule for continuous training.

Deming Point #7

- The traditional dictatorial supervisory role must change to a proactive leadership role.
- Make the organization flexible so that supervisors may become part of the quality team.

- The new supervisor is responsible for ensuring that quality action is taken in all areas impacting quality.

Deming Point #8

- Create a management environment where people feel secure, confident, responsible and fulfilled.
- Everyone in the organization should be able to express ideas/opinions, ask questions, suggest system deficiencies and improvements, and have pride in their workmanship.
- Create a climate of trust and openness.
- The management must be open-minded and responsive to suggestions.

Deming Point #9

- Break down inter and intra-departmental barriers.
- Establish a cross-functional interface to encourage communication.
- Establish a well-coordinated and integrated system.
- Institute a participative team approach.
- Try to eliminate or minimize psychological and emotional barriers to job performance such as: jealousy, ambition, fear, personality conflicts, fear of change, etc.

Deming Point #10

- Eliminate arbitrary goals and slogans.
- Do not judge performance by numbers. Instead, encourage people to be productive and innovative.
- Do not set targets that may cause workers to compromise and make sacrifices at the altar of quality.

Deming Point #11

- Eliminate work standards that prescribe numerical quotas.
- Eliminate those goals and objectives that hinder performance.
- Learn, teach and institute methods of process improvement.

Deming Point #12

- Eliminate inhibitors (physical, environmental, psychological, emotional) to the improvement of quality and productivity.
- Involve and empower people to do the job well.
- Remove barriers that stand between workers and their pride of workmanship.

Deming Point #13

- Identify training needs and institute a vigorous program of education and self-improvement.
- Emphasize and encourage educational opportunities.
- Create a climate of personal growth and achievement.
- Train employees in statistical methods used for process improvement.

Deming Point #14

- Create a dedicated and committed management structure that will make the transformation succeed.
- Create a quality culture.
- Make people responsible for and proud of their work.
- Recognize achievement.
- Make quality everyone's business.

Deming: Theory of Profound Knowledge

To further elucidate his 14-point theory, Deming has identified what he calls "a system of profound knowledge", the understanding of which he considers imperative for the effective implementation of a TQM System. The essential elements of this system include:

- **Knowledge of Variation**

  - Understand the role of variation.
  - Improve processes by reducing/eliminating variability.
  - Use statistical process control methods to control, monitor and improve processes.

- **Knowledge of Loss Function**

  - Identify critical quality characteristics and their associated costs.
  - Identify costs/losses incurred due to poor quality by the organization, by the customer or through sub-optimization.
  - Improve quality by minimizing/optimizing costs.

- **Knowledge of Win-Win Philosophy**

  - Success comes through cooperation rather than competition.
  - Establish a partnership with the suppliers and customers.

- **Knowledge of Psychology**

  - Understand the role of intrinsic and extrinsic motivation.
  - Understand the psychology of change.
  - Involve and empower the workforce.
  - Create a joy of work.
  - Improve inter/intra-communication.

- **Knowledge of Reliability**

  - Understand the operational functionality of the system.
  - Improve the dependability of the system.
  - Emphasize product performance rather than just the intended design or usage.

- **Theory of Knowledge**

  - Understand the organizational operational and communication systems.
  - Understand the theory of prediction.
  - Use theory and experience together.
  - Obtain data.
  - Use statistical methods for analyzing information for effective decision-making.

◆ TQM SYSTEM: JURAN APPROACH

Dr. Joseph M. Juran is another famous quality expert with a powerful message. The basic premise of Juran's philosophy can be summarized as follows:

- Quality means fitness for use.
- Quality holds the key to competitive survivability.
- There is a new world order for quality. To do business in this new Quality/Productivity Era would require excellence in the quality of products and services.
- Quality improvement requires relinquishing the traditional approaches and charting a new course with the following attributes:
  - Constancy in improvement, ie., an ongoing annual improvement in quality, year after year
  - Hands-on leadership by upper management
  - A universal way of thinking about quality, ie., a quality culture that permeates and applies to all levels of the organization.
  - Establishment of new policies, goals, plans, organizational measures and controls throughout the organization. These quality management measures and activities must be designed with great care so as to allow a smooth transition and acceptance within the company.

- Creation of cross-functional unity in the organization so that everyone will be aware of the new directions
- Massive training in quality at all levels of the organization

The basic components of the TQM System, according to Juran, involves quality planning, quality control and quality improvement. The elements of this trilogy as outlined by Dr. Juran are appended in Table 29.

The planning process is essential for delineating a quality road map. It prepares the company to meet and achieve quality goals. A well-planned process is always capable of meeting quality goals under operating conditions. Some of the basic elements of quality planning involve the following:

- Identifying the customer requirements
- Developing the product vis-à-vis these requirements
- Identifying the processes that impact quality
- Establishing quality goals
- Ensuring process capability to meet these quality goals

Quality control activities ensure that the conduct of operations is in accordance with the stipulated quality plans and procedures. A well-controlled production process is guaranteed to yield a consistently high quality product that is predictable, reliable, fit for use, and meeting the customer's needs and requirements. Quality control activities involve the following elements:

- Identifying the areas requiring controls
- Implementing control procedures
- Establishing a measurement system
- Setting performance standards
- Measuring actual against expected performance
- Taking action on the deviations

Quality improvement activities lead a company towards excellence and provide a competitive edge. They realize unprecedented levels of performance that achieve customer delight. Continuous quality improvement is the key to expanded markets, higher profits and long-term survival. Quality improvement activities include the following:

- Determining improvement needs, opportunities and initiatives
- Identifying specific projects for improvement

Table 29. Basic Quality Process: Juran

Quality Planning

Identify the customers, both external and internal.

Determine customer needs.

Develop product features that respond to customer needs. (Products include both goods and services.)

Establish quality goals that meet the needs of customers and suppliers alike, and do so at a minimum combined cost.

Develop a process that can produce the needed product features.

Prove process capability - prove that the process can meet the quality goals under operating conditions.

Quality Control

Choose control subjects - what to control.

Choose units of measurement.

Establish measurement.

Establish standards of performance.

Measure actual performance.

Interpret the difference (actual versus standard).

Take action on the difference.

Quality Improvement

Prove the need for improvement.

Identify specific projects for improvement.

Organize to guide the projects.

Organize for diagnosis - for discovery of causes.

Diagnose to find the causes.

Provide remedies.

Prove that the remedies are effective under operating conditions.

Provide for control to hold the gains.

"The Juran Trilogy © Chart."
Reproduced with permission of Juran Institute, Inc., 11 River Road, Wilton, CT 66897, U.S.A., from *Quality Progress*, August, 1986, pp. 19-24.

- Establishing improvement teams
- Implementing improvement strategies
- Identifying deficiencies
- Instituting remedial measures
- Assessing improvement
- Controlling the processes to maintain gains.

A careful and systematic implementation of the elements identified above would result in an effective TQM System. For a more serious application and use of Juran's methods, the reader is advised to consult other appropriate sources and references.

◆ TQM SYSTEM: CROSBY APPROACH

Philip B. Crosby, another well-known quality management expert, bases his approach to implementing a TQM System on his "Four Absolutes of Quality" and his 14-step implementation plan. The four absolutes are:

- The definition of quality is conformance to requirements.
- The system of quality is prevention.
- The performance standard is zero defects.
- The measurement of quality is the price of nonconformance.

Crosby's 14-step plan, appended in Table 30, needs careful understanding and interpretation for an effective TQM System implementation. The basic premise of Crosby's approach is as follows:

Step 1: Management Commitment

- Management must display personal commitment and participation in the quality program.
- Define and establish the quality policy and objectives.
- Make sure that the policy and commitment is understood, implemented and maintained at all levels of the organization.

Step 2: Quality Improvement Team

- Establish an inter/intra-departmental and cross-functional quality improvement team.
- The team must clearly understand the task at hand and should have all the necessary tools to do the job.

Table 30. Fourteen Steps: Crosby

1. Management Commitment

2. Quality Improvement Team

3. Measurement

4. Cost of Quality

5. Quality Awareness

6. Corrective Action

7. Zero Defects Planning

8. Education

9. Zero Defects Day

10. Goal Setting

11. Error Cause Removal

12. Recognition

13. Quality Councils

14. Do It Over Again

Step 3: Measurement

- Establish a formal and well-structured quality measurement system/procedures for all areas of activity. Revise/review these procedures as appropriate.
- Measurement data should be properly recorded.
- The quality improvement status should be identified.
- Corrective action should be taken where required.
- Make use of charts to identify and display the quality improvement results.

Step 4: Cost of Quality

- Establish a quality cost system. Evaluate the total costs necessary to achieve the desired quality.
- Use the cost data to optimize the corrective action strategy.

Step 5: Quality Awareness

- Foster quality awareness programs.
- Educate employees on the:
  - Costs of poor quality
  - Concern for quality improvement
  - Positive attitude towards quality
  - Importance of quality related discussions, interface and cross-functional dialogue

Step 6: Corrective Action

- Quality awareness, attitude and discussions lead to the identification of quality problems and opportunities for corrective action.
- Quality problems should be identified at the team meetings and appropriate corrective action should be initiated.

Step 7: Zero Defects Planning

- The emphasis should be on doing things right, the first time.
- Establish a Zero Defects program and make sure that everyone clearly understands its purpose, scope and importance. Ensure the complete participation of everyone.
- Identify improvements made through the program and repeat the continuous cycle.

Step 8: Education

- Identify the total training needs at all levels of the organization.
- Provide appropriate education and training in each area of activity.

Step 9: Zero Defects Day

- Establish a formal Zero Defects Day.
- Emphasize the company's commitment to the Zero Defects program.
- Explain the Zero Defects program to everyone and expound it as the company's performance standard.

Step 10: Goal Setting

- Encourage employees to set up short-term and long-term goals for themselves.
- The goals should be specific and measurable.
- Employees should be encouraged to monitor their performance and progress in realizing their goals.

Step 11: Error Cause Removal

- Establish a system whereby employees can identify problems that hinder performing their work without deficiencies.
- Ensure that appropriate functional groups continuously provide prompt solutions and remedies to these designated problems.

Step 12: Recognition

- Establish a viable system to recognize the outstanding achievements of employees.
- The prizes and awards should not be financial in nature but rather serve as expressions of praise and appreciation.

Step 13: Quality Councils

- Establish councils comprised of quality professionals and team chairpersons.
- Schedule regular council meetings to study the efficacy of the quality program, to identify the system's strengths and weaknesses and to generate continuous improvement strategies.

Step 14: Do It Over Again

- Most programs tend to loose their drive, prowess and impact over extended periods of time. Every so often, at appropriate intervals, re-energize the quality program by doing it all over again.
- Maintain a continuous cycle of improvement.

◆ TQM: THE JAPANESE PERSPECTIVE

For the sake of comparison, let us briefly outline the Japanese approach to quality. Japanese-style total quality control is referenced by the phrase "Company-Wide Quality Control" (CWQC) and is a bit broader in scope than its U.S. counterpart. The late Karoa Ishikawa, one of the leading pioneers of quality control in Japan, has defined and differentiated the U.S. and Japanese styles of total quality control as follows:

> **"Total Quality Control (TQC)**: A system for integrating quality technologies into various functional departments (ie., engineering, production, sales and service) to achieve customer satisfaction."

> **"Company-Wide Quality Control (CWQC)**: A means to provide good and low cost products, dividing the benefits among consumers, employees, and stockholders while improving the quality of people's lives."

The Japanese emphasis of quality is on customer satisfaction and value for money. This is evidenced by the definition of quality control given in the Japanese Industrial Standard Z8101-1981:

> **"Quality Control**: A system of means to economically produce goods or services which satisfy the customer's requirements."

Some of the key characteristics of the Japanese approach to quality can be summarized as follows:

- "Quality control is a thought revolution in management" - Ishikawa
- While the North American emphasis is limited to the product, process and system, the Japanese approach goes further to also include a focus on cost, employee involvement, customer satisfaction and welfare of society at large.
- Specifically, the Japanese approach puts greater onus on:
  - Design improvement
  - Extensive testing
  - Higher production levels
  - No compromise on quality
  - Extensive internal auditing
  - Total employee involvement
  - Problem-solving
  - Use of statistical methods
  - Partnering with suppliers and customers

◆ THE TQM EPILOGUE

Whatever method, approach or philosophy may be used to achieve quality, it would be unrealistic to expect quality to spring up overnight with a big bang. Quality comes through small increments, step by step, piece by piece. Since quality is fundamental to improved profitability, credibility, marketability, growth and survival, the two quality imperatives are then:

- **Customer Focus:** total customer satisfaction/delight by meeting/exceeding their requirements/expectations.
- **Long-Term Total Quality Focus:** concern for the quality of all aspects of the organization with constancy of purpose. This involves supplier/customer partnering; employee involvement, empowerment, and recognition; quality of processes, procedures, products and services; etc.

Briefly summarizing our discussion on quality, the following axiomatic commonalities may be worthy of recapitulation:

- **Management Responsibilities/Action**
  - Management to display active commitment and leadership.
  - Management to identify a committed mission, vision, quality policy/objectives.
  - Management to inspire a shared vision, model the way, be approachable, enable and encourage everyone to contribute, act and achieve.
  - The quality policy and strategy to be clear, simple, direct and applicable to all.
  - The quality organization to be supportive of quality activities and inter/intra-communication and interfacing.
  - Total cross-functional coordination is required between sales, marketing, design, procurement, production, and other administrative/organizational elements.

- **Supplier-Customer Partnering**
  - Creating trust and a lasting relationship with suppliers
  - Effectively communicating requirements to suppliers with continued mutual input into each other's process control activities
  - Clearly understanding customer's requirements, expectations, and service standards
  - Seeking total customer commitment, satisfaction and partnering

- **Employee Involvement**

  - Totally integrated work environment
  - Participative management: Steering Committee, Process Improvement Teams, etc.
  - Employee empowerment, recognition and rewards
  - Free and open inter/intra-functional communication and coordination.
  - Management concern for employee welfare, pride of workmanship and quality of work-life

- **Disciplined and Structured Systems**

  - Process control and management
  - Improvement projects
  - Effective measurement, evaluation and verification systems
  - Education and training

Total quality improvement is a game collectively played by four teams of players: the suppliers, customers, management and employees. The game may be played in any number of ways but the result must be the same: all four teams as winners; there must not be any losers. Quality is a win-win game.

PART THREE

THE

QUALITY

CERTIFICATION

11

QUALITY SYSTEM ACCREDITATION

◆ DEMONSTRATION OF QUALITY ACHIEVEMENT

When a company has successfully implemented a TQM System and achieved a certain level of quality, it would like to seek means of announcing their achievement. This recognition allows the company:

- To demonstrate their ability to provide high quality products and services.
- To assure present and prospective customers of their continued commitment to quality.
- To achieve market reputation and credibility.
- To realize expanded and continued market share.

Some of the many ways of achieving recognition include:

- Certification/registration to the ISO 9000 series
- Achieving and meeting the requirements of one of the quality awards, such as the:
  - Malcolm Baldrige National Quality Award
  - Deming Prize for Quality
  - George M. Low Award: NASA's Quality and Excellence Award
  - Canada Award for Business Excellence
  - Shingo Prize for Excellence in Manufacturing
  - Presidential Award for Quality

Certification to ISO 9000 means that a company's total quality system has been assessed by an independent, third-party accredited certifying organization, known as the Registrar, and found to meet the applicable requirements of the chosen level/quality system standard from the ISO 9000 series. Similarly, qualification to any of the other quality awards is also achieved by meeting the requisite evaluation criteria established for this award.

In as much as there are subtle differences in the approach, focus and emphasis of these quality accreditation processes, there are some fundamental commonalities, such as the following, required by all of these awards:

- Establishment, implementation and maintenance of a total quality management program
- Objective evidence of quality policy, systems, procedures and processes physically and functionally operating in the company
- Evidence of maintenance and continuous quality improvement efforts and results
- Customer satisfaction and delight

The generic procedural steps for accreditation to these awards are as follows:

- Establish, implement and maintain an effective TQM System.
- Select the appropriate award for accreditation consideration.
- Prepare the requisite quality system documentation addressing all the requirements and evaluation criteria of the selected award, eg. quality manual, procedures manuals, work instructions and suitable forms, records, books and files.
- Make an application for third-party accreditation.
- Complete the total audit/assessment process with the accreditor and meet all the requisite requirements.
- Achieve accreditation and maintain/improve the quality status.

The details regarding the process of certification to the ISO 9000 series of quality system standards are covered extensively throughout the book. As for the other quality system accreditation awards already mentioned, only a brief outline with its requisite evaluation criteria elements are presented here. For more extensive details, the reader is advised to contact the organization administering the specific award.

This chapter is included only to provide a collective and comprehensive package of information for a comparative evaluation of quality system requirements across various quality accreditation programs. It has been noticed from experience that many companies, while seeking or preparing for accreditation to some program or award, would also like to be aware of other similar accreditation programs and their requisite criteria. This chapter will, therefore, prove useful in providing:

- An awareness of various quality accreditation programs and awards
- A comparative evaluation of the quality system requirements for these various awards
- An additional source of information for augmenting the development/implementation of a self-directed TQM System.

From a comparative evaluation of the various quality awards criteria, some intriguing observations can be made:

- That there is an underlying commonality in terms of requirements for establishing a quality management system.
- That the criteria in itself can serve as guidelines for implementing a TQM system.

Consequently, an organization searching for a TQM model can either use the award criteria of any one of the awards as guidelines for implementing TQM or develop its own TQM model based on the collective knowledge and information of all the awards.

◆ MALCOLM BALDRIGE NATIONAL QUALITY AWARD

This award is granted annually to U.S. companies who excel in quality achievement and quality management. There are three eligibility categories for the award: manufacturing companies, service companies and small businesses. Generally, up to two awards are given in each category per year.

To receive the Baldrige Award, a company has to establish a total quality management system and satisfy the evaluation criteria dictated by the award. As a specific example, Table 31 lists the 1995 examination categories/items for the Baldrige Award.

The Malcolm Baldrige Award is managed by the National Institute of Standards and Technology (NIST) and administered by the American Society for Quality Control (ASQC). The eligibility of the award is limited only to companies operating within the United States of America. Further details regarding this award can be obtained from the following:

Table 31. Malcolm Baldrige National Quality Award

EVALUATION CRITERIA ELEMENTS (1995)

1.0 **Leadership**

    1.1   Senior Executive Leadership
    1.2   Leadership System and Organization
    1.3   Public Responsibility and Corporate Citizenship

2.0 **Information and Analysis**

    2.1   Management of Information and Data
    2.2   Competitive Comparisons and Benchmarking
    2.3   Analysis and Uses of Company-Level Data

3.0 **Strategic Planning**

    3.1   Strategy Development
    3.2   Strategy Deployment

4.0 **Human Resource Development and Management**

    4.1   Human Resource Planning and Evaluation
    4.2   High Performance Work Systems
    4.3   Employee Education, Training, and Development
    4.4   Employee Well-Being and Satisfaction

5.0 **Process Management**

    5.1   Design and Introduction of Products and Services
    5.2   Process Management: Product and Service Production and Delivery
    5.3   Process Management: Support Services
    5.4   Management of Supplier Performance

6.0 **Business Results**

    6.1   Product and Service Quality Results
    6.2   Company Operational and Financial Results
    6.3   Supplier Performance Results

7.0 **Customer Focus and Satisfaction**

    7.1   Customer and Market Knowledge
    7.2   Customer Relationship Management
    7.3   Customer Satisfaction Determination
    7.4   Customer Satisfaction Results
    7.5   Customer Satisfaction Comparison

- United States Department of Commerce
  Technology Administration
  National Institute of Standards and Technology
  Route 270 and Quince Orchard Road
  Administration Building, Room A537
  Gaithersburg, MD 20899-0001, U.S.A.
  Telephone: 301-975-2036
  Telefax: 301-948-3716

- American Society for Quality Control
  611 East Wisconsin Avenue
  P.O. Box 3005
  Milwaukee, WI 53202-3005, U.S.A.
  Telephone: 414-272-8575
  Telefax: 414-272-1734

◆ DEMING PRIZE FOR QUALITY

The Deming Prize was instituted in 1951 by the Union of Japanese Scientists and Engineers (JUSE) in recognition of Dr. Deming's contributions to the quality improvement and achievement efforts in Japan. There are three different categories for the award: The Deming Prize for Individual Person; the Deming Application Prize; and the Quality Control Award for Factory adjudged by the Deming Prize Committee.

The Deming Application Prize is awarded each year by the Deming Prize Committee to an applicant adjudged meritorious by the committee. Originally, the Deming Prize was restricted to Japanese companies; however, since 1984, it has been extended to allow candidate acceptance of overseas companies.

The evaluation criteria elements for the Deming Application Prize for Quality are listed in Table 32. Further details regarding the Deming Prize can be obtained from the following:

- Union of Japanese Scientists and Engineers
  5-10-11 Sendagaya
  Shibuya - Ku
  Tokyo 151, Japan
  Telephone: +81-3-5379-1212
  Telefax: +81-3-5378-1220

Table 32. Deming Application Prize for Quality

EVALUATION CRITERIA ELEMENTS

1. Policy and Objectives

1) Policy with regard to management, quality and quality control
2) Methods in determining policy and objectives
3) Appropriateness and consistency of the contents of objectives
4) Utilization of statistical methods
5) Deployment, dissemination and permeation of objectives
6) Checking objectives and their implementation
7) Relationship with long-range and short-range plans

2. Organization and its Operation

1) A clear-cut line of responsibilities
2) Appropriateness of delegation of power
3) Cooperation between divisions
4) Activities of committees
5) Utilization of the staff
6) Utilization of QC Circle activities
7) Quality control audit

3. Education and its Extension

1) Education plan and actual accomplishment
2) Consciousness about quality and control, understanding of quality control
3) Education concerning statistical concepts and methods, and degree of permeation
4) Ability to understand the effects
5) Education for subcontractors and outside organizations
6) QC Circle activities
7) Suggestion system and its implementation

4. Assembling and Disseminating Information, and its Utilization

1) Assembling outside information
2) Disseminating information between divisions
3) Speed in disseminating information (use of computer)
4) (Statistical) analysis of information and its utilization

5. Analysis

1) Selection of important problems and themes
2) Appropriateness of the analytical method
3) Utilization of statistical methods
4) Tying in with own engineering technology
5) Quality analysis, process analysis
6) Utilization of results of analysis
7) Positiveness of suggestions for improvement

Table 32. Deming Application Prize for Quality (continued)

EVALUATION CRITERIA ELEMENTS

6. Standardization

1) System of standardization
2) Method of establishing, revising, and withdrawing standards
3) Actual records in establishing, revising and withdrawing standards
4) Contents of standards
5) Utilization of statistical methods
6) Accumulation of technology
7) Utilization of standards

7. Control (KANRI)

1) Control systems for quality and in related areas such as cost, delivery and quantity
2) Control points and control items
3) Utilization of statistical methods such as the control chart, and general acceptance of the statistical way of thinking
4) Contributions of QC Circle activities
5) Actual conditions of control activities
6) Actual conditions of control state

8. Quality Assurance

1) Procedures for new product development - quality deployment (breakdown of quality function) and its analysis, reliability, design review, etc.
2) Safety and product liability prevention
3) Process design, control and improvement (KAIZEN)
4) Process capabilities
5) Measurement and inspection
6) Control of facilities/equipment, subcontracting, purchasing, services, etc.
7) Quality assurance system and its audit
8) Utilization of statistical methods
9) Evaluation and audit of quality
10) Practical conditions of quality assurance

9. Effects

1) Measuring effects
2) Visible effects, such as quality, serviceability, date of delivery, cost, profit, safety, environment, etc.
3) Invisible effects
4) Compatibility between prediction of effects and actual records

10. Future Plans

1) Understanding of the status-quo, and concreteness
2) Policies adopted to solve shortcomings
3) Plans of promotion of TQC for the future
4) Relations with the company's long-range plans

◆ GEORGE M. LOW AWARD: NASA'S QUALITY AND EXCELLENCE AWARD

While all the other quality awards are open to any manufacturing company, the George M. Low Award is awarded only to NASA's current or prospective contractors, subcontractors and suppliers in the aerospace industry. The award is a recognition of those companies who have demonstrated sustained excellence and outstanding achievements in quality and productivity for three or more years. The award program is managed by NASA's Office of Continual Improvement, and is jointly administered by NASA and the American Society for Quality Control (ASQC).

The general evaluation criteria elements for the 1994 George M. Low Award are appended in Table 33. For additional details, contact the ASQC (address given above) or NASA's office as follows:

- National Aeronautics and Space Administration (NASA)
  Office of Continual Improvement
  Washington, D.C. 20546, U.S.A.
  Telephone: 202-358-2157
  Telefax: 202-358-4165

◆ CANADA AWARD FOR BUSINESS EXCELLENCE

This award was created in 1984 by the Government of Canada to honour businesses in all industry sectors for their outstanding achievements. The award covers achievement in eight categories: Entrepreneurship, Environment, Industrial Design, Innovation, Invention, Marketing, Small Business, and Total Quality.

The award for the "Total Quality" category is given in recognition of outstanding achievement in overall business quality through a commitment to continuous quality improvement. Emphasis is placed on the total involvement of the company, including all business functions and all employees, on the competitiveness of the products or services in the marketplace and on a high level of customer satisfaction.

Table 33. George M. Low Award: NASA's Quality and Excellence Award

EVALUATION CRITERIA ELEMENTS (1994)

1. **NASA Contract Performance**

   1.A. Provide evidence of how performance requirements are determined and communicated throughout the organization.
   1.B. Provide objective data demonstrating the level of performance in all areas of activity. Award fees, or other objective criteria should demonstrate degree of customer satisfaction.
   1.C. Document continual improvement with objective data.
   1.D. Provide evidence of initiatives which improved the value of products, processes, and services.
   1.E. Identify the processes used to determine and measure customer needs and satisfaction.

2. **NASA Schedule Performance**

   2.A. Provide sufficient data to demonstrate the degree to which schedule requirements have been met over the three-year period.
   2.B. Describe how schedule requirements are evaluated, documented, and disseminated.
   2.C. Describe how the scheduling system is used to analyze past and anticipated schedule performance over the life of the contract.
   2.D. Provide examples, as applicable, demonstrating exceptional responsiveness to rescheduling, work-arounds, and reprioritized work activities.

3. **NASA Cost Performance**

   3.A. Document that actual costs are at or below the estimated contract cost, taking customer-initiated changes into account.
   3.B. Demonstrate an ability to accurately and consistently forecast costs.
   3.C. Describe the system that ensures that the customer is advised of pending cost changes or cost risks in a timely manner.
   3.D. Document savings from cost reduction/avoidance programs.

4. **NASA Problem Prevention and Resolution**

   4.A. Describe the processes used for problem resolution and provide an example of how a <u>major</u> problem would be identified, resolved, and communicated to the customer.
   4.B. Demonstrate the processes used to prevent, as opposed to resolve, problems.

5. **Innovation and Technology Achievements**

The evaluation criteria elements for the "Total Quality" category of the 1994 Canada Award for Business Excellence are appended in Table 34. Further information on the award can be obtained from the following:

- Canada Award for Business Excellence
  Industry Canada
  235 Queen Street
  Ottawa, Ontario, Canada K1A 0H5
  Telephone: 613-954-4079
  Telefax: 613-954-4074

Table 34. Canada Award for Business Excellence

Category: Total Quality

EVALUATION CRITERIA ELEMENTS (1994)

Quality Improvement Policy and Plan

1.a   Policy and Definitions
1.b   Development and Content of Quality Improvement Plan
1.c   Planned Measurements of Quality

Implementation of Policy and Plan

2.a   Communication of Quality Policy and Plan
2.b   Leadership, Deployment and Tracking
2.c   Customer Needs and Assurance of these Needs
2.d   Employee Involvement, Coaching and Training
2.e   Innovative Quality Improvement Techniques

Results Achieved

3.a   Product or Service Improvement and Customer Satisfaction
3.b   Employee Involvement and Satisfaction
3.c   Supplier Partnering/Performance
3.d   Further Results and Benefits

Future Planning

4.a   Future Planning for Quality Improvement
4.b   Planning New Products or Services

◆ SHINGO PRIZE FOR EXCELLENCE IN MANUFACTURING

Established in 1988, the Shingo Prize for Excellence in Manufacturing promotes world class manufacturing and recognizes American companies and plants which excel in productivity, quality, customer satisfaction, and their manufacturing processes. The Shingo Prize may be awarded to as many as three businesses in each of the two prize categories: large manufacturing companies, subsidiaries or plants and small manufacturing companies. The evaluation criteria elements for the prize are appended in Table 35.

Table 35. Shingo Prize for Excellence in Manufacturing

(Utah State University's College of Business)

EVALUATION CRITERIA ELEMENTS (1994)

I. Total Quality and Productivity Management Culture and Infrastructure

    A. Leading
    B. Empowering
    C. Partnering

II. Manufacturing Strategies, Processes and Systems

    A. Manufacturing Vision and Strategy
    B. Manufacturing Process Integration
    C. Quality and Productivity Methods Integration
    D. Manufacturing and Business Integration

III. Measured Quality and Productivity

    A. Quality Enhancement
    B. Productivity Improvement

IV. Measured Customer Satisfaction

V. Summary of Achievements

The Shingo Prize is administered by the Office of Business Relations at Utah State University's College of Business. For further information, contact the following:

- The Shingo Prize
  College of Business
  Utah State University
  Logan, UT 84322-3521, U.S.A.
  Telephone: 801-750-2279
  Telefax: 801-750-3440

◆ PRESIDENTIAL AWARD FOR QUALITY

The President's Quality Award Program, created in 1988, is administered by the Federal Quality Institute and includes two awards:

- **Presidential Award for Quality** - designed for organizations that have mature quality management efforts (at least 3-6 years), and are well-advanced in the quality transformation process. Applicants must be part of the Federal Government, and have at least 500 Federal employees. The award may be given to as many as two organizations each year.
- **Quality Improvement Prototype (QIP) Award** - designed for organizations that have recently begun the quality transformation process. Applicants must be a part of the Federal Government, and have at least 100 Federal employees. The QIP Award may be given to as many as six organizations each year.

The Presidential Award criteria are an adaptation of the Malcolm Baldrige National Quality Award criteria, but reflect the unique Federal environment and culture. The evaluation criteria elements for the award are appended in Table 36. For further information, contact the following:

- Federal Quality Institute
  P.O. Box 99
  Washington, D.C. 20044-0099, U.S.A.
  Telephone: 202-376-3747
  Telefax: 202-376-3765

Table 36. Presidential Award for Quality

EVALUATION CRITERIA ELEMENTS (1994)

1.0 **Leadership**

- 1.1 Executive Leadership
- 1.2 Managing for Quality
- 1.3 Public Responsibility and Community Citizenship

2.0 **Information and Analysis**

- 2.1 Scope and Management of Quality and Performance Data and Information
- 2.2 Similar Provider Comparisons and Benchmarking
- 2.3 Analysis and Uses of Organization-Level Data

3.0 **Strategic Quality Planning**

- 3.1 Quality and Operational Performance Planning Process
- 3.2 Quality and Operational Performance Plans

4.0 **Human Resource Development and Management**

- 4.1 Human Resource Planning and Management
- 4.2 Employee Involvement
- 4.3 Employee Education and Training
- 4.4 Employee Performance and Recognition
- 4.5 Employee Well-Being and Satisfaction

5.0 **Management of Process Quality**

- 5.1 Design and Introduction of Quality Products and Services
- 5.2 Process Management: Product and Service Production and Delivery Processes
- 5.3 Process Management: Business Processes and Support Services
- 5.4 Supplier and Intermediary Quality
- 5.5 Quality Assessment

6.0 **Quality and Operational Results**

- 6.1 Product and Service Quality Results
- 6.2 Operational Performance Results
- 6.3 Business Process and Support Service Results
- 6.3 Supplier and Intermediary Quality Results

7.0 **Customer Focus and Satisfaction**

- 7.1 Customer Expectations: Current and Future
- 7.2 Customer Relationship Management
- 7.3 Commitment to Customers
- 7.4 Determination of Customer Satisfaction
- 7.5 Customer Satisfaction Results
- 7.6 Customer Satisfaction Comparison

12

ISO 9000 CERTIFICATION

◆ STANDARDS-DRIVEN MARKETS

As globalization continues and international trading blocks are formed, like the one in Europe, access to international markets will become especially important. The rules of the game on the international playing field seem to be conformance to the ISO 9000 series of quality system standards. There is a standards-driven quality revolution. The market forces are directing companies to seek third-party evidence of conformance to one of the contractual standards in the ISO 9000 series. Quality system accreditation and registration will become one of the basic requirements before a business contract is awarded.

About ninety countries have accepted the ISO 9000 standards. There is a world-wide political and trade policy trend towards quality system registration. A "certificate of registration" acknowledges that the quality system operated by the firm meets specific requirements. The European markets are attempting to put mandated requirements for ISO 9000 certification. Increasingly, it seems that accreditation will become more and more a requirement for international trading, as well as domestic markets.

◆ ISO 9000 CERTIFICATION

Registration/certification to ISO 9000 means that a company's total quality system has been assessed and has been found to meet the applicable requirements of the chosen level of the ISO 9000 standards. There are two types of certification: two-party certification and third-party certification.

Originally, when the standards were developed, they were intended to be used as a second-party contractual document between the buyer and the seller to assure the buyer that the seller can furnish an acceptable product or service at the stipulated level of quality.

Today, however, most organizations are using the series for third-party certification, that is, seeking an independent accreditation of their quality system in general, without any reference to the current or prospective customer(s). Third-party certification is done by independent accredited Registrars who carry out a comprehensive audit of the company's quality system and provide a seal of approval of its effectiveness.

It should be noted that, in a third-party certification, the auditors of the accredited registrar do not audit the quality of the finished product but rather only carry out a comprehensive quality system audit. Consequently, even when a company may achieve third-party ISO 9000 certification and establish a global credibility, it may still have to comply with all the requisite product inspection/verification requirements stipulated in a bilateral two-party contractual agreement between the buyer and the seller.

It must be clearly understood that the process of certification is not a means to an end. Some companies, due to market-driven pressures, may be tempted to myopically implement only cosmetic systems to simply achieve accreditation/certification status and keep their customers satisfied. Again, having achieved certification status, some companies may also neglect to pursue their emphasis on continuous improvement. The ultimate goal must be continuous improvement of the system as well as the product, with or without the certification.

◆ BENEFITS OF ISO 9000 CERTIFICATION

Over and above the numerous advantages of quality system certification inadvertently mentioned throughout this book, some very specific and direct benefits include the following:

Intrinsic

- Improved control of operations
- Improved internal quality system

- Cost containment through reduced rework, scrap, overtime
- Improved efficiency and productivity
- Improved conformance and compliance
- Decreased liability
- Reduction of costly multiple customer audits
- Increased customer confidence and employee morale

Extrinsic

- World-wide recognition and credibility
- Common denominator of business quality around the world
- Access to European and world markets
- Use of certification label as a status symbol
- Qualification to bid on contracts in new markets
- Expanded and continued market share
- Improved partnership with suppliers and customers

◆ CERTIFICATION START-UP QUESTIONS/ANSWERS

Notwithstanding the market demands for certification or its benefits, most organizations would be willing to achieve accreditation as long as they can justifiably identify value-addedness of certification. consequently, before committing to this mammoth undertaking, managers are generally insistent on being fully cognizant of the pros and cons of the certification process. Through an extensive consulting experience in facilitating and helping companies to achieve ISO 9000 certification, we have come across a number of commonly asked questions that we are appending in Table 37.

We shall attempt to provide some basic answers and experiential guidelines pertaining to these questions. Note that some questions require detailed discussion and methodology; these are expounded at length either in this chapter and/or in several other chapters of the book. The nature and extent of some of these questions is such that the answer, typically, depends on the specific characteristics of the organization's operability framework, such as: its size, nature of business, existing quality initiatives, current state of procedures and documentation, resource base, nature of customers, marketability aspects, etc.

Table 37: ISO Certification Start-Up Questions

Questions

1. Why do we need certification when we already have good quality?
2. Would certification further improve the quality of our products and services?
3. What tangible gains can be expected from certification?
4. How would certification process impact our current operability?
5. How would certification requirements affect our current systems, procedures and processes?
6. What type of preparation is required for certification?
7. How would the ISO system be implemented?
8. What type of resources are required to achieve/maintain certification?
9. Is the certification for product quality or system quality?
10. Can the certificate logo/stamp be affixed onto the products?
11. How long would it take to achieve certification?
12. How long is the certification valid for?
13. With more than one plant/site in the organization, do we need plant-by-plant certification or can we get a single certificate for the entire corporation?
14. What are the total costs of certification?
15. Do we need the assistance of an outside consultant?
16. How do employees feel about ISO certification?
17. How can the certification process be ameliorated in a unionized work environment?
18. How do we select the appropriate Registrar for certification?
19. What are the post-certification activities/requirements?

Answers to Questions in Table 37

Q.1 - Why do we need certification when we already have good quality?

If a company has high standards of quality, it is more the reason to achieve certification, because:

- It will provide tangible evidence and credibility of quality via accreditation by an independent third-party organization.
- It will enhance its competitive position against other registered and non-registered companies.
- It will add structure, regimentation and discipline to the current quality activities.
- The employees will be able to tangibly realize the results of their quality improvement efforts.

Q.2 - Would certification further improve the quality of our products and services?

ISO 9000 certification is no panacea for all the quality issues. Quality is not certificate-dependent. Quality comes through a dedicated continuous improvement strategy and a performance mindset.

Typically, ISO 9000 standards only serve as a baseline process through which companies document internal quality programs and respond to customer needs. However, the disciplined approach, regimentation and standardization of procedures and processes vis-à-vis the certification exercise would, indeed, help in achieving substantial long-term improvements in quality.

Q.3 - What tangible gains can be expected from certification?

The certification process can provide numerous tangible and intangible benefits, some of which can be realized over the short term while others may take a long time to actualize. In addition to the many intrinsic and extrinsic benefits outlined in the preceding section, the certification exercise can be instrumental in enhancing a company's operability in a diversity of ways, as follows:

- It can provide an opportunity and means for initiating internal quality management and continuous improvement activities, if they are not already in place.
- It allows you to examine your processes and procedures to ensure that you document what you do and do what you document.
- It helps to simplify, control, and discipline the processes and allows a critical examination at the non-value adding entities.
- The process promotes quality awareness and teamwork.
- It permits standardization of operations and allows employees to better understand the overall nature of work processes and their role into it.
- The system infuses transparency into the operations which ultimately helps to control the processes more effectively.
- The payback can be direct and spontaneous in terms of improved production processes, increased efficiency and productivity, and a decrease in errors or nonconforming product as a result of internal audits and corrective and preventive actions.

Q.4 - How would certification process impact our current operability?

Certification can have significant impact on the company's operations as follows:

- Quality becomes everyone's responsibility.
- Everyone has to, unequivocally, follow the established and documented procedures. There is no turning back to the old non-disciplined way of doing business.
- The certification status has to be maintained. It would be virtually disastrous for a company to achieve certification and then loose it in the subsequent attempts. A company must be prepared to expend resources for continuous improvement and maintenance of the systems or else it should not even bother to go for certification.
- The workforce will have to become more and more empowered.

Q.5 - How would certification requirements affect our current systems, procedures and processes?

The extent of realignment or redevelopment of the current systems and procedures vis-à-vis the format, structure and requirements of ISO standards is dependent on the extent of their present orderliness and the span of their applicability.

Q.6 - What type of preparation is required for certification?

For ISO certification, the following set of tasks have to be accomplished:

- Preparation of Quality System Documentation:
  - Quality Manual - outlines the company's quality policies, objectives, system, and brief description of procedures while addressing the format requirements of the standard.
  - Quality System Procedures - these documents outline the detailed procedure for each system element, with requisite proformas, forms, etc.
  - Manufacturing Procedures - outlines task instructions for specific activities throughout the production cycle.
- Step-by-step implementation and control of the system elements
- Continuous review and audit of the system effectiveness
- Compliance with the requirements of the certification process

Q.7 - How would the ISO system be implemented?

The system implementation requires the following actions:

- Continuous management involvement and monitoring of the system
- Provision of adequate resources by the management
- The appointment of a Quality Manager, who has the responsibility and authority to facilitate system implementation, conduct reviews, monitor programs and maintain the system

- The development of teams to implement various aspects of the system and to carry-out day-to-day problem solving and quality improvement activities

Q.8 - What type of resources are required to achieve/maintain certification?

The entities and resources required to achieve and maintain certification include, as a minimum, the following:

- Human resources:
  - A Quality Manager or ISO/TQM coordinator
  - Trained Lead Auditor and auditors
  - Teams to develop procedures, implement the system, and monitor effectiveness.
- Financial resources:
  - Funds for entities required to implement the system and achieve certification, such as:
    - Training: ISO 9000, TQM, Auditing, Process Management, etc.
    - External consultant fees, if required
    - Development of documentation
    - Requisite software/hardware entities
    - Registrar's fees for certification
    - Expenses for employee activities related to certification

Q.9 - Is the certification for product quality or system quality?

ISO 9000 is not a product certification standard, but a quality system standard. Registration is granted for the effective implementation of the quality system only. The auditors of the Registrar would not evaluate the quality of products per sé.

Q.10 - Can the certificate logo/stamp be affixed onto the products?

The certification logo/stamp cannot be affixed on to the product itself, because it is not the product that gets certified but the quality system that produces the product. The company can, however, declare the certification status in their company profile, brochure or literature.

Q.11 - How long would it take to achieve certification?

The average time to obtain certification is about 18 months; however, some companies have done it in less than 6 months, while others have spent more than 24 months.

Estimates of the amount of time and money required to achieve certification depends on many diverse factors, such as:

- Nature and extent of business
- Company's preparedness, commitment and enthusiasm
- State of existing systems and documentation
- Whether registration is for one plant or multiple sites
- Effectiveness and precision of the implemented system

Q.12 - How long is the certification valid for?

Normally, a certificate is valid for a period of three years, starting from the time when the certificate was awarded on the basis of successful compliance to the first complete on-site audit requirements. During the three years, several surveillance audits are carried out by the Registrar. If a company fails to meet the acceptance criteria on any one of these follow-up audits, the certificate can be withdrawn. At the end of the three-year certification period, the company has to make a fresh application for registration. However, if a company maintains its quality system effectively, the recertification exercise should not be overly strenuous.

Q.13 - With more than one plant/site in the organization, do we need plant-by-plant certification or can we get a single certificate for the entire corporation?

Normally, certification is awarded for individual plants, sites, divisions, facilities, operations, or production processes. In some cases, a single registration may cover multiple functions, sites or even an entire corporation, if it can be justifiably evidenced that a central corporate quality system is effectively functioning at each of the sites. Even for multiple corporate certification, each site has to be audited.

Q.14 - What are the costs of certification?

The total cost of certification can be compartmentalized into two main categories: external costs, internal costs.

External Costs

- Registrar's Fees: the normal range of certification costs for each plant/facility, is as follows:
    - Certification to ISO 9001: $12,000 - $17,000

- Certification to ISO 9002: $8,000 - $12,000
- Certification to ISO 9003: $4,000 - $10,000
- Sometimes a pre-registration audit, either through the services of the Registrar, or from independent sources, is recommended. This would cost approximately $500 - $1,500.
- Costs for hiring an outside consultant to help facilitate the certification process could range from $30,000 - $50,000.

Internal Costs

- Estimating the internal costs would be a mammoth undertaking. Many companies do not count the internal costs of preparation, documentation, implementation and training under a quality system. Indeed, when existing employees are used in the process, the costs often are considered part of normal personnel expenses for employee activities related to necessary business functions.

Training is an important aspect and should be handled carefully. Training is required in at least the following major areas:

- ISO 9000/TQM principles and processes
- Process Management
- Team Approach
- Auditing

Training cost can be substantially reduced by bringing-in a trainer to do in-house training rather than sending a large number of employees outside to external training course.

Q.15 - Do we need the assistance of an outside consultant?

If a company does not have sufficient in-house capability, seeking the help of an outside consultant would be highly recommended. A good consultant can save time, money and aggravation for the company. However, a word of advice would be in order:

- Do not hire an "ISO awareness type" consultant just because he/she is less expensive. Hire a good, credible consultant, who has hands-on experience of physical implementation of ISO certification system.
- The consultant or consulting company must not do the writing or preparation of documentation or implementation of the system. The control and ownership of all of these processes must be in the hands of the employees. The consultant should only act as a catalyst to facilitate the process.

Q.16 - How do employees feel about ISO certification?

Depending on the existing operability framework of the company, ISO certification process will certainly have an impact on the employees. We carried out post-ISO certification surveys in the plants that we helped for the certification process and found the following key comments coming out of the employees:

Negative comments:

- The process is an inconvenience and it is putting a strangle-hold on production.
- There is too much paperwork.
- It drives in fear to be always thinking "is it ISO appropriate".
- I am being forced into it; ISO should be more voluntary.
- Because auditors do not use the same rules, people do not know the boundaries of operation.
- Writing, maintaining and following procedures as per ISO requirements is cumbersome, because there is too much detail.

Positive comments:

- The process has created uniformity of operation, because everyone follows the same procedures as per ISO format.
- The operation is more disciplined and orderly.
- ISO helps me understand why I am doing things the way I am doing.
- ISO made me pay better attention to doing things.
- The process has helped in an equitable delineation of responsibilities; ISO is everybody's responsibility.
- We are now able to identify problems in production at a much earlier stage and a timely corrective/preventive action can be taken.
- Overall, ISO has had a positive influence on the plant.

Q.17 - How can the certification process be ameliorated in a unionized work environment?

Unless the process is poorly managed, the certification exercise should run smoothly even when the plant workforce is unionized. From my personal experience of having consulted in an unionized environment, I can provide some basic guidelines as follows:

- Provide sufficient and effective information on the certification process and requirements to everyone.
- Involve and empower people to develop procedures through teamwork.

- Use Visual Factory approach (see Chapter 23) to make the communication process open, transparent, and informatory.
- Follow the commandments appended in Table 21, Chapter 6.

Q.18 - How do we select the appropriate Registrar for certification?

The details pertaining to the selection of a Registrar are outlined in the proceeding section.

Q.19 - What are the post-certification activities/requirements?

Some of the key post-certification activities should be the following:

- Identify areas where the system is creating hinderance or burden on the operations and try to simplify the process.
- Obtain continuous feedback from people who are typically involved in the system implementation and maintenance.
- Establish means of measuring system effectiveness.
- Keep a strong focus on the maintenance and continuous improvement of the system.

◆ REGISTRATION PROCESS

The process of registration/certification is not complicated but requires careful planning and preparation. The basic steps are as follows:

- Obtain management commitment.
- Establish a steering team.
- Appoint an ISO 9000 coordinator.
- Review the existing quality system to identify:
  - the state and level of the total quality system functionally operating within the company.
  - the structure and format of the company's quality system vis-à-vis the format and guidelines outlined in ISO 9004-1.
  - the company's state of preparedness.
  - the format of the current internal quality system documentation, ie., the quality manual, procedures manuals, work instructions, etc.
- Select the appropriate level, ie., ISO 9001, ISO 9002 or ISO 9003, for registration.

- Identify what needs to be done to be able to meet the requirements of the selected standard.
- Conduct in-house awareness/training sessions.
- Develop, compile or revise the quality system documentation vis-à-vis the chosen standard.
- Conduct ongoing quality audits.
- Define, develop and implement new/revised quality system procedures and instructions.
- Implement corrective/preventive actions.
- Select a suitable Quality Registrar, make an application for registration and submit the quality manual for assessment.
- Implement improvements recommended by the pre-assessment audit, if any.
- Complete the total on-site audit/assessment process with the Registrar and meet all the specified requirements.
- Take requisite action to remove all discrepancies, as per the Registrar's recommendations.
- Obtain certification status.
- Conduct frequent checks and maintain the certification status.

From the registration process appended above, we can now identify the major action items as follows:

- Selection of appropriate quality model
- Preparation of quality system documentation
- Selection of suitable Registrar
- Implementation of the system
- Compliance/certification with the Registrar

The topics will now be discussed, at length, in the proceeding sections and chapters.

◆ SELECTING THE APPROPRIATE QUALITY MODEL

The selection of the appropriate quality model typically depends on what the company does.

Companies whose operations involve the entire cycle of design, development, production, installation, and servicing would normally be seeking certification to the ISO 9001 level. Since ISO 9001 is the most comprehensive model of the three, it is applicable to organizations with a more comprehensive operational scope, especially where a substantial part of the internal activity relates to the technical design and development of specifications for products or services. Although ISO 9001 commonly applies to manufacturing or processing industries, it can be equally applied to a wide range of other organizations, such as construction or even professional consulting services.

Companies who are not involved in any design function but only produce to an already established design or specification would seek certification to the ISO 9002 model. ISO 9002 applies to manufacturing, processing and even service organizations which work to the technical designs and specifications provided by their customers.

Since the ISO 9003 level concerns itself only with requirements relating to final inspection and testing, this model has a rather limited scope. It applies to organizations whose products or services are quite simple in nature and, as such, their quality can be simply assessed by routine testing and inspection.

The numbering in the three-tier model may give the impression that there is some kind of progression among the tiers and hence organizations seeking certification should start for example, with ISO 9003 and move up to ISO 9001 over a period of time or vice versa. It may also give the impression that certification to ISO 9001 is better than certification to ISO 9002 or ISO 9003. The three models are complete in themselves and the company should select the level that best reflects its activities. Moving from one model to another is possible and reasonable but should occur only when the organization has changed in some way or altered the profile of its total activity for certification purposes.

ISO 9001 and ISO 9002 are much alike in their quality system requirements. The ISO 9001 certification requirements involve twenty elements (see Table 10, Chapter 4) whereas those for ISO 9002 involve nineteen of these twenty. The one element that is part of ISO 9001 but not ISO 9002 is "Design Control". Experience has indicated that there are many companies who, even though not directly involved in the "Design" function, still keep a close watch on and provide significant input into the design activities of their suppliers. Thus, even when such companies would normally go for ISO 9002 certification, they should include references to the design aspects of their operations in their quality system documentation.

In much the same way, companies who are heavily involved in the "Design" function would normally choose to go for ISO 9001 certification. However, if these companies attempt to seek ISO 9002 certification just because it may be easier to achieve, it would really indicate a lack of commitment to quality or a lack of confidence in their design capabilities.

◆ QUALITY SYSTEM DOCUMENTATION

A quality system needs to be established, maintained and documented. The system covers the organization, allocation of responsibilities, procedures, processes and resources which would jointly lead to the provision of goods and services in accordance with the quality policy and objectives. Normally, any company who has a well-established quality management system would have the proper requisite documentation for the system. Preparing the quality system documentation for ISO 9000 certification simply amounts to developing or modifying the existing documentation so as to systematically address and accommodate all the requisite system elements of the applicable ISO 9000 standard.

A quality system is normally documented by means of one or several tiers of documents. One such hierarchy is schematically shown in Figure 4.

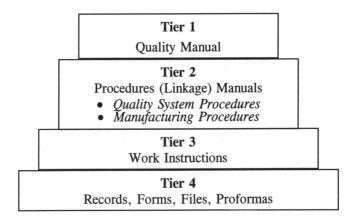

Figure 4: Documentation Hierarchy Pyramid

Tier 1: Quality Manual

Following the format, structure and requirements of ISO 9000 standards, the Quality Manual outlines the management policies, objectives, organizational structure, quality plans, systems and procedures.

Tier 2: Procedures (Linkage) Manuals

The *Quality System Procedures* contains detailed set of instructions for each of the ISO system elements addressed in the Quality Manual. This repetitive exercise is necessary because the Quality Manual, being brief, does not elucidate how each system element is implemented and what procedures are followed. These procedures also clarify who does what, in liaison with whom, and under what authority.

The *Manufacturing Procedures* are the typical Standard Operating Procedures (SOPs) by which the company runs its manufacturing functions. These procedures form the linkage between system elements and manufacturing operations.

Tier 3: Work Instructions

They are the basic operating instructions identifying how the manufacturing procedures are to be carried out for an effective day-to-day functioning of the system. Work Instructions are typically the task instructions for specific activities on the shop floor or in the office, such as work schedules, job descriptions, plant operating instructions, testing/inspection methods, financial reporting instructions, records of quality control activities, records of quality system audits, safety instructions, etc.

Tier 4: Proformas

The fourth tier simply consists of all the requisite form, proformas, books, files and records essential for the documentation and maintenance of the quality system and the effective running of the organization.

This format and structure of the quality system documentation hierarchy as described above should only be viewed as an overall generic documentation framework. By no means should any organization force-fit its operational activities into this framework.

For instance, experience has indicated that some small organizations with few procedural details may be able to accommodate their system elements into only one or two levels of documentation: a quality manual and/or a procedural manual containing all their procedures, instructions and proformas. In some situations, it has been observed that Work Instructions are used for training purposes only. What is important to realize is that the quality documentation should accurately describe the organization's quality policy and operating procedures. Basically, quality system documentation serves the following fundamental purposes:

- They make sure that everyone involved knows what they should be doing, how that should be done and by whom.
- They provide objective evidence to a third-party assessor or to customers that the system is comprehensive and that the organization truly does operate according to the stated management policies and objectives.

♦ CHOOSING A REGISTRAR FOR CERTIFICATION

The certification to ISO 9000 standards is carried out by independent third-party certifying organizations, known as Registrars. Most of the industrialized countries have a host of registrars carrying out the certification task, and this list is growing daily as the demand for certification increases. Companies are free to choose any registrar they wish either from within the country or outside; however, the difficulty is not in finding a registrar, but finding the right one.

In this section, we shall cover the following three essential aspects:

- Process of selection
- Accreditation of registrars
- List of registrars

Process of Selection

In selecting a suitable registrar, a company should consider the following items:

- Find out if there are any regulatory or marketplace requirements that would influence the choice of registrar.
- Investigate if the registrar's certificates are recognized or accepted in markets where the company wishes to sell.

- How competent is the registrar? Check his track record of competency and registrations.
- How broad are his range of knowledge and capabilities? Does the registrar possess capabilities in the area of those functions that your company is engaged in?
- What kind of certification procedures and processes are used by the registrar? For example: process for protecting confidential information; appeal process or complaint resolution procedure; policy and procedure regarding suspensions and withdrawal of the registration; responding to complaints or questions in a timely manner; information and guidance on the deficiencies in the quality system; etc.
- What is the total cost structure of the registrar for certification and how does it compare with that of other registrars? Such costs include: application fee; fee associated with document preparation; fees for quality manual review, as well as for the subsequent review of any other relevant documents and their revisions; cost of the initial visit, including travel and living costs; cost of any follow-up visits; cost of pre-certification audit, if required; cost of modifying the scope of registration, if desired; cost of surveillance audits; cost of reassessment upon expiration of the original registration, etc.
- Find out the range of credibility and recognition that the registrar enjoys - national, international, or both. What organizations have accredited/recognized the registrar. More importantly, what is the scope of accreditation, i.e. for what product or industry area has the registrar achieved accreditation?

Accreditation of Registrars

In searching for a suitable registrar, a question that is often asked by companies is: who accredits the accreditors (registrars)? Indeed, the registrars have to have the credibility to conduct the certification process.

There are some well-established government or quasi-government bodies in several countries who have undertaken the responsibility for accreditation of registrars. Following is a partial list of the bodies:

- Australia

  JAS-ANZ: Joint Accreditation System of Australia and New Zealand

- Belgium

  Comité National pour l'Accréditation des Organismes de Certification (NAC-QS)

- Canada

  Advisory Committee on Quality (ACQ) - Standards Council of Canada, Ottawa

- China

  China State Bureau of Technical Supervision (CSBTS), Beijing

- France

  Association Française pour l'Assurance de la Qualité (AFAQ), France
- Germany

  Deutschen Akkreditierungs Rat (DAR), Berlin
- Hong Kong

  Hong Kong Quality Assurance Agency, Kowloon
- Italy

  Sistema Nazionale per l'Accreditamento (SINCERT), Milano
- Netherlands

  Raad Voor de Certificatie (RVC), Netherlands
- Spain

  Asociación Espanola de Normalización Y Certificación (AENOR), Spain
- Sweden

  SWEDAC, Sweden
- U.K.

  National Accreditation Council for Certification Bodies (NACCB), London
- U.S.A.

  Registration Accreditation Board (RAB) - Jointly administered by the American National Standards Institute (ANSI) and the American Society for Quality Control (ASQC), Milwaukee, Wisconsin

It should be noted that each of these bodies utilize their own criteria for accrediting the Registrars. There is, as yet, no universal agreement between these registrar accreditation bodies to recognize each other's accreditation criteria. Any agreement or mutual recognition is still limited to bilateral MOUs (Memorandum of Understanding) either between the accrediting organizations or between the Registrars themselves on a one-to-one basis. Attempts are, however, now underway, through the international committee: "ISO: Committee on Conformity Assessment (ISO/CASCO)", to develop a single internationally acceptable criteria for the certification of Registrars, that all accreditation bodies can use.

The following points should also be noted:

- Registrars are not bound to get accreditation from these accrediting bodies. They can operate without such accreditation. However, market-driven pressures would probably force most registrars to seek accreditation status.
- The validity of the accreditation status is normally 4 years.

List of Registrars

The list of registrars operating in a country can generally be obtained from the national standards body of the country. In Canada, U.S.A. and the U.K., contact the following:

- Canada

  Standards Council of Canada
  45 O'Connor Street
  Ottawa, Ontario, Canada K1P 6N7
  Telephone: 613-238-3222
  Telefax: 613-995-4564

- U.S.A.

  Registrar Accreditation Board
  American Society for Quality Control
  611 East Wisconsin Avenue
  P.O. Box 3005
  Milwaukee, WI 53202-3005, U.S.A.
  Telephone: 414-272-8575
  Telefax: 414-272-1734

- U.K.

  The National Accreditation Council for Certification Bodies
  19 Buckingham Gate
  London, U.K. SWI E6LB
  Telephone: +44-71-233-7111
  Telefax: +44-71-233-5115

A partial (unofficial) list of the quality system registrars operating in the U.S.A. and Canada is appended below for reference. We have also included the telephone and telefax numbers of these registrars for easy reference, as available at the time of this writing.

Quality System Registrars

U.S.A.

- ABS Quality Evaluations, Inc., Houston, TX
  Telephone: 713-873-9400   Telefax: 713-874-9564
- A.G.A. Quality, A Division of A.G.A. Laboratories, Cleveland, OH
  Telephone: 216-524-4990 ext. 8349   Telefax: 216-642-3463
- AIB Registration Services, Manhattan, KS
  Telephone: 913-537-4750   Telefax: 913-537-1493
- American Association for Laboratory Accreditation (AALA). Gaithersburg, MD
  Telephone: 301-670-1377   Telefax: 301-869-1495
- American European Services, Inc. (AES), Washington, DC
  Telephone: 202-337-3214   Telefax: 202-337-3709
- American Quality Assessors, Columbia, SC
  Telephone: 803-254-1164   Telefax: 803-252-0056
- American Society of Mechanical Engineers, New York, NY
  Telephone: 212-605-4796   Telefax: 212-605-8713
- AT&T's Quality Registrar, Union, NJ
  Telephone: 908-851-3058   Telefax: 908-851-3360
- Bellcore Quality Registration, Piscataway, NJ
  Telephone: 908-699-3739   Telefax: 908-336-2244
- Bureau Veritas Quality International (NA) Inc. (BVQI), Jamestown, NY
  Telephone: 716-484-9002   Telefax: 716-484-9003
- Davy Registrar Services (DRS), Pittsburgh, PA
  Telephone: 412-566-3402   Telefax: 412-566-3407
- Det norske Veritas (DnV) Industry, Inc., Houston, TX
  Telephone: 713-579-9003   Telefax: 713-579-1360
- DLS Quality Technology Associates, Inc., Camillus, NY
  Telephone: 315-468-5811   Telefax: 315-468-5811
- Entela, Inc., Q.S.R.D., Grand Rapids, MI
  Telephone: 616-247-0515   Telefax: 616-247-7527
- Hartford Steam boiler Inspection and Insurance Company, Hartford, CT
  Telephone: 203-722-5394   Telefax: 203-722-5530
- Intertek Services Corporation, Fairfax, VA
  Telephone: 703-476-9000   Telefax: 703-273-4124
- KEMA Registered Quality Inc., Chalfont, PA
  Telephone: 215-822-4281   Telefax: 215-822-4271
- KPMG Quality Registrar, Short Hills, NJ
  Telephone: 800-716-5595   Telefax: 201-912-6050
- Lloyd's Register Quality Assurance Ltd., Hoboken, NJ
  Telephone: 201-963-1111   Telefax: 201-963-3299
- MET Electrical Testing Company, Baltimore, MD
  Telephone: 410-354-2200   Telefax: 410-354-1624

- NSF International, Ann Arbor, MI
  Telephone: 313-769-5197   Telefax: 313-769-0109
- National Quality Assurance, U.S.A., Boxborough, MA
  Telephone: 508-635-9256   Telefax: 508-266-1073
- National Standards Authority of Ireland (NSAI), Merrimack, NH
  Telephone: 603-424-7070   Telefax: 603-429-1427
- Performance Review Institute Registrars Inc., Warrendale, PA
  Telephone: 412-772-1616   Telefax: 412-772-1699
- Perry Johnson Registrars Inc., Southfield, MI
  Telephone: 810-358-3388   Telefax: 810-356-4822
- Quality Systems Registrars Inc.(QSR), Herndon, VA
  Telephone: 703-478-0241   Telefax: 703-478-0645
- SGS International Certification Services, Inc., Hoboken, NJ
  Telephone: 201-792-2400   Telefax: 201-792-2558
- Steel Related Industries, Wexford, PA
  Telephone: 412-935-2844   Telefax: 412-935-6825
- TRA Certification, Elkhart, IN
  Telephone: 219-264-0745   Telefax: 219-264-0740
- Tri-Tech Services, Inc., Danvers, MA
  Telephone: 412-884-2290   Telefax: 412-884-2268
- TUV Rheinland of North America, Inc., Newtown, CT
  Telephone: 203-426-0888   Telefax: 203-426-3156
- Underwriters Laboratories, Inc. Melville, NY
  Telephone: 516-271-6200   Telefax: 516-271-8259
- Vincotte USA inc., Houston, TX
  Telephone: 713-465-2850   Telefax: 713-465-1182

CANADA

- Bureau Veritas Quality International (North America), Inc., Jamestown, NY
  Telephone: 716-484-9002   Telefax: 716-484-9003
- Canadian Gas Association (CGA) Approvals, Inc., Don Mills, ON
  Telephone: 416-447-6465   Telefax: 416-447-7067
- Canadian General Standards Board (CGSB), Ottawa, ON
  Telephone: 613-941-8709   Telefax: 613-941-8706
- Groupement Québecois de Certification de la Qualité, Québec City, PQ
  Telephone: 418-643-5813   Telefax: 418-646-3315
- Litton Systems Canada Limited, Etobicoke, ON
  Telephone: 416-249-1231   Telefax: 416-245-0324
- MGQA Certification Ltd., Oshawa, ON
  Telephone: 905-433-2955   Telefax: 905-432-9308
- Quality Certification Bureau Inc., Edmonton, AB
  Telephone: 403-496-2463   Telefax: 403-496-2464
- Quality Management Institute (QMI), Mississauga, ON
  Telephone: 905-272-3920   Telefax: 905-272-3942

- Quality Systems Assessment Registrar (QUASAR), Mississauga, ON
  Telephone: 905-542-1323   Telefax: 905-542-1318
- SGS International Certification Services Canada Inc., Markham, ON
  Telephone: 905-479-1160   Telefax: 905-479-9452
- Underwriters' Laboratories of Canada (ULC), Scarborough, ON
  Telephone: 416-757-3611   Telefax: 416-757-9540
- Underwriters' Laboratories, Inc., Melville, NY
  Telephone: 516-271-6200   Telefax: 516-423-5657
- Warnock Hersy Professional Services Limited, Lasalle, PQ
  Telephone: 514-366-3100   Telefax: 514-366-5350

13

ISO 9001 (1994)
QUALITY SYSTEM GUIDELINES

◆ INTRODUCTION

A quality assurance manual for ISO 9000 certification needs to have at least the following characteristics:

- The manual has to address and accommodate, with precision, all the requirements stipulated in the chosen level of the ISO 9000 quality system standard.
- The manual has to describe, adequately and accurately, all the systems and procedures being physically functionally operated, followed and implemented in the company.
- The company should be in a position to produce documented objective evidence to validate the contents of the manual.

In order to develop and prepare a good manual, the manual-writing team must have:

- A clear understanding of the requirements of the chosen ISO 9000 level of standard.
- A knowledge of all the systems and procedures operating in the company.
- The ability to write well and professionally.

Accurately deciphering and interpreting the requirements stipulated in any of the ISO 9000 series is almost imperative as preparation for ISO 9000 certification. Undoubtedly, the best way to achieve this is by studying the documents diligently over and over again. Preparing a checklist and guidelines on what is required to be addressed and how and in what sequence it will be accommodated, can facilitate the process. In this chapter, we are appending a set of guidelines that we have developed from our understanding, interpretation and experience and we hope this would help the companies toiling to develop effective interpretation of the quality system requirements for ISO 9000 certification. We have chosen ISO 9001 as example because this is the level with the highest set of requirements.

To be able to give an accurate and precise description of the system elements, the team members have to be well-informed about the systems and procedures operating in the company. Firstly, it is hoped that the make-up of the team is from those personnel who are well versed with the functioning of the organization. Notwithstanding however, no one person or group is expected to possess the complete understanding of all systems and procedures of the company. Therefore, in this regard the team would be continuously seeking assistance from other qualified personnel or functions of the organization either to obtain/validate information or to get the portions of the manual written. This also reinforces a need for conducting ISO 9000 awareness/training sessions for all employees so as to enable them to provide proper input and accurate information to the team and ultimately to the manual.

Finally, it is highly desirable that the team members would be thoroughly proficient and competent in the style of writing and command of language. The manual has to be written with utmost tenacity and professionalism. Besides being required for company use or ISO 9000 certification, the manual is an important marketing tool. To expedite the process and save time and resources, it may even be cost-effective for a company to consider hiring the services of a competent outside professional consultant. However, it must be clearly understood that a consultant can only act as a catalyst - the driving force must come from within the organization.

◆ QUALITY SYSTEM GUIDELINES

As indicated above, the most crucial tasks for ISO 9000 Certification is the preparation of the quality manual. However, before this mammoth task can be undertaken, it is imperative to have an absolutely thorough understanding of the requirements of the standard. In this section, we are providing a detailed package of guidelines describing the requirements stipulated in each clause of ISO 9001. We have specifically chosen a sequential step-by-step format of presentation of the guidelines so as to facilitate clause-by-clause writing of the manual. Note that in some cases, our interpretation simply amounts to rewording of the ISO 9001 clause element - it is because the clause interpretation is simple but has been included as a reminder to ensure that the manual would adequately cover the requisite element.

For each clause of ISO 9001, the guidelines identify what must be addressed and included in the quality manual. The personnel or team writing the manual should, therefore, take each item one by one and identify the corresponding systems and procedures that are or should be operating in the company. Continuing in this manner, it should not be difficult to complete the Quality Manual that adequately and accurately describes the company's quality system while effectively addressing all the requirements stipulated in ISO 9001.

The guidelines for the clause-by-clause interpretation of the systems elements have been particularly presented in a bullet format to facilitate the writing of the manual. The bullets identify the requirements of the clause and as such the manual should follow the sequence of short, precise and accurate paragraphs addressing each requirement. For each clause, therefore, the manual should adequately address all the requirements of the clause while describing the requisite system element physically and functionally operating in the company. Long descriptions of the system or procedures or any motherhood statements about them should be avoided as far as practical.

ISO 9001 (1994): QUALITY SYSTEM REQUIREMENTS

SYSTEM ELEMENTS (Clause)
Manual Guidelines

4.1 MANAGEMENT RESPONSIBILITY

- Define quality policy and objectives.
- Establish quality organizational structure.
- Provide requisite resources.
- Appoint a management representative.
- Plan for management review of the quality system.

4.1.1 Quality Policy

The supplier's management with executive responsibility shall define and document its policy for quality, including objectives for quality and its commitment to quality. The quality policy shall be relevant to the supplier's organizational goals and the expectations and needs of its customers. The supplier shall ensure that this policy is understood, implemented and maintained at all levels of the organization.

- Define and document policy and objectives.
- Policy to include: elements of management commitment; approach to product/service quality.
- Policy to be consistent with the company's goals and expectations.
- Policy means: total customer satisfaction; product/service quality constancy and conformance to specified requirements.
- Policy to be: understood by everyone; implemented and maintained at all levels within the organization.
- Objectives to be: measurable; ambitious; achievable.
- Commitment can be demonstrated by: ensuring that everyone understands and implements the quality policy; initiating, managing and following-up on the implementation of quality policy and system; not accepting deviations from policy, poor quality or wasted resources.

- Policy and objectives should be such as to address all requisite ISO-9001 system elements.

4.1.2   Organization

4.1.2.1   Responsibility and Authority

The responsibility, authority and the inter-relation of personnel who manage, perform and verify work affecting quality shall be defined and documented, particularly for personnel who need the organizational freedom and authority to:

a)   initiate action to prevent the occurrence of any nonconformities relating to product, process and quality system;

b)   identify and record any problems relating to the product, process and quality system;

c)   initiate, recommend or provide solutions through designated channels;

d)   verify the implementation of solutions;

e)   control further processing, delivery or installation of nonconforming product until the deficiency or unsatisfactory condition has been corrected.

- Define and document responsibility and authority of people who manage, perform and verify the work.
- Prepare the organizational chart identifying their interrelationship.
- Ensure that the responsibility and authority is in line with company policy and objectives, and all relevant personnel are fully aware of the channels of responsibility.
- Ensure that the designated personnel have the freedom and authority to: identify and record quality problems relating to the product, process and quality system; initiate, recommend and provide solutions through the system; verify the implementation of solutions; institute further control mechanisms to prevent nonconformities.
- Responsible persons must constantly interface with all activities and links which influence the achievement of quality, such as: purchasing, design development, production, process control, inspection, marketing, sales, delivery, servicing.
- Quality is everyone's responsibility through: effective and timely work habits; checking and inspection of all requisite documentation, procedures, specifications, tools and material; identification of output deficiencies and taking of prompt corrective and preventive action.

- The ultimate responsibility for quality rests with the management: to display commitment; to promote awareness; to organize work; to provide resources; to ensure customer satisfaction.

4.1.2.2   Resources

The supplier shall identify resource requirements and provide adequate resources, including the assignment of trained personnel (see 4.18), for management, performance of work and verification activities including internal quality audits.

- Identify in-house verification requirements.
- Provide trained personnel and adequate resources.
- Verification activities include, for example: inspection, test and monitoring of the design, production, installation and servicing processes and/or product; design reviews and audit of the quality system processes and/or product.
- Verification resources may involve: proper information regarding verification activities and arrangements; awareness of existing standards; training for the people involved; necessary equipment; sufficient time to do the work; documented procedures; cooperation of everyone involved in verification work.

4.1.2.3   Management Representative

The supplier's management with executive responsibility for quality shall appoint a member of the supplier's own management who, irrespective of other responsibilities, shall have defined authority for:

a)   ensuring that a quality system is established, implemented and maintained in accordance with this International Standard, and

b)   reporting on the performance of the quality system to the supplier's management for review and as a basis for improvement of the quality system.

NOTE 5   The responsibility of a management representative may also include liaison with external bodies on matters relating to the supplier's quality system.

- Executive management to appoint a member of its own management team with the authority and responsibility to ensure that: the quality system is developed, implemented and maintained in all functions; quality strategy and improvement programs are prepared and followed up; inspection/audit of products, processes and quality system is carried out effectively.
- The representative is not responsible for the quality of the product per sè, but ensures effective implementation of quality improvement systems and processes.
- The representative reports to the management on the performance of the quality system for review and improvement.
- The appointment of the management representative is recorded in the Quality Manual and all relevant personnel are made aware of this appointment and its associated authority and responsibility.

4.1.3 Management Review

The supplier's management with executive responsibility shall review the quality system at defined intervals sufficient to ensure its continuing suitability and effectiveness in satisfying the requirements of this International Standard and the supplier's stated quality policy and objectives (See 4.1.1). Records of such reviews shall be maintained (See 4.16).

- Identify the company's quality review process in the manual.
- Management should review the quality system at regular intervals to ensure its continuing suitability and effectiveness.
- Reviews should identify the effectiveness of the quality policy and objective.
- Results of these reviews should be: documented, analyzed for deficiencies and problems; discussed with responsible personnel.
- Suitable and appropriate corrective/preventive action should be taken to eliminate system deficiencies.
- Management reviews should include details of: adequacy of organizational structure and resources for the effective implementation of quality system; the extent and degree of implementation of the quality system; the performance status of processes and systems; and the actual product/service quality status.

4.2 QUALITY SYSTEM

4.2.1 General

The supplier shall establish, document and maintain a quality system as a means of ensuring that product conforms to specified requirements. The supplier shall prepare a quality manual covering the requirements of this International Standard. The quality manual shall include or make reference to the quality system procedures and outline the structure of the documentation used in the quality system.

NOTE 6 Guidance on quality manuals is given in ISO 10013.

- This clause is meant to provide guidelines for establishing a quality system to meet ISO 9001 requirements.
- A quality system needs to be established, maintained and documented. The system covers the organization, allocation of responsibilities, procedures, processes and resources which would jointly lead to the provision of goods and services in accordance with the quality policy and objectives.
- The quality system normally is documented by means of one or several tiers of documents, eg., a Quality Manual as an overall system manual; one or more specific procedural manuals for each component of the production process; requisite work instructions; and suitable forms, books, files and records.
- The Quality Manual defines and identifies the scope of quality plans, quality system procedures and review mechanism as per requirements of ISO 9001.

4.2.2 Quality System Procedures

The supplier shall:

a) prepare documented procedures consistent with the requirements of this International Standard and the supplier's stated quality policy, and

b) effectively implement the quality system, and its documented procedures.

For the purpose of this International Standard, the range and detail of the procedures that form

*part of the quality system shall be dependent upon
the complexity of the work, the methods used, and
the skills and training needed by personnel
involved in carrying out the activity.*

*NOTE 7   Documented procedures may make reference
to work instructions that define how an activity
is performed.*

- All elements, requirements and provisions adopted for the quality system should be documented properly.
- Documented procedures should be established consistent with the requirements of ISO 9001.
- The format and extent of documented quality system procedures (eg. design, purchasing, process work instructions), supporting the quality manual, would take various forms, considering:
  - size of the organization
  - specific nature of the activity
  - intended scope and structure of the quality manual
- Documented procedures should be established for making changes, modifications, revisions or additions to the contents of a quality manual. The procedures may apply to one or more parts of the organization.

4.2.3   Quality Planning

*The supplier shall define and document how the
requirements for quality will be met. Quality
planning shall be consistent with all other
requirements of a supplier's quality system and
shall be documented in a format to suit the
supplier's method of operation. The supplier
shall give consideration to the following
activities, as appropriate, in meeting the
specified requirements for products, projects or
contracts:*

a)   the preparation of quality plans;
*b)   the identification and acquisition of any
      controls, processes, equipment (including
      inspection and test equipment), fixtures,
      resources and skills that may be needed to
      achieve the required quality;*
*c)   ensuring the compatibility of the design, the
      production process, installation, servicing,
      inspection and test procedures and the
      applicable documentation;*

> d) *the updating, as necessary, of quality control, inspection and testing techniques, including the development of new instrumentation;*
> e) *the identification of any measurement requirement involving capability that exceeds the known state of the art, in sufficient time for the needed capability to be developed;*
> f) *the identification of suitable verification at appropriate stages in the realization of product;*
> g) *the clarification of standards of acceptability for all features and requirements, including those which contain a subjective element;*
> h) *the identification and preparation of quality records (see 4.16).*
>
> NOTE 8   *The quality plans referred to (see 4.2.3a) may be in the form of a reference to the appropriate documented procedures that form an integral part of the supplier's quality system.*

- Prepare and maintain documented quality plans consistent with all other requirements of the quality system. A quality plan may be a part of a larger overall plan and may be included or referenced in the quality manual.
- Quality plans should define:
  - quality objectives
  - standard operating practices
  - specific responsibilities and authority
  - specific documentation procedures and instructions
- Quality planning activities should give timely consideration to activities such as:
  - developing quality plans
  - implementing controls
  - acquiring cross-functional compatibility
  - evaluating and reviewing system effectiveness
  - keeping appropriate quality records

4.3 CONTRACT REVIEW

4.3.1 General

The supplier shall establish and maintain documented procedures for contract review and for the coordination of these activities.

- Establish and maintain documented procedures for review and coordination of activities relating to contracts.
- A review process plan/checklist should be developed to standardize and improve the contract review process.

4.3.2 Review

Before submission of a tender, or the acceptance of a contract or order (statement of requirement), the tender, contract or order shall be reviewed by the supplier to ensure that:

a) the requirements are adequately defined and documented; where no written statement of requirement is available for an order received by verbal means, the supplier shall ensure that the order requirements are agreed before their acceptance;

b) any differences between the contract or order requirements and those in the tender are resolved;

c) the supplier has the capability to meet the contract or order requirements.

- Review the contract to ensure that: the purchase order requirements are clear, adequately defined and properly documented; any discrepancy between the requirements and tender is resolved; the supplier has the capability and capacity to meet the contractual requirements.

4.3.3 Amendment to contract

The supplier shall identify how an amendment to a contract is made and correctly transferred to functions concerned within the supplier's organization.

- Establish procedures for amending the contract.
- Results of the review/amendment should be discussed with the purchaser in order to achieve agreement.
- All requisite findings of the review/amendment should be communicated to the departments that needs it.

4.3.4 Records

Records of contract reviews shall be maintained (see 4.16).

NOTE 9   Channels for communication and interfaces with the customer's organization in these contract matters should be established.

- Contact review/amendment records must be maintained.

4.4 DESIGN CONTROL

4.4.1 General

The supplier shall establish and maintain documented procedures to control and verify the design of the product in order to ensure that the specified requirements are met.

- Identify, clause by clause, all the requisite design control procedures operating in the company.
- Design function may comprise various facets: product design, process design, service design.
- Develop, document and maintain control and verification procedures for all phases of the design function process.

4.4.2 Design and Development Planning

The supplier shall prepare plans for each design and development activity. The plans shall describe or reference these activities, and define responsibility for their implementation. The design and development activities shall be assigned to qualified personnel equipped with adequate resources. The plans shall be updated as the design evolves.

- Establish and document a plan for all activities relating to design and development work.
- The plan should identify work schedules, verification activities, as well as assignment of the relevant responsibilities.
- Integrate the plan with other relevant plans and verification procedures.
- The plans must be updated as the design evolves.
- Assign qualified personnel, with responsibilities for specific work functions, to the planned design and verification activities.
- Provide adequate resources.

4.4.3 Organizational and Technical Interfaces

Organizational and technical interfaces between different groups which input into the design process shall be defined and the necessary information documented, transmitted and regularly reviewed.

- Establish inter and intra-organizational and technical interface between various design work groups associated with the process as well as product.
- Ensure that the necessary design information is documented, transmitted and reviewed on a regular basis.

4.4.4 Design Input

Design input requirements relating to the product, including applicable statutory and regulatory requirements, shall be identified, documented and their selection reviewed by the supplier for adequacy. Incomplete, ambiguous or conflicting requirements shall be resolved with those responsible for imposing these requirements.

Design input shall take into consideration the results of any contract review activities.

- The manual should indicate all design input procedures.
- Identify, review and record all pertinent design inputs related to the product in a design description document.
- Design description should be all encompassing, to include design aspects; materials and processes requiring development and analysis, including any prototype testing, verification, installation and service; and applicable statutory and regulatory requirements.

- Incomplete, ambiguous or conflicting requirements must be resolved and agreements reached between purchaser and supplier, or with those responsible for imposing these requirements, on how the design requirements will be met.
- Establish a schedule for verification, review and update of design requirements, taking also into consideration the results of any contract review activities.

4.4.5 Design Output

Design output shall be documented and expressed in terms that can be verified and validated against design input requirements.

Design output shall:

a) meet the design input requirements;
b) contain or make reference to acceptance criteria;
c) identify those characteristics of the design that are crucial to the safe and proper functioning of the product (e.g. operating, storage, handling, maintenance and disposal requirements);

Design output documents shall be reviewed before release.

- Identify and document design output in terms of requirements, calculations and analyses that can be verified, such as drawings, specifications, instructions, software, installation, service procedures, and bills of materials.
- Design outputs should exhibit how they embody design input requirements, including a reference acceptance criteria.
- Design outputs must identify those characteristics that are crucial to the safe functioning of the product.
- Design output must include a review of output design documents before release.

4.4.6 Design Review

At appropriate stages of design, formal documented reviews of the design results shall be planned and conducted. Participants at each design review shall include representatives of all functions concerned with the design stage being reviewed, as well as other specialist personnel, as required. Records of such reviews shall be maintained (see 4.16).

- Conduct documented reviews of the design results at all stages of design development.
- Design review teams should include all requisite personnel associated with the function concerned.
- Maintain records of the design reviews.

4.4.7 Design Verification

At appropriate stages of design, design verification shall be performed to ensure that the design stage output meets the design stage input requirements. The design verification measures shall be recorded (see 4.16).

NOTE 10   In addition to conducting design reviews (see 4.4.6), design verification may include activities such as:

- performing alternative calculations;
- comparing the new design with a similar proven design, if available;
- undertaking tests and demonstrations; and
- reviewing the design stage documents before release.

- Plan, establish and document design verification activities to ensure that the design output meets design input requirements at each stage of the design.
- Verification is done to check that the design: satisfies all specified product/service requirements; meets functional and operational requirements (eg., performance, reliability, maintainability); covers safety and other environmental considerations; ensures compatibility and interfaces of materials, components, and/or service elements; has considered selection of appropriate materials and facilities; has ensured technical feasibility of plans for implementing the design portions of the contract (eg., procurement, production, inspection, testing); will allow consistent achievement of tolerances.
- Ensure that proper design verification methods are employed, such as: undertaking qualification tests and demonstrations; carrying out alternative calculations; comparison of new designs with similar proven designs (if available); reviewing design stage documents before release.

4.4.8   Design Validation

Design validation shall be performed to ensure that product conforms to defined user needs and/or requirements.

NOTES

11   Design validation follows successful design verification (see 4.4.7).

12   Validation is normally performed under defined operating conditions.

13   Validation is normally performed on the final product, but may be necessary in earlier stages prior to product completion.

14   Multiple validations may be performed if there are different intended uses.

- Establish procedure for design validation to ensure that product conforms to defined user needs and requirements.
- Design verification leads to design validation . Validation is normally performed under operating conditions on the final product, however, it may be performed at any stage as per requirements.

4.4.9   Design Changes

All design changes and modifications shall be identified, documented, reviewed and approved by authorized personnel before their implementation.

- Establish procedures to ensure that all changes and modifications have been identified, documented, reviewed, approved, and effectively disseminated.
- Design changes/modifications can arise due to: omissions, errors, material selection, manufacturing difficulties, improvement requirements, safety considerations, purchaser requested changes.
- Design changes must be approved by authorized personnel prior to their implementation.

4.5 DOCUMENT AND DATA CONTROL

4.5.1 General

The supplier shall establish and maintain documented procedures to control all documents and data that relate to the requirements of this International Standard including, to the extent applicable, documents of external origin such as standards and customer drawings.

NOTE 15   Documents and data can be in the form of any type of media, such as hard copy, or electronic media.

- List all document and data control procedures in the manual.
- Establish and maintain procedures to control all documentation and data pertaining to the quality system.
- Document and data control system can be in the form of hard copy media or electronically maintained.

4.5.2 Document and Data Approval and Issue

The documents and data shall be reviewed and approved for adequacy by authorized personnel prior to issue. A master list or equivalent document control procedure identifying the current revision status of documents shall be established and be readily available to preclude the use of invalid and/or obsolete documents.

The control shall also ensure that:

a)   the pertinent issues of appropriate documents are available at all locations where operations essential to the effective functioning of the quality system are performed;

b)   invalid and/or obsolete documents are promptly removed from all points of issue or use, or otherwise assured against unintended use;

c)   any obsolete documents retained for legal and/ or knowledge-preservation purposes are suitably identified.

- Documents and data to be reviewed and approved for adequacy by authorized personnel prior to issue; especially the following:
  - Quality Manual and System Procedures
  - Quality Plans
  - Documents pertaining to: Design, Purchasing, Process Control, Audit
- Establish a master list or document control procedure, electronically or otherwise, to identify all documents/data and their current revision status.
- Ensure the availability of pertinent issues of all appropriate documents at all essential locations.
- Obsolete documents should be promptly removed from all points of issue or use. If there is a need to retain obsolete documents for some legal and/or knowledge purposes, make sure that they are suitably identified.

4.5.3 Document and Data Changes

Changes to documents shall be reviewed and approved by the same functions/organizations that performed the original review and approval, unless specifically designated otherwise. The designated functions/organizations shall have access to pertinent background information upon which to base their review and approval.

Where practicable, the nature of the change shall be identified in the document or the appropriate attachments.

- Establish and maintain a continuous and viable mechanism for controlling document changes/revisions.
- Changes must be reviewed/approved by the same functions/ organizations who performed the original review/approval (unless specifically designated otherwise). Pertinent background information must be available on which to base changes/reviews/ approvals.
- Assessment of the effect of changes on other related procedures, systems, product/service must be made and appropriate action taken. The nature of these changes must be identified in the document or appropriate attachments.
- Notice of changes must be sent, and confirmation received through transmittal record form, to all persons who have been issued a copy of the Quality Manual.

4.6 PURCHASING

4.6.1 General

The supplier shall establish and maintain documented procedures to ensure that purchased product (see 3.1) conforms to specified requirements.

- List, in the manual, all requisite procurement procedures of the company.
- Plan and establish a system/procedure to control all procurement activity to ensure that purchased products meets specified requirements.

4.6.2 Evaluation of Subcontractors

The supplier shall:

a) *evaluate and select sub-contractors on the basis of their ability to meet subcontract requirements including the quality system and quality assurance requirements;*

b) *define the type and extent of control exercised by the supplier over subcontractors. This shall be dependent upon the type of product, the impact of subcontracted product on the quality of final product and, where applicable, on the quality audit reports and/or quality records of the previously demonstrated capability and performance of subcontractors.*

c) *establish and maintain quality records of acceptable sub-contractors (see 4.16).*

- Establish and maintain a system for evaluating and selecting sub-contractors on the basis of their ability to meet sub-contract requirements, including quality capability.
- Define the type and extent of controls to be exercised over the sub-contractors. Controls to be commensurate with:
  - Complexity and technical requirements of the product and its impact on the quality of final product.
  - Quality audit reports and/or quality records of sub-contractors' past performance in supplying similar products/services.
- Establish and maintain quality records of acceptable sub-contractors.

4.6.3 Purchasing Data

Purchasing documents shall contain data clearly describing the product ordered, including where applicable:

a) *the type, class, grade or other precise identification;*

b) *the title or other positive identification, and applicable issues of specifications, drawings, process requirements, inspection instructions and other relevant technical data, including requirements for approval or qualification of product, procedures, process equipment and personnel;*

c) *the title, number and issue of the quality system standard to be applied.*

The supplier shall review and approve purchasing documents for adequacy of the specified requirements prior to release.

- Establish and maintain an effective procurement data system.
- Purchasing documents should clearly describe all the technical requirements (type, class or other precise information) to ensure the quality of the procured products/services.
- The purchase order should reference to the quality standard applied and identify all technical requirements, including testing/process requirements.
- Review and approve purchasing documents for adequacy of specified requirements prior to release.

4.6.4 Verification of Purchased Product

4.6.4.1 Supplier verification at subcontractor's premises

Where the supplier proposes to verify purchased product at the sub-contractor's premises, the supplier shall specify verification arrangements and the method of product release in the purchasing documents.

- When verifying product at sub-contractors' premises, the purchasing documents must identify/specify verification arrangements and methods of product release.

4.6.4.2 Customer verification of subcontracted product

Where specified in the contract, the supplier's customer or the customer's representative shall be afforded the right to verify at the subcontractor's premises and the supplier's premises that subcontracted product conforms to specified requirements. Such verification shall not be used by the supplier as evidence of effective control of quality by the sub-contractor.

Verification by the customer shall not absolve the supplier of the responsibility to provide acceptable product, nor shall it preclude subsequent rejection by the customer.

- When specified in the contract, procedure should be established to allow customers to verify, at sub-contractor's and/or supplier's premises, that product conforms to specified requirements.
- Such verification cannot be used by the supplier as evidence of effective control of quality by the sub-contractor.
- Verification by the customer does not absolve the supplier of the responsibility to continuously provide acceptable product nor shall it preclude subsequent rejection by the customer.

4.7 CONTROL OF CUSTOMER-SUPPLIED PRODUCT

The supplier shall establish and maintain documented procedures for the control of verification, storage and maintenance of customer-supplied product provided for incorporation into the supplies or for related activities. Any such product that is lost, damaged or is otherwise unsuitable for use shall be recorded and reported to the customer (see 4.16).

Verification by the supplier does not absolve the customer of the responsibility to provide acceptable product.

- "Purchaser supplied products" are products owned by the customer and furnished to the supplier for inclusion into the final product to meet the requirements of the contract. It may be a product or service, for example, the use of a customer's transport for delivery, use of machine tools or equipment, etc.

- The purchaser bears the responsibility of providing acceptable product or service.
- The supplier should establish and maintain documented procedures for product/service verification, storage, and maintenance of these "purchaser supplied products".
- The supplier must report to the purchaser, any loss, damage or unsuitability of the supplied product/service.

4.8 PRODUCT IDENTIFICATION AND TRACEABILITY

Where appropriate, the supplier shall establish and maintain documented procedures for identifying the product by suitable means from receipt and during all stages of production, delivery and installation.

Where and to the extent that traceability is a specified requirement, the supplier shall establish and maintain documented procedures for unique identification of individual product or batches. This identification shall be recorded (see 4.16).

- Establish, maintain and document the process of identification and traceability of the product during all stages of procurement, production, delivery and installation.
- Identification is made to the applicable drawings, specifications or part number.
- Establish individual batch or lot identification when specifically required.
- Record the identification needed for traceability at all pertinent stages.

4.9 PROCESS CONTROL

The supplier shall identify and plan the production, installation and servicing processes which directly affect quality and shall ensure that these processes are carried out under controlled conditions. Controlled conditions shall include the following:

a) *documented procedures defining the manner of production, installation and servicing, where the absence of such procedures could adversely affect quality;*
b) *use of suitable production, installation and servicing equipment, and a suitable working environment;*
c) *compliance with reference standards/codes, quality plans and/or documented procedures;*
d) *monitoring and control of suitable process parameters and product characteristics;*
e) *the approval of processes and equipment, as appropriate;*
f) *criteria for workmanship, which shall be stipulated in the clearest practical manner (e.g. written standards, representative samples or illustrations);*
g) *suitable maintenance of equipment to ensure continuing process capability.*

Where the result of processes cannot be fully verified by subsequent inspection and testing of the product and where, for example, processing deficiencies may become apparent only after the product is in use, the process shall be carried out by qualified operators and/or shall require continuous monitoring and control of process parameters to ensure that the specified requirements are met.

NOTE 16   Such processes requiring pre-qualification of their process capability are frequently referred to as special processes.

Records shall be maintained for qualified processes, equipment and personnel, as appropriate (See 4.16).

- Identify all process control activities pursued in the company.
- Quality has to be manufactured in, and this is accomplished through effective process control systems.
- Plan and operate production, installation and servicing processes under controlled conditions.
- Implementing controlled conditions imply:
  - Documented procedures, process flow charts, standardized criteria for workmanship, suitable equipment and working environment.
  - Use of statistical process control (SPC) techniques.
  - Approval of processes before and during use.
  - Monitoring and control of product and process characteristics during production in order to prevent nonconformities.

- Suitable maintenance of equipment.
- Special processes are those that the results of which cannot be verified by subsequent inspection or test, but deficiencies may become apparent during use.
- Identify special processes in the Quality Manual.
- Plan, implement and monitor controlled conditions for special processes the same way as done for other processes.
- Specify requirements for any qualifications and maintain records of qualified processes, personnel and equipment.

4.10 INSPECTION AND TESTING

4.10.1 General

The supplier shall establish and maintain documented procedures for inspection and testing activities in order to verify that the specified requirements for product are met. The required inspecting and testing, and the records to be established, shall be documented in the quality plan or documented procedures.

- Procedures for inspection and testing activities of product at all stages must be established, maintained and documented in the quality plan.
- Identify how records shall be maintained.

4.10.2 Receiving Inspection and Testing

4.10.2.1   *The supplier shall ensure that incoming product is not used or processed (except in the circumstances described in 4.10.2.3) until it has been inspected or otherwise verified as conforming to specified requirements. Verification of the conformance of specified requirements shall be in accordance with the quality plan and/or documented procedures.*

4.10.2.2   *In determining the amount and nature of receiving inspection, consideration shall be given to the amount of control exercised at the sub-contractor's premises and the recorded evidence of conformance provided.*

4.10.2.3 *Where incoming product is released for*
urgent production purposes prior to
verification, it shall be positively
identified and recorded (see 4.16) in order
to permit immediate recall and replacement
in the event of nonconformity to specified
requirements.

- Establish a quality plan or documented procedures (sampling inspection plans, etc.) to verify incoming product before it is used for processing.
- Establish procedures to handle nonconforming product as per clause 4.13 of ISO 9001 pertaining to control of nonconforming product.
- The intensity and frequency of receiving inspection can be minimized by ensuring and exercising controls at the source.
- Product may be released, without incoming inspection, under positive recall. Product is to be identified and recorded for traceability or inspection at a later date as per quality plan.

4.10.3   In-process Inspection and Testing

The supplier shall:

a)   inspect and test the product as required by
the quality plan and/or documented procedures;
b)   hold product until the required inspection and
tests have been completed or necessary reports
have been received and verified, except when
product is released under positive-recall
procedures (see 4.10.2.3). Release under
positive-recall procedures shall not preclude
the activities outlined in 4.10.3a).

- Establish and identify in the manual, the quality plan or documented procedures for in-process inspection and testing.
- Hold product until all requisite inspections and tests have been completed or released and tests have been completed or release product under positive recall procedures.
- Handle nonconformities as per procedures established in the Quality Manual.

4.10.4   Final Inspection and Testing

The supplier shall carry out all final inspection
and testing in accordance with the quality plan
and/or documented procedures to complete the
evidence of conformance of the finished product to
the specified requirements.

The quality plan and/or documented procedures for final inspection and testing shall require that all specified inspection and tests, including those specified either on receipt of product or in-process, have been carried out and that the results meet specified requirements.

No product shall be dispatched until all the activities specified in the quality plan and/or documented procedures have been satisfactorily completed and the associated data and documentation are available and authorized.

- Establish and identify, in the manual, all procedures for final inspection and testing.
- The quality plan or documented procedures should require that all of the following inspections have been carried out:
  - Incoming inspection
  - In-process inspection
  - Final inspection
- The inspection results and data must indicate product conformance to specified requirements.
- Product should not be shipped until the inspection results are complete and specified requirements are met.
- Conformance results/data/documentation must be available and authorized.

4.10.5   Inspection and Test Records

The supplier shall establish and maintain records which provide evidence that the product has been inspected and/or tested. These records shall show clearly whether the product has passed or failed the inspections and/or tests according to defined acceptance criteria. Where the product fails to pass any inspection and/or test, the procedures for control of nonconforming product shall apply (See 4.13).

Records shall identify the inspection authority responsible for the release of product (see 4.16).

- Establish and maintain records to verify that the product has passed inspection and meets acceptance criteria.
- Handle nonconformities as per procedures established in the Quality Manual.
- Records should identify the inspection authority responsible for the release of product.

4.11   CONTROL OF INSPECTION, MEASURING AND TEST EQUIPMENT

4.11.1   General

The supplier shall establish and maintain documented procedures to control, calibrate and maintain inspection, measuring and test equipment (including test software) used by the supplier to demonstrate the conformance of product to the specified requirements. Inspection, measuring and test equipment shall be used in a manner which ensures that measurement uncertainty is known and is consistent with the required measurement capability.

Where test software or comparative references such as test hardware are used as suitable forms of inspection, they shall be checked to prove that they are capable of verifying the acceptability of product, prior to release for use during production, installation, or servicing, and shall be rechecked at prescribed intervals. The supplier shall establish the extent and frequency of such checks and shall maintain records as evidence of control (see 4.16).

Where the availability of technical data pertaining to the inspection, measuring and test equipment is a specified requirement, such data shall be made available, when required by the customer or customer's representative, for verification that the inspection, measuring and test equipment is functionally adequate.

- Establish and identify in the manual, procedures for the control, calibration and maintenance of all inspection, measuring and test equipment. Ensure that the measurement uncertainty of the equipment is known and is consistent with the required measurement capability.
- If test hardware or test software is used for inspection, make sure that they are capable of verifying the product acceptability. Also, recheck such equipment at regular intervals.
- Establish and maintain a schedule and records of checks and rechecks of equipment to demonstrate evidence of control.
- Make available to the customer, when required, technical data pertaining to the measurement devices for verification to ensure that it is functionally adequate.

4.11.2   Control Procedure

The supplier shall:

a)   *determine the measurements to be made, the accuracy required, and select the appropriate inspection, measuring and test equipment that is capable of the necessary accuracy and precision;*

b)   *identify all inspection, measuring and test equipment that can affect product quality, and calibrate and adjust them at prescribed intervals, or prior to use, against certified equipment having a known valid relationship to internationally or nationally recognized standards. Where no such standards exist, the basis used for calibration shall be documented;*

c)   *define the process employed for the calibration of inspection, measuring and test equipment including details of equipment type, unique identification, location, frequency of checks, check method, acceptance criteria and the action to be taken when results are unsatisfactory;*

d)   *identify inspection, measuring and test equipment with a suitable indicator or approved identification record to show the calibration status;*

e)   *maintain calibration records for inspection, measuring and test equipment (see 4.16);*

f)   *assess and document the validity of previous inspection and test results when inspection, measuring and test equipment is found to be out of calibration;*

g)   *ensure that the environmental conditions are suitable for the calibration, inspections, measurements and tests being carried out;*

h)   *ensure that the handling, preservation and storage of inspection measuring and test equipment is such that the accuracy and fitness for use is maintained;*

i)   *safeguard inspection, measuring and test facilities, including both test hardware and test software, from adjustments which would invalidate the calibration setting.*

NOTE 18   The metrological confirmation system for measuring equipment given in ISO 10012 may be used for guidance.

- Identify the measurements to be made, and the level of accuracy/ precision required. Select appropriate inspection/measuring/test equipment that has the precision/accuracy required for the task.
- Calibrate all equipment and devices at regular intervals or prior to use.
- The equipment must be calibrated against certified equipment having a known valid relationship to a recognized national/international standard. Where no standards exist, identify and document the basis used for calibration.
- Establish and maintain calibration procedures to include details of equipment type, identification number, location, frequency of checks, check method, acceptance criteria and action on nonconformances.
- Identify the calibration status by a suitable indicator or approved identification record.
- Maintain calibration records.
- If the equipment is found to be out of calibration, check to ensure the validity of preceding measurements taken by the same equipment.
- Establish adequate environmental conditions for calibration.
- Provide suitable storage facilities for the equipment to maintain a high degree of accuracy and fitness for use.
- Guard the equipment (software as well as hardware) against unauthorized tampering or adjustment.

4.12   INSPECTION AND TEST STATUS

The inspection and test status of product shall be identified by suitable means, which indicate the conformance or nonconformance of product with regard to inspection and tests performed. The identification of inspection and test status shall be maintained, as defined in the quality plan and/or documented procedures, throughout production, installation and servicing of the product to ensure that only product that has passed the required inspections and tests [or released under an authorized concession (see 4.13.2)] is dispatched, used or installed.

- Establish, either in the quality plan or through documented procedures, a system of identification of the product conformance/ nonconformance with regard to inspection/tests performed. The status can be identified using stamps, tags, markings, labels, routing cards, inspection records, test software, physical location, etc.

- Identify the inspection/test status throughout production cycle - from receipt to shipment.
- Maintain inspection and test status to ensure that only suitable product is dispatched, used or installed.

4.13   CONTROL OF NONCONFORMING PRODUCT

4.13.1   General

The supplier shall establish and maintain documented procedures to ensure that product that does not conform to specified requirements is prevented from unintended use or installation. This control shall provide for identification, documentation, evaluation, segregation (when practical), disposition of nonconforming product, and for notification to the functions concerned.

- Establish and list in the manual, all procedures regarding control of nonconforming product.
- Establish and maintain a system:
    - To ensure that nonconforming material is identified, documented and segregated, if possible.
    - To prevent the unintended use or installation of nonconforming material or product.
    - To evaluate the nature of nonconformity.
    - To notify the functions concerned.
    - To take appropriate action for the disposition of nonconforming material/product.

4.13.2   Review and Disposition of Nonconforming Product

The responsibility for review and authority for the disposition of nonconforming product shall be defined.

Nonconforming product shall be reviewed in accordance with documented procedures. It may be

a)   reworked to meet the specified requirements,
b)   accepted with or without repair by concession,
c)   regraded for alternative applications, or
d)   rejected or scrapped.

Where required by the contract, the proposed use or repair of product (see 4.13.2b) which does not conform to specified requirements shall be reported for concession to the customer or customer's representative. The description of the nonconformity that has been accepted, and of repairs, shall be recorded to denote the actual condition (see 4.16).

Repaired and/or reworked product shall be re-inspected in accordance with the quality plan and/or documented procedures.

- Define, establish and identify the responsibility, authority, and procedures for review and disposition of nonconforming product.
- Possible modes of disposition can be:
  - Rework to meet specified requirements
  - Acceptance by concession
  - Re-grading for alternative use
  - Rejecting or scrapping
- If required by the contract, the proposed use or repair of the nonconforming product should be reported to the customer for concession. Also, the nature and description of nonconformity or repair, that has been mutually accepted by both parties, should be recorded to denote actual condition.
- Repaired/reworked product must be re-inspected.

4.14 CORRECTIVE AND PREVENTIVE ACTION

4.14.1   General

The supplier shall establish and maintain documented procedures for implementing corrective and preventive action.

Any corrective or preventive action taken to eliminate the causes of actual or potential nonconformities shall be to a degree appropriate to the magnitude of problems and commensurate with the risks encountered.

The supplier shall implement and record any changes to the documented procedures resulting from corrective and preventive action.

- Establish and maintain documented procedures for implementing corrective and preventive action.
- Corrective/preventive action must be commensurate with:
  - magnitude of the problem
  - risks encountered
- Establish procedures to ensure implementation and recording of changes resulting from corrective/preventive action.

4.14.2   Corrective Action

The procedures for corrective action shall include:

a)   *the effective handling of customer complaints and reports of product nonconformities;*
b)   *investigation of the cause of nonconformities relating to product, process and quality system, and recording the results of the investigation (see 4.16);*
c)   *determination of the corrective action needed to eliminate the cause of nonconformities;*
d)   *application of controls to ensure that corrective action is taken and that it is effective.*

- Develop procedures for corrective action to include:
  - means to effectively handle customer complaints
  - reports of product nonconformities
  - investigating and recording of causes of nonconformities
  - determination of corrective action to be taken to eliminate nonconformities
  - monitoring/auditing/follow-up on corrective action implementation and its effectiveness.

4.14.3   Preventive Action

The procedures for preventive action shall include:

a)   *the use of appropriate sources of information such as processes and work operations which affect product quality, concessions, audit results, quality records, service reports and customer complaints to detect, analyze and eliminate potential causes of nonconformities;*

   b)   *determination of the steps needed to deal with*
          any problems requiring preventive action;
   c)   *initiation of preventive action and*
          application of controls to ensure that it is
          effective;
   d)   *ensuring that relevant information on actions*
          taken is submitted for management review
          (see 4.1.3).

- Develop procedures for preventive action to include:
  - analysis of all available information to identify and eliminate potential causes of nonconformities.
  - outlining protocol to deal with problems requiring implementation and its effectiveness.
  - initiating/monitoring/controlling preventive action implementation and its effectiveness.
  - submitting, for management review, all pertinent information on actions taken and/or changes made to procedures as a result of corrective/ preventive action.

4.15 HANDLING, STORAGE, PACKAGING, PRESERVATION AND DELIVERY

4.15.1 General

The supplier shall establish and maintain
documented procedures for handling, storage,
packaging, preservation and delivery of product.

- Plan, develop and maintain documented procedures for handling, storage, packaging, preservation and delivery of incoming material, materials in process, and finished goods.

4.15.2 Handling

The supplier shall provide methods of handling
product that prevent damage or deterioration.

- Develop appropriate methods of handling materials to ensure prevention of damage or deterioration.

4.15.3 Storage

The supplier shall use designated storage areas or stock rooms to prevent damage or deterioration of product, pending use or delivery. Appropriate methods for authorizing receipt to and dispatch from such areas shall be stipulated.

In order to detect deterioration, the condition of product in stock shall be assessed at appropriate intervals.

- Plan and secure suitable designated storage facilities, physical as well as environmental, to prevent deterioration of the product.
- Receipt and issue of material from stock areas must be controlled.
- Carry out periodical review of material in stock to detect deterioration.

4.15.4 Packaging

The supplier shall control packing, packaging and marking processes (including materials used) to the extent necessary to ensure conformance to specified requirements.

- Establish procedures for the control of packing, packaging and marking processes to provide appropriate protection against damage or deterioration to ensure conformance to specified requirements.

4.15.5 Preservation

The supplier shall apply appropriate methods for preservation and segregation of product when the product is under the supplier's control.

- Establish methods for preservation and segregation of product during all phases of manufacturing - from the time of receipt until delivery.

4.15.6 Delivery

The supplier shall arrange for the protection of the quality of product after final inspection and test. Where contractually specified, this protection shall be extended to include delivery to destination.

- Provide suitable means of protecting the quality of product during all phases of delivery.

4.16 CONTROL OF QUALITY RECORDS

The supplier shall establish and maintain documented procedures for identification, collection, indexing, access, filing, storage, maintenance and disposition of quality records.

Quality records shall be maintained to demonstrate conformance to specified requirements and the effective operation of the quality system. Pertinent quality records from the subcontractor shall be an element of these data.

All quality records shall be legible and shall be stored and retained in such a way that they are readily retrievable in facilities that provide a suitable environment to prevent damage or deterioration and to prevent loss. Retention times of quality records shall be established and recorded. Where agreed contractually, quality records shall be made available for evaluation by the customer or the customer's representative for an agreed period.

NOTE 19   Records can be in the form of any type of media, such as hard copy or electronic media.

- Establish and maintain documented procedures to identify, select, index, access, file, store, maintain and dispose of quality records.
- Quality records are used to demonstrate product quality and effective implementation of the quality system. Records to verify product quality include: quality plans; records of identification, traceability, inspection/test, and positive recall; records of nonconformance; document numbers; revision numbers; sub-contractors quality records. Records to verify effective system implementation include records pertaining to all the requisite system elements of ISO-9001.
- Quality records are to be legible and identifiable to the relevant product.
- Quality records are to be stored and maintained in such a way as to prevent deterioration and facilitate ease of retrieval.
- Establish, record, and implement procedures for retention times of the records.

- Arrangements should be established for making the records available to the customer or his representative for evaluation. Accordingly, relevant personnel should be notified of the agreed period for the storage of records.
- Records can be maintained electronically or in the form of hard copy.

4.17 INTERNAL QUALITY AUDITS

The supplier shall establish and maintain documented procedures for planning and implementing internal quality audits to verify whether quality activities and related results comply with planned arrangements and to determine the effectiveness of the quality system.

Internal quality audits shall be scheduled on the basis of the status and importance of the activity to be audited and shall be carried out by personnel independent of those having direct responsibility for the activity being audited.

The results of the audits shall be recorded (see 4.16) and brought to the attention of the personnel having responsibility in the area audited. The management personnel responsible for the area shall take timely corrective action on deficiencies found during the audit.

Follow-up audit activities shall record the implementation and effectiveness of the corrective action taken (see 4.16).

NOTES

20   The results of internal audits form an integral part of the input to management review activities (see 4.1.3.).

21   Guidance on quality system audits is given in ISO 10011.

- Establish and maintain documented procedures for planning and implementing internal quality audits to verify compliance of quality activities/results with planned arrangements and effectiveness of the quality system.
- Establish appropriate audit schedules.

- Audits must be conducted by personnel independent of the activity audited.
- Audit findings must be documented and communicated to the responsible personnel as well as management for a timely corrective action.
- Follow-up audits must identify and record implementation and effectiveness of the corrective action taken.

4.18 TRAINING

The supplier shall establish and maintain documented procedures for identifying training needs and provide for the training of all personnel performing activities affecting quality. Personnel performing specific assigned tasks shall be qualified on the basis of appropriate education, training and/or experience, as required. Appropriate records of training shall be maintained (see 4.16).

- Establish and maintain a system for identifying training needs.
- Provide training for all personnel whose activities effect quality and system implementation.
- For specific tasks, the assigned personnel must be qualified on the basis of appropriate education, training and experience.
- Maintain records of training activities.

4.19 SERVICING

Where servicing is a specified requirement, the supplier shall establish and maintain documented procedures for performing, verifying and reporting that the servicing meets the specified requirements.

- If service function is part of the requirements, establish and maintain documented procedures for performing and verifying that the service meets the specified requirements.
- Continuously check the quality of service provided.
- Service also includes: customer complaints and service to internal functions.

4.20   STATISTICAL TECHNIQUES

4.20.1   Identification of Need

The supplier shall identify the need for statistical techniques required for establishing, controlling and verifying process capability and product characteristics.

- Identify needs for statistical techniques required for establishing, controlling and verifying process capability and product characteristics.

4.20.2   Procedures

The supplier shall establish and maintain documented procedures to implement and control the application of the statistical techniques identified in 4.20.1.

- Establish and maintain documented procedures for the implementation and control of application of requisite statistical techniques.
- Statistical techniques include such methods as: sampling inspection plans, statistical process control, control charts, process capability analysis, design of experiments and other analytical problem solving techniques.

Note: The text of ISO 9001 have been reproduced with permission of the Standards Council of Canada.

14

ISO 9000: QUALITY SYSTEM DOCUMENTATION

◆ INTRODUCTION

As indicated earlier, for the effective operation of a quality system, its contents must be properly structured and documented. Any company which has a well-established quality management system would normally have the proper requisite documentation for the system, such as the Quality Manual, the Procedures Manuals and the Work Instructions.

The quality manual is the most important item of the system documentation. It is a silent, but powerful, spokesperson for the company. It clearly identifies, to everyone, the company's commitment to quality through its management mission/vision, quality policy and objectives, systems, procedures and methodologies. This is the document that a company would like to display up-front to identify its commitment to quality. It is, therefore, fundamentally important to ensure that the quality manual is developed with utmost tenacity and professionalism.

The procedures manuals and work instructions, on the other hand, are internal to the company and need not be disclosed to anyone except during a mutually consented, requisite quality system audit. These manuals contain operating procedures for the day-to-day functioning of the organization. Although the whole system is dynamic and responsive to the changing conditions, the detailed procedures and area work instructions are the ones most subject to regular revision, often because the organization's position and operating methods keep developing and changing. Therefore, the development of procedures, their review and revision require continuous support from all the personnel and functions impacting quality.

◆ QUALITY SYSTEM DOCUMENTATION

As indicated earlier, some or all of the following documents are required for the process of certification. To facilitate our discussion, we shall use analogy to ISO 9001 standard.

- Quality Manual
- Quality System Procedures Manual
- Quality Plans
- Manufacturing Procedures Manuals or Standard Operating Procedures
- Work Instructions
- Proformas, files, forms, books, records

Quality Manual

The following key elements regarding the quality manual should be clearly noted:

- The quality manual must:
  - Be brief
  - Not contain any detailed operating procedures
  - Address all requisite system elements of ISO 9001
  - Outline the overall framework of company's operations and quality system.
- From experience, we have observed that even when most companies have a quality manual, it does not specifically address the format and structure of ISO 9001 requirements. Companies generally have to develop the quality manual right from the start.
- Early in the manual development phase, it is important to first establish the format and structure of the manual. There are no fixed rules as such - any type of structure is acceptable. Perhaps, it would be more germane to use the same structure that the company is currently using for its other documentations. Having decided on the format and structure, it would be good to consistently follow the same approach throughout the quality manual and other procedure manuals to maintain uniformity.
- As a matter of information, it should be noted that, during the process of certification, when the quality manual is sent to the Registrars' auditors for review, the auditors typically do the following two things:
  - They conduct a thorough review to unsure that the manual adequately addresses all the system elements of ISO 9001.
  - They prepare a checklist of functions and procedures that the company outlines vis-à-vis the twenty system elements of ISO 9001. This checklist is, then, used by the auditors during the comprehensive on-site audit for certification to ensure that the company is doing what it says.

In the next few sections, we shall provide some basic guidelines for developing the quality manual. The same approach can be utilized for developing the quality system procedures manuals as well as the manufacturing manuals. The suggested format, structure and contents of the manual are perhaps only one example of the many different ways such a manual can be developed. Another good source of information on quality manual development is the newly developed international standard by the technical committee ISO/TC176: "ISO 10013: Preparation of Quality Manual".

Quality System Procedures Manuals

As an extension to the quality manual, these constitute a set of twenty second level system procedures manuals providing greater details on how each system element, addressed in the quality manual, is implemented. Although the exercise of developing this second set of procedures separately, rather than including the detailed procedures in the quality manual itself, seems repetitive, it is necessary for the following reasons:

- The quality manual is generally brief and generic in nature. Copies of the manual can be made available to anyone upon request. Detailed operating procedures are normally confidential and internal to a company. By combining the detailed system level procedures into the quality manual, the company would run the risk of divulging their internal procedures to outside agencies.
- Secondly, the operational procedures are always continually evolving and changing. That is a normal part of business/manufacturing process. If these procedures are included into the quality manual, then whenever a change is made in the procedures, it has to be reported to the Registrar as well as to all whom a copy of the manual has been issued. This can create an unwarranted burden on the system. On the other hand, if the system level procedures are developed as a separate entity, routine changes in the procedures can be easily accommodated and managed.

It must be clearly understood, however, that if the quality manual is kept brief and generic, then the system level procedures have to be developed, because the company has to identify the means and methods by which the system is implemented, operated, and maintained. The quality system procedures manuals could follow the same basic approach and format as for the quality manual, which is outlined in the next section. However, for these procedures, the most fundamental need is to have everyone's involvement and participation in the developmental process.

Quality Plans

The international standard: "ISO 8402 - Quality vocabulary" defines a *quality plan* as follows:

> "**Quality plan**: Document setting out the specific quality practices, resources and sequence of activities relevant to a particular product, project or contract."

Clause "4.2: Quality System" of the ISO 9001 stresses the need and requirement for quality planning and the preparation of quality plans. We have observed from experience, that some companies have developed separate documents for quality plans while others have the quality planning framework incorporated with their system level procedures manuals. Each approach is fine as long as there is clear evidence of a proper sequence of activities outlining the quality procedures and practices followed for the functional activity undertaken. The ISO/TC176, technical committee has developed an internal standard: "ISO 9004-5: Guidelines for Quality Plans" which can be gainfully used to develop quality plans.

Manufacturing Procedures Manuals

These documents contain the operating procedures that every company utilizes to produce products and services. Although there is no specific requirement of ISO certification process for the format, structure and extent of these procedures per sé; however, there is a need to interface these procedures with the quality system requirements of the standard. Some companies, we have observed, have gone through the exercise of rewriting these manufacturing procedures or standard operating procedures in the same format as the quality manual and quality system procedures so as to create uniformity, precision and efficiency in the system.

Work Instructions

Work Instructions are really a summary of the manufacturing procedures. They present a brief, step-by-step set of operational instructions on how to handle a task. These can be presented in the form of a flow chart also. Many companies have video-taped theses instructions for daily usage and learning or have set aside these for training purposes only.

Proformas

The forms, proformas, books, records and files forms the tangible backbone of the quality system. Some of the important ones needed for the implementation and functioning of the system are as follows:

- "Revision Transmittal Record" for changes/revision to the controlled copies of the quality manual.
- "Request for Document Change" form
- "Issuance of Change" form
- "Nonconformance and Corrective/Preventive Action Report" form
- "Internal Audit Nonconformance Report" form
- "Training Record" matrix
- "Equipment Calibration" matrix
- Etc.

◆ QUALITY MANUAL FUNDAMENTALS

What is a quality manual? The definition given in the international standard "ISO 8402 (1994): Quality Vocabulary" is as follows:

> "**Quality Manual**: Document stating the quality policy and describing the quality system of an organization."

Basically, a quality manual describes the documented quality system procedures intended for the overall planning and administration of activities which impact the quality of an organization's products and services. The manual generally serves the following purposes:

- It serves as a means of communicating a company's policy, procedures and commitment to quality.
- It formalizes and documents the quality system.
- It assists in the effective implementation and maintenance of the quality system.
- It establishes effective inter- and intra-organizational interfaces.
- It provides an improved control of operations.
- It serves as the basis for auditing quality system performance.
- It provides consistency and uniformity in the application of system procedures.
- It provides an objective evidence that the company is truly operating a quality system as per the stated policies and objectives.

Since manuals are indispensable tools and guidebooks for both inexperienced and expert workers, they must be developed with great care. Manuals are meant to make things easier, not more difficult. Therefore, they should be precise, accurate, and simple to understand. They should not be unnecessarily thick or bulky nor contain confusing or complicated instructions and procedures. Manuals should help the worker in finishing the job quickly and right the first time. If the manual is so complicated or long-winded that a worker has to spend time figuring out the manual itself rather than its outlined procedures in order to do a job, then tasks will go unfinished, machines will simply not work and the workers will become unduly demoralized.

The quality manual should be very precise, accurate and to the point. The quality manual should only contain the management mission, the quality policies, objectives, plans and an overall description of the system elements operating in the company. It should not contain procedural details; they should be left for the procedural manuals and work instructions.

Similarly, the procedures manuals should also be precise and not too bulky. They should not be too complicated to be read by the operating personnel. They are not meant to be glossy ornamental pieces to be put on bookshelves; they are to contain practical methods and procedures described in such a way as to let its users work with speed and accuracy to save time, effort, materials and utilities while at the same time protect the worker and the organization from every conceivable risk and danger. An instructions manual for a certain process or piece of equipment is no different. It should be written with clarity and precision. The operator should not be wasting time deciphering the instructions or be forced to remember unnecessary things.

Following are some guidelines for the development of quality manuals:

- The manual should be simple, clear, precise, practical and specific to the elements addressed. Even when each user may have a different level of education and/or experience, the manual should be understandable by all and easy to follow.
- The format and structure should be well thought out and followed consistently and uniformly throughout the manual.
- The sequence of requirements/procedures/instructions should be in line with the sequence of operations.

- The information should be precise, error free, necessary, pertinent and directly applicable. There is no need to give long explanations and complicated theories. The illustrations, flow diagrams or sketches should be simple and not crowded with details. The definitions, abbreviations and terminology should be correct and uniformly acceptable to all. Remember that the user needs to read the manual, apply it and get the job done properly and efficiently.

◆ QUALITY MANUAL PREPARATION

When a quality manual has to be prepared to document the system elements vis-à-vis ISO 9000 certification from either an existing company quality system documentation or from scratch, any or all of the following recommended procedures may be used:

- Establish a team of competent personnel to coordinate and develop the manual.
- Identify the pertinent standard and study its applicable requirements.
- Identify the existing applicable quality system procedures operating in the company.
- Obtain an up-to-date status of the quality system from each function and activity in the organization.
- Establish the format and structure of the intended manual.
- The team, under its leader, starts the actual writing activity. The team leader may:
  - use the services of an outside consultant, if needed.
  - delegate portions of the manual writing activity to other functional units, as appropriate.
  - continually seek up-to-date information from various functions, as required.
- When the draft of the manual is ready, it should be reviewed by:
  - the steering committee or management to ensure accuracy of the statements relating to management commitment, quality policies and objectives.
  - the various Process Management Teams or functions of the organization to ensure completeness and accuracy of the system elements, procedures, processes and methodologies.
  - other essential personnel, as appropriate.
- The ultimate responsibility for ensuring the completeness and accuracy of the manual as well as of its contents and writing style lies with the appointed team.
- Before issuing the manual, the document should be subjected to a final review by the appropriate responsible personnel.
- Finally, procedures must be established for the distribution, control, development, review and revision of the manual.

◆ QUALITY MANUAL: FORMAT AND STRUCTURE

Although there is no required structure or format for the quality manual, the following guidelines should provide sufficient assistance in developing a suitable manual. For the specific purpose of ISO 9000 registration, a quality manual should be prepared, chapter by chapter, responding to all the clauses outlined in the selected ISO standard and identifying clearly and accurately the systems and procedures operating in the company. For the purpose of illustration, the ISO 9001 level is selected as an example to elucidate the method of developing the format, structure and content of a quality manual.

Typically, the manual would include, as a preamble, a series of introductory chapters such as:

- Cover Page
- Table of Contents
- Foreword - Company Profile
- Introduction to Manual
- Certification
- Copyrights
- Document Distribution
- Manual Revision
- Definitions and Abbreviations
- Vision
- Mission

Next, the manual continues to address, clause by clause, all the twenty chapters of the system elements of ISO 9001 describing the quality system and procedures operating in the company. The quality system elements are appended in Table 11, Chapter 4.

Preamble of the Quality Manual

- **Cover Page:** sets out company's name/address; manual revision number; controlled copy number; person/organization to whom issued; signature/date of authority approving/reviewing the manual.
- **Table of Contents:** provides a total list of contents addressed in the manual.
- **Foreword - Company Profile:** present a brief profile of the company and its operations: nature of business of the specific plant/location/Division to which the manual pertains to; company's overall quality philosophy.

- **Introduction to Manual:** identifies scope and applicability of the manual: overall framework of quality system and responsibilities.
- **Certification:** certification to the effect that the quality manual adequately and accurately describes the quality system in use within the company. This page must be signed and dated by the Chief Executive officer and the Quality Manager.
- **Copyrights:** clearly stipulates the rights for the distribution and reproduction of the manual.
- **Document Distribution:** identifies document distribution policy regarding controlled and uncontrolled copies; responsibility/authority for document control system; and record keeping.
- **Manual Revision:** stipulates how often the manual will be reviewed/revised and how would the revisions be transmitted to everyone concerned.
- **Definitions and abbreviations:** provides the relevant definitions, abbreviations, and terminology used in the manual.
- **Vision:** sets out company's business vision, if any. (Optional - not required by ISO).
- **Mission:** Presents company's mission statement. (Optional - not required by ISO).

Format and Structure

The format and structure of the manual also requires careful consideration. A standardized format can be developed to achieve consistency and uniformity. For instance, the top of each page in the manual should bear the company name and logo (if practical), the title of the ISO 9001 clause being addressed and the document control information, such as: page number, section, issue, date, and approving authority.

The description of the system elements for each clause can also be categorized (see Table 38) under standardized headings, such as:

- Purpose
- Scope
- Responsibility
- General Procedures
- References

After the introductory chapters of the quality manual have been developed, the manual then addresses, clause by clause, the system elements of ISO 9001. Each clause describes what is required to be included in the Quality Manual to meet the ISO 9001 requirements vis-à-vis what is being done within the company. One should follow each clause, item by item, and identify all the management systems, procedures and processes operating in the company. To facilitate the development of the quality manual, a useful "manual checklist" is presented in chapter 16. The checklist identifies a step-by step list of requirements for each clause of ISO 9001. By writing the quality manual with the help of this checklist, a company can guarantee the accuracy of adequately addressing the requirements.

Table 38. Quality Manual: Sample Format		
LOGO 　ABC Company, Inc. 　Lovers Lane 　Quality Land	**Quality Manual**	Section:　4.5 Issue:　1 Page:　1 of 3 Date:　1994-07-27 Approved by:

DOCUMENT AND DATA CONTROL

Purpose

Scope

Responsibility

General Procedures

- General
- Document and Data Approval and Issue
- Document and Data Changes

References

15

ISO 9000: QUALITY SYSTEM IMPLEMENTATION

◆ IMPLEMENTATION PHASES

As indicated earlier, it generally takes between ten to fifteen months for a company to achieve certification. During this period, there is a lot of apprehension, inquisitiveness, and a general state of perplexity among employees. Management cannot afford to be oblivious to such idiosyncratic overtures - they must make concerted efforts to provide ample opportunity for workers to understand, question and participate effectively in the whole process. The leadership role in this scenario is normally played by the designated ISO coordinator or quality manager.

The overall process of ISO 9000 quality system implementation can be compartmentalized into six distinct phases: Awareness, Documentation, Implementation, Audit, Certification, and Maintenance. Each phase has its own unique difficulties and predicaments. We shall attempt to outline some of the most fundamental concerns and difficulties of the process and provide guidelines for their resolution. Detailed guidelines on each aspect of system implementation are also adequately covered in several other chapters of this book.

Phase 1: Awareness

In this phase, the question most predominantly asked is: what is ISO 9000 quality system? Most of the fears and apprehensions stems from the lack of knowledge about the subject. People cannot willingly participate in the process unless they understand it clearly. Consequently, the focus of this phase is on the provision of awareness about ISO 9000. The following action plan is suggested:

- The Quality Manager/ISO Coordinator and a few key personnel should undertake the initial training in ISO 9000/TQM implementation from some reputable source/institution.
- The Quality Manager should find a good consultant to provide in-house training, initially as follows:
  - A one or two-day session on the detailed content of ISO 9000 to various groups of people in the organization from the ranks of Directors, Managers and Supervisors.
- The managers and supervisors who have been trained should now be given responsibility to prepare mini-awareness sessions and conduct these sessions themselves onto the working level people under their supervision. These sessions will continue over time so as to sequentially cover the following topics:
  - ISO 9000 awareness
  - Quality system documentation
  - Quality system implementation
  - Audit procedures
  - Maintenance of the quality system
- It is imperative to ensure that everyone in the company receives some training, commensurate with the needs.

Phase 2: Documentation

The "awareness phase" identifies the need for documenting the system, and as a consequence, the obvious questions pertaining to this phase are:

- What documents need to be developed?
- Who would develop them?
- How does everybody input into the process?

As indicated earlier, the following documents need to be established:

- Quality Manual
- Quality System Procedures Manual
- Manufacturing Procedures/Work Instructions

The Quality Manual is generic in nature. It addresses the ISO 9000 elements while outlining the quality system and procedures of the company. We would recommend that, for the sake of coherence and uniformity, the quality manual should be written exclusively by the Quality Manager or designated ISO Coordinator. However, it must be categorically understood that this task cannot be completed without the help of other key personnel. If the Quality Manager lacks experience in the subject, it would be germane for him to seek the assistance of a qualified outside consultant.

The second tier, i.e. the system level procedures, are really an expanded version of the quality manual. However, since they are the ones that need to be superimposed onto the working level business/manufacturing procedures, they have to be developed in conjunction with the people responsible for the day-to-day production of products. The Quality Manager can either undertake the task of developing these procedures with the help of production people or he can provide the leadership role and direction while the divisional process management teams can develop these procedures.

The Manufacturing Procedures and/or Work Instructions are, typically, the operating procedures through which the company is or has been running its business. If they are not in an up-to-date manner or lack a disciplined structure, they can be replenished and/or reproduced in a more precise manner on the same lines as the system level procedures. Notwithstanding, however, these will normally be developed or augmented by the technical/production people. What is important to realize is that these procedures have to have a linkage to the system level procedures in several areas, such as: document control system, process control, identification and traceability, inspection, identification of nonconformances, taking of corrective and prevention action, etc. Once again, the Quality Manager can provide a leadership role and assistance to the technical people to generate/augment these manufacturing procedures while establishing a linkage to the system elements.

Phase 3: Implementation

This is the most crucial phase in the certification process. Developing a set of fine looking documents is not as difficult as implementing the system. Hoe does the system get physically implemented or functioning? How do various operating elements get interconnected and integrated?

Although system implementation takes time, it is by no means intractable. A systematic set of actions, such as the following, should facilitate the implementation process.

- Assess the status of the operating and manufacturing procedures to ensure that each station/division has well established procedures and everyone follows them.
- Each of these procedures should include the various requisite aspects of the quality system, such as:
  - Procedures for making changes and approval of documents
  - System for controlling all documentation
  - System for identification of nonconformances and taking of correction/ prevention action
  - Suitable means of keeping records
  - System for identification and traceability
  - Etc.
- Establish procedures for audit and review of the system effectiveness.

A more detailed discussion on system implementation is appended in the next section.

Phase 4: Audit

This phase is typically associated with the fear of auditing. Most people who have never before witnessed or experienced a system audit, annotate this exercise with, perhaps, revenue/taxation audit. The prevailing apprehension generates the following queries:

- What is a system audit?
- Is there a pass/fail in the audit? What will happen if I fail the audit?
- What kind of questions would the Registrar's auditors ask? Do I have to answer all the questions? What would happen if I cannot answer a question?

Auditing is the most essential entity of the system. The success of a system is totally dependent on the effectiveness of the audit function. A detailed discussion on the subject has been appended in Chapter 17; however, the following requisites should be noted:

- Depending on the size of the organization, there is a need to have at least one or two qualified Lead Auditors and between three to ten auditors. However, more trained auditors means better system maintenance.
- Several audit awareness sessions should be conducted by the qualified auditors to explain the process of internal and external auditing.
- Numerous internal audits need to be conducted for each Division prior to the first full audit by the Registrar, and this exercise is continued throughout the certification period.
- Full system audit should also be conducted at least once or twice each year.
- Continuous audit training/retraining should be an integral part of the system.

Phase 5: Certification

Once the system has been adequately documented, implemented and internally audited for conformance, it is time for certification audit by the Registrar. There are two options available in this regard: the company can arrange for an informal pre-certification audit to be conducted by the registrar before the full certification audit, or the company can go for full formal certification audit right away. Some essential elements of the certification audit are appended below:

- Depending on the size of the organization, the on-site full certification audit would involve between 1 to 3 auditors of the registrar, auditing for a period of 2 to 5 days. For example, a company with 250 employees can expect a team of two auditors for a period of three days.
- The audit generally covers the entire plant/facility for which certification is being sought. The basic premise is that anything that impacts quality would be a part of the audit process. Notwithstanding, however, there are always some segments of the business that may not or need not be included within the scope of the audit, e.g. accounting/administration functions; machine maintenance section; utilities; any specific research project or facility that has no direct bearing on the product design and/or manufacturing; etc. These entities should be clearly identified to the audit team prior to starting the full audit. It must be understood, however, that the audit team has the prerogative to assess/audit any aspect of work that they deem important vis-à-vis the quality system implementation.

The certification audit also requires proper planning. The employees should be suitably informed and/or trained for the overall external audit process. Besides the technical aspects, these awareness sessions should also emphasize the role of effective communication, cooperation, and helpfulness towards the audit team.

Phase 6: Maintenance

Once a certificate has been awarded, the next most important task is the maintenance of the quality system. A poorly maintained system would have a high chance of failing a follow-up audit, and a company can easily loose its certificate, and hence its credibility, at any time during or after the certification period. The basic activities associated with system maintenance include:

- Maintenance of procedures
- Regular audits
- Continuous training

- Effective control of nonconformances
- Implementation of preventative measures

The system effectiveness can generally be measured by continuously analyzing the following information:

- Rate of nonconformances
- Nature and type of defects
- Audit reports
- System nonconformances
- Customer complaints
- Rate of rejects/returns

◆ IMPLEMENTATION ROAD-MAP

In line with the activities associated with the six implementation phases identified above, we can now outline an overall sequential plan for the certification process. The following order of events is recommended for the implementation of ISO 9000 quality system.

- Top management undergoes ISO 9000 orientation.
- The Quality Manager/ISO Coordinator and the steering group receives training in ISO 9000 system.
- The Quality Manager and the steering group develops a strategic plan.
- A decision is made whether to hire an outside consultant to facilitate the implementation process.
- ISO 9000 training seminars are provided to Directors, Managers and Supervisors.
- The Quality Manager starts the development of the quality manual.
- The Quality Manager and key Technical Managers identify Process Management Teams to start development of system level procedures and manufacturing procedures. The Quality Manager provides the leadership role.
- Regular ISO 9000 awareness sessions are given to employees at all levels in the organization.
- The steering group undertakes the responsibility of developing quality policy, objectives, vision/mission statements.
- Key personnel are identified to take responsibility for various important system elements, e.g. training, calibration, audit, records, document control, etc.
- All quality system documentation is reviewed by key personnel.
- The Quality Manager and another key personnel undergoes Lead Auditor training.
- Auditing training is provided to a select group of people who will manage the audit function.

- System implementation begins.
- Routine internal audits are performed.
- System deficiencies are identified and corrected.
- Contact is established with the chosen Registrar for the conduct of a pre-certification audit.
- A final evaluation is made to ensure that the system is functioning effectively.
- Registrar performs the complete on-site certification audit.
- Deficiencies identified through the external audit, if any, are corrected.
- Company is awarded the certification.
- System is maintained and assessed continuously for compliance to surveillance audits by the Registrar during the span of certification.

Based on the implementation steps identified above, Table 39 presents a ten-phase ISO 9000 Implementation road-map.

Table 39: ISO 9000 Implementation: Road-Map

Phase 1:   Management Readiness
- Executive/Senior management orientation/awareness
- Top management approval/support
- Establish a steering committee/council
- Identify ISO/TQM coordinator/project leader

Phase 2:   Strategic Planning - Needs Analysis
- Select appropriate standard level (e.g. ISO 9001)
- Identify total ISO 9001 requirement
- Develop a master plan
- Formulate time schedule
- Identify expenditure of resources
- Identify need for external consultant

Phase 3:   Current Systems: Evaluation
- Identify current systems/procedures/processes
- Identify current documentation: Quality Manual, Procedures Manuals, Work Instructions
- Outline current infrastructure/responsibilities
- Perform a gap-analysis

Phase 4:   Implementation Framework
- Delineate responsibilities
- Establish Process Management Teams
- Organize Quality Manual writing team
- specify coordinators/teams for Procedures Manuals/Work Instructions

Phase 5:   ISO 9000 Training
- Management training
- Team leader and team member training
- General ISO awareness training for everyone
- Internal lead-auditor/auditor training

Table 39: ISO 9000 Implementation: Road-Map (Continued)

Phase 6:   Documentation Preparation
- Steering committee to develop:
  - Mission/Vision Statement
  - Quality policy/objectives/plans
- Development of Quality System Procedure
- Development and/or augmentation of:
  - Manufacturing Procedures
  - Standard Operating Procedures
  - Work Instructions

Phase 7:   System Implementation
- Implement all requisite procedures
- Integrate/interface the system
- Document the system implementation activities
- Eliminate system deficiencies, if any

Phase 8:   System Conformance Audits
- Develop internal audit schedule
- Conduct section-by-section audits
- Conduct a full system audit
- Take corrective/preventive action on deficiencies
- Document the audit findings
- Execute management review/evaluation of the system

Phases 9:   Registrar Certification
- Establish registration protocol with the Registrar
- Submit Quality Manual and/or system level procedures for assessment
- Complete documentation/system compliance for observations/nonconformances identified by the Registrar
- Undergo an on-site pre-registration audit (optional)
- Complete the comprehensive on-site registration with the Registrar
- Take requisite action to remove all discrepancies
- Obtain certification status

Phase 10:   System Maintenance
- Conduct frequent checks/audits
- Maintain and control procedures, systems and documentation
- Maintain compliance to surveillance audits by the Registrar
- Maintain focus on continuous improvement

◆ ISO 9001: IMPLEMENTATION GUIDELINES

Much has already been said above on the subject; here we shall present some fundamental user-friendly guidelines for hands-on implementation of the system. To clearly understand what is involved, the following should be noted:

- The primary objective and function of companies is to produce products and services.
- The secondary objective is to put into place some kind of quality system to help accomplish the primary objective in the most effective manner.
- For the primary objective, the companies have standard operating procedures for the day-to-day functioning and operability.
- The ISO 9001 quality system accommodates the secondary objectives. It helps to superimpose a disciplined structure on the company's operating framework to achieve consistently high quality products.
- The ISO 9001 quality system elements, by nature, are generic and almost totally meaningless by themselves. Their meaningfulness can only be realized and appreciated when they are meshed into the company's business operability. Consequently, it must be understood that companies are not in the business of designing quality system per sé; they are in the business of producing products, and for them, that is the most important function. For this function, the companies have, both, the short-term pressures and demands which must be adequately addressed and accommodated, and, also they must maintain a focus on longer-term growth and excellence. Any quality implementation exercise must, therefore, be fully cognizant of this basic reality and must be acted in a manner that would help and not hinder the company's business operations.
- Typically then, what happens when we implement ISO 9001? Simply put, we look at the company's operating procedures and assess the gaps and deficiencies vis-à-vis the disciplined structure and approach outlined in the ISO 9001 quality system. We, then, combine, enmesh, and harmonize the two systems to augment the effectiveness of the business systems.

Let us now elucidate the implementation process, and as before, for this purpose, we shall consider, as an example, the requirements of ISO 9001 (1994) level (see Tables 10/11, Chapter 4). A pictorial representation of ISO 9001 implementation network is appended in Figure 5.

As can be observed from Figure 5 (see page 260), the implementation network can be compartmentalized into the following categories:

- Management related aspects of the system that span over the entire system, e.g. Quality Manual; Quality policy/plan/objectives; training; management review.
- Stand-alone clauses, such as: contract review; design control; purchasing; servicing.
- Elements that impact the entire system, such as: documents and data control; quality records; internal quality audits.
- Elements associated with production that comprise the remainder of the system elements.

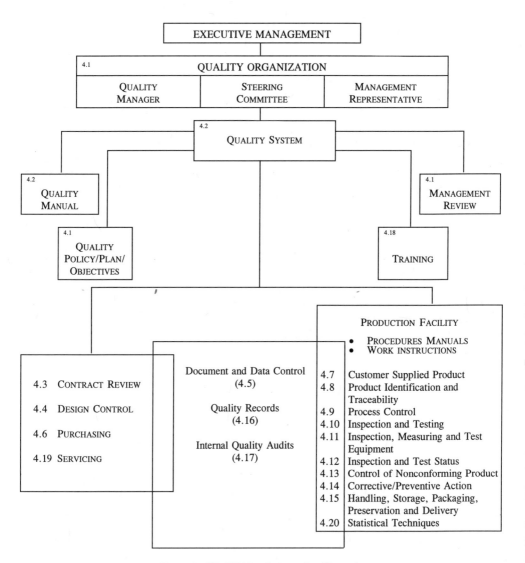

Figure 5: ISO 9001 Implementation Network

We shall now describe the implementation framework by considering either each element or group of elements. We shall identify the requirements, their impact and inter-relationship, and point out what needs to be done for implementing the system and what does the registrar's auditors look for in terms of system implementation and compliance.

Firstly, as an overall general requirement of the system, the following needs to be done:

- The Quality Manual must outline the company's procedures for each element of ISO 9001.
- The second tier system level procedures need to provide greater details of the procedures, element by element, substantiating and expanding on what has been said in the Quality Manual.
- Each Division in the organization produces its own operating procedures describing detailed instructions for carrying out the company's business, while identifying linkage to the system elements of ISO 9001.

Clause 4.1: Management Responsibility

This clause sets the stage for the quality system. The auditors are generally looking for:

- Statement of quality policy and objectives in the quality manual.
- Evidence that quality policy is understood and followed by everyone.
- Identification of responsibilities and authority for all aspects of quality in any or all tiers of documentation.
- Identification of a Quality Manager and Management Representative.
- Assurance that the executive management reviews the effectiveness of quality system at defined intervals.

Clause 4.2: Quality System

This clause is not directed to any specific entity; it is a general clause that emphasizes the need for the system to be properly documented via the various levels of documentation, viz., Quality Manual, Procedures Manual, Work Instructions, Quality Plans, and all requisite forms, records, etc. Typically, there is no need of any evidence in this clause per sé because the contents of this clause really consist of the whole system, which will be evidenced through all other clauses. We would recommend that you should systematically and briefly describe, in the Quality Manual, what constitutes your quality system. The auditors are, generally, anxious to see that you have developed effective Quality Plans.

Clauses 4.3, 4.4., 4.6, 4.19: Contract Review; Design Control; Purchasing; Servicing

For each of these stand-alone clauses, the following is recommended:

- Each Division responsible for these functions would develop detailed and documented operating procedures, with effective linkage to all other system elements.
- Evidence of all aspects of implementation of the procedures outlined in these clauses would be required during external audit.

Clause 4.5: Document and Data Control

From the system's point of view, this is the most important of all clauses. It impacts all other clauses as well as the whole business operability. The following action plan is recommended:

- Develop a master file (log), to be controlled by the Quality Manager, identifying all documents, their approval/authority, revision status, location, etc.
- Establish proformas for issue, approval, modifications and changes to documents.
- Each document in the system shall have a log identifying the document status.

Clause 4.7: Control of Customer-Supplied Products

This clause applies to situations where the customer provides material to be incorporated into the product. A system level procedure has to be established for the control of such products.

Clause 4.8: Product Identification and Traceability

This clause simply requires that products be traceable so that deficiencies can be identified and corrected. The auditors generally use this clause to trace the final product backwards through the entire life cycle of the product by virtue of which almost the whole system can be verified and evaluated.

Clause 4.9: process Control

The auditors need evidence of procedures by which the company controls processes. In assembly-line production situation, processes can be easily controlled by the use of Statistical Process Control (SPC) methods. However, the difficulty of showing evidence of process control arises in a non-assembly-line production situation. In such cases, the company should identify all those means by which the control of production is exercised. Also, it can be stressed that effective control of processes is done by ensuring that there are documented procedures for all entities and that they are followed to the rule. The emphasis is on evaluating process capability and maintenance of the system and equipment.

Clause 4.10: Inspection and Testing

For this clause, the auditors are looking for evidence of the procedures and methods by which incoming, in-process and final inspection is carried out. Records must be kept to show that the requisite inspection and testing is carried out. The incoming raw material inspection part of this clause should also be interconnected to clause 4.6 on "Purchasing".

Clause 4.11: Control of Inspection, Measuring and Test Equipment

The following action plan is recommended:

- Develop a master list of all equipment in the company that: i) requires calibration; ii) does not require calibration.
- For equipment that requires calibration, the following need to be done:
    - If the equipment is calibrated by an external agency, make sure that you have proper documentation to validate your claim. Also, the records must identify that calibration has been done against known national or international standards.
    - For equipment that is calibrated in-house, you must have documented procedures to identify how the calibration has been done. Also, all other conditions for calibration as stipulated in clause 4.11 must also be met.
- The equipment that does not require calibration should be identified as such. The auditors might require a valid reason as to why such equipment does not require calibration.
- Make sure that all other requirements of clause 4.11 are adequately addressed in the procedures.

Clause 4.12: Inspection and Test Status

- The inspection and test status should be appropriately identified on the product.

Clauses 4.13, 4.14: Control of Nonconforming Product: Corrective and Preventive Action

The following action plan is recommended:

- Develop a form for identification of nonconformances.
- Record only major nonconformances or else if you start recording all minor day-to-day observations/nonconformances also, the system will be overwhelmingly burdensome.
- Make sure that proper action is taken on nonconformances.

Clause 4.15: Handling, Storage, packaging, Preservation and Delivery

This clause simply requires the establishment of suitable operating procedures for these entities.

Clause 4.16: Control of Quality Records

- The type of quality records to be maintained and controlled are clearly specified in each requisite clause of ISO 9001. There are basically sixteen different types of records identified in ISO 9001.
- A decision should be made on how long the quality records are to be kept and this should be strictly controlled. The auditors generally wish to confirm that you are doing what you say.

Clause 4.20: Statistical Techniques

Typically, the use of statistical methods is not mandatory but is highly recommended for process improvement. For some companies who can feasibly use statistical methods, meeting the requirements of this clause is not so difficult. However, there are many companies where the viability of using statistical method is almost nil. These companies should come forth and categorically state whatever extent of usage of statistical methods they have, while at the same time attempt to institute and encourage the application of these analytical techniques.

◆ ISO 9001 (1994): IMPACT OF CHANGES FROM 1987 TO 1994

This section has been introduced especially for those companies who have already achieved ISO 9000 certification on the 1987 version of the standards and who would now like to update their systems to the revised 1994 version of the standards. The following clause-by-clause description outlines the impact of these changes. As the material in this edition of the book has been developed for the revised version, the reader would be able to find guidelines and assistance in many other chapters, such as: Chapter 13, 14 and 16.

4.1 Management Responsibility

4.1.1 Quality Policy

- Identify and extend responsibility/involvement up to the executive management level.
- Identify and ensure that company's quality policy is commensurate with its objectives and customer's needs.

4.1.2 Organization

- Quality-related responsibility/authority is to be extended from "product" to include "product, process and system".
- Emphasize/ensure provision of adequate resources for: quality management, performance of work, verification activities (especially internal quality audits).
- Management representative should be a member of the management team.
- Management representative to report to management on performance of quality system for review and improvement.

4.1.3 Management Review

- Management with executive responsibility to review the quality system at defined intervals.

4.2. Quality System

4.2.1 General

- Quality system must be documented in a Quality Manual

4.2.2 Quality System Procedures

- Quality System Procedures must be documented and referenced in the Quality Manual.

4.2.3 Quality Planning

- Quality plans must be prepared to identify means of taking timely corrective action for quality-related problems.

4.3 Contract Review

4.3.1 General

- Requires documented procedures.

4.3.2 Review

- When contracts are accepted verbally, there should be a mechanism to indicate agreement.

4.3.2 Amendment to Contract

- Identify procedure how contracts are amended and communicated to all concerned.

4.4 Design Control

4.4.1 General

- Requirement for establishing/maintaining documented procedures for all design control activities.

4.4.4 Design Input

- Design input must take into account:
  - Regulatory/statutory requirements
  - Results of any contract review activities

4.4.5 Design Review

- Formalize the design review process.
- Review process to include representations from all concerned.
- Design stage reviews to be conducted/documented and records kept.

4.4.6 Design Output

- Output to be documented and expressed in terms of requirements that can be verified.
- Output to include a review of the design output documents before release.

4.4.7 Design Verification

- Verification must take place at each appropriate design stage and results recorded.
- Design stage documents must be reviewed prior to release.

4.4.8 Design Validation

- New requirement: stipulates design validation activities to be performed.

4.5   Document and Data Control

4.5.1   General

- Requires documented procedures.
- Document control is extended to include documents of external origin, such as international standards, customer drawings, etc.
- Document control system can be in hard copy or electronic media.

4.5.2   Document and Data Approval and Issue

- Obsolete documents can be retained for legal and/or knowledge purposes but should be suitably identified.

4.6   Purchasing

4.6.1.   General

- Requires documented procedures.

4.6.2   Evaluation of Subcontractors

- Identify/define the extent of controls exercised over the subcontractors.
- Quality records of acceptable subcontractors should be maintained.

4.6.4   Verification of Purchased Product

- If purchased products are verified at the subcontractor's premises, the supplier should specify verification arrangements and the method of product release.
- The customer has the right to verify material/product at the supplier's as well as subcontractor's premises, if specified in the contract.

4.7   Control of Customer-Supplied Product

- Requires documented procedures.

4.8   Product Identification and Traceability

- Requires documented procedures.

4.9   Process Control

- Clause expanded to include process control procedures for installation and servicing processes in addition to production processes.
- Requires documented procedures.
- Requirement for suitable maintenance of equipment to ensure continuing capability of the process.
- "Special processes" is now an integral part of process control rather than a separate sub-clause. Requirement expanded to include assignment of qualified operators to perform these operations and continuous monitoring and control of process parameters. Also, verification of the process operation, including equipment and personnel, must be specified.

4.10 Inspection and Testing

4.10.1   General

- Requires documented procedures.
- The required inspection and testing, and the records to be established, should be documented in the quality plan or documented procedures.

4.10.5   Inspection and Test Records

- Records must identify authority responsible for the release of product. (Requirement originally in 4.12 and now moved to 4.10.5).

4.11 Control of Inspection, Measuring and Test Equipment

4.11.1   General

- Requires documented procedures.
- Where test software or comparative references such as test hardware is used for acceptance, they shall be checked prior to release for use during production, installation, or servicing and shall be rechecked at prescribed intervals.

4.12 Control of Nonconforming Product

4.13.1   General

- Requires documented procedures.

4.13.2   Review and Disposition of Nonconforming Product

- Repaired or reworked product should be reinspected in accordance with the quality plan or documented procedure requirements.

4.14 Corrective and Preventive Action

4.14.1   General

- The clause has been expanded to include requirement for "preventive action". The corrective and preventive action will be commensurate with the level of risk encountered.
- Requirement for establishing/maintaining documented procedures.

4.12.2   Corrective Action

- Corrective action extended from "product" to include "product, process and quality system".
- Corrective action relating to "customer complaints" to be addressed.

4.14.3   Preventive Action

- New requirement: stipulates establishing procedures for taking preventive action.
- Procedures should identify the use of appropriate records and information for analysis of problems for preventive action.

- Requires that the preventive action taken, including changes to procedures, be submitted for management review.

4.14 Handling, Storage, Packaging, Preservation and Delivery

4.15.1 General

- New requirement regarding "preservation" aspects have been added.

4.15.5 Preservation

- Preservation aspects as originally addressed in 4.15.4 have been dropped and readdressed into a separate sub-clause, 4.15.5.
- Requirement stipulates that the product must be appropriately preserved and segregated.

4.16 Control of Quality Records

- Requires documented procedures.
- Allowance has been made to keep records in any form: hard copy, electronic or any other media.

4.17 Internal Quality Audit

- Requirement stipulates the establishment/maintenance of documented procedures for planning and implementing internal quality audits.
- Internal audits must be performed by personnel independent of those having direct responsibility for the activity being audited.
- Follow-up activities must record the implementation and effectiveness of corrective action taken.

4.18 Training

- Requirement for establishing/maintaining documented procedures.

4.19 Servicing

- "Servicing" has been added to the requirements for ISO 9002.
- Requires documented procedures.

4.20 Statistical Techniques

- Requirement stipulates:
  - The identification of need for statistical techniques for establishing, controlling and verifying process capability and product characteristics.
  - The establishment and maintenance of documented procedures to implement and control the application of statistical techniques.

16

ISO 9001 (1994):
SYSTEM CHECKLIST

◆ INTRODUCTION

A checklist is a simple but extremely effective tool for ensuring propriety, validity and authenticity of a document, process or procedure. For ISO 9000 certification process, a checklist can be an invaluable tool to ensure adequate and accurate coverage of system elements and their effective implementation. Basically, the checklists can identify systems strengths and weaknesses and assists in taking a prompt corrective action wherever appropriate to eliminate deficiencies.

◆ ISO 9000 CERTIFICATION: SYSTEM CHECKLIST

In so far as possible, a detailed checklist for the system elements of the chosen ISO-9000 level of standard should be prepared for use during the process of manual development and for the purpose of internal auditing. For the manual, the checklist can quickly identify if any system element has been either inadvertently missed or misrepresented. For the internal audit, the checklist makes the process of verification easier and ensures that all systems are properly implemented and are functioning effectively and efficaciously. The checklists are an essential and invaluable tool for external audits also. Normally, the external auditors have a very exhaustive checklist against which they would audit the quality system of the organization for certification. Some checklists for auditing purposes are included in chapter 17.

In this chapter, we are including a checklist for the system elements of ISO 9001 developed from our own understanding and experience. We hope that this checklist will provide sufficient basic framework for manual development and internal auditing process. The users may modify this checklist and develop their own commensurate with their needs.

ISO 9001 (1994): ACTION CHECKLIST

LEGEND

****	Adequate coverage
***	Improvement needed in system development/implementation
**	Fails to meet criteria in system development/implementation
*	Not applicable

SYSTEM ELEMENTS	****	***	**	*
4.1 MANAGEMENT RESPONSIBILITY				
4.1.1 Quality Policy				
• Quality policy defined/documented.				
• Quality objectives defined/documented.				
• Commitment to quality demonstrated.				
• Policy consistent with company's goals/expectations/ customer's needs.				
• Policy/objectives understood by all.				
• Policy/objectives implemented.				
• Policy/objectives maintained at all levels.				
4.1.2 Organization				
4.1.2.1 Responsibility and Authority				
• Quality responsibility/authority defined/ documented.				
• Responsible personnel designated/announced.				
• Organizational chart established.				
• Organizational structure developed to ensure its support for the achievement of quality goals.				
• Designated personnel has freedom/authority to:				
• Take action to prevent nonconformity				
• Identify and record quality problems				
• Recommend/provide solutions				

SYSTEM ELEMENTS	****	***	**	*
• Verify implementation of solutions • Control/monitor further nonconformances. **4.1.2.2 Resources** • In-house verification requirements identified/documented. • Adequate verification resources provided. • Trained personnel designated. • Verification activities to include management performance of work, internal quality audits. **4.1.2.3 Management Representative** • Management representative appointed/authorized to ensure implementation/maintenance of quality system requirements. • Appointment announced and recorded in Quality Manual. • Representative to report to management on quality system performance. **4.1.3 Management Review** • Senior management carries out review of quality system implementation/effectiveness at regular intervals. • Records of reviews maintained.				
4.2 QUALITY SYSTEM				
• Quality system established/maintained/documented as per ISO-9001. • Quality plans documented. • Quality Manual prepared/maintained. • Quality procedures/instructions documented. • Quality records/forms/books/files prepared and maintained. • Quality system being implemented as per Quality Manual.				

SYSTEM ELEMENTS	****	***	**	*
4.3 CONTRACT REVIEW				
• Contracts reviewed for adequacy of requirements. • Discrepancies satisfactorily resolved. • Contracts reviewed to ensure that company is capable of meeting requirements. • Contract review records maintained. • Procedures established for amending contract. • Inter/intra communication maintained for contract review/amendment activities.				
4.4 DESIGN CONTROL				
4.4.1 General				
• Control/verification procedures for all phases of design function developed/maintained.				
4.4.2 Design and Development Planning				
• Plans for design/development activity prepared/ documented/referenced. • Qualified personnel assigned for design/development activity. • Adequate resources provided to design personnel. • Design plans integrated with other relevant plans. • Plans updated as design evolved.				
4.4.3. Organizational and Technical Interfaces				
• Organizational/technical interfaces established. • Information documented/transmitted/reviewed regularly.				
4.4.4 Design Input				
• All pertinent design input requirements identified/ reviewed/recorded. • Ambiguities appropriately resolved. • Results of contract review activities accommodated in design output.				

SYSTEM ELEMENTS	* * * *	* * *	* *	*
4.4.5 Design Output • Design output documented/expressed in terms of requirements that can be verified. • Design output meets input requirements. • Design output contains reference acceptance criteria. • Design output identifies critical product safety factors. • Design output includes a review of design output before release.				
4.4.6 Design Review • Design results reviewed/documented at all stages of design development. • Review teams to include all requisite personnel. • Records of design reviews maintained.				
4.4.7 Design Verification • Design review/verification activities scheduled. • Competent personnel designated to verify design activities. • Design qualification tests/demonstrations carried out. • Design input/output capability and compatibility evaluated/verified. • New designs compared with similar proven designs.				
4.4.8. Design Validation • Design validated to ensure conformance to user requirements. • Design validation ensured at any/all stages of design development.				
4.4.9 Design Changes • Procedures for design changes/modifications established. • Design changes reviewed/approved by appropriate persons. • Changes approved by authorized personnel before utilization.				

SYSTEM ELEMENTS	* * * * *	* * *	* *	*
4.5 DOCUMENT AND DATA CONTROL				
4.5.1 General				
• Document/data control procedures established/ maintained.				
4.5.2 Document and Data Approval and Issue				
• Procedures established to control, electronically or otherwise, all quality system documents/data and current revstatus. • All documents pertaining to ISO-9001 system requirements reviewed/approved before issue. • Pertinent documents available at appropriate locations. • Obsolete documents promptly removed.				
4.5.3 Document and Data Changes				
• Changes to documents reviewed/approved by the same person who originally approved changes. • Designated persons have access to all requisite information upon which to base their review/approval. • Nature of changes identified in the document.				
4.6 PURCHASING				
4.6.1 General				
• System/procedure established to ensure purchased product conforms to specified requirements.				
4.6.2 Evaluation of Subcontractors				
• Sub-contractors evaluated and selected on the basis of their ability to meet specified requirements, including quality capability.				

SYSTEM ELEMENTS	*****	***	**	*
• Controls exercised over sub-contractors to be commensurate with complexity of product and past performance. • Quality records of acceptable sub-contractors kept. **4.6.3 Purchasing Data** • Procurement data system established. • Purchasing documents clearly describe detailed information/data regarding ordered product. • Purchasing documents reviewed/approved for adequacy prior to release. **4.6.4 Verification of Purchased Product** **4.6.4.1 Supplier Verification at Subcontractors' Premises** • Procedures for verification and product release specified in purchasing documents. **4.6.4.2 Customer Verification of Subcontracted Product** • Customer afforded the right to verify product at sub-contractor's/supplier's premises.				
4.7 CONTROL OF CUSTOMER-SUPPLIED PRODUCT • Procedures for verification/storage/maintenance of customer supplied product established/maintained. • Customer supplied product lost, damaged, or unsuitable for use recorded/reported to purchaser.				
4.8 PRODUCT IDENTIFICATION AND TRACEABILITY • Procedures established and maintained for identification/traceability of product during all stages of production.				

SYSTEM ELEMENTS	* * * * *	* * * *	* *	*
• When traceability is a requirement, individual product or batches will have unique identification which is recorded.				
4.9 PROCESS CONTROL • Production and installation operations performed under controlled conditions. • Documented procedures, process flow charts established for each process. • All processes controlled through process control tools/methods, (including SPC methods), workmanship criteria, suitable equipment and working environment. • All processes approved before and during use. • Special processes employed are identified in the Quality Manual. • Control conditions exercised for special processes. • Special processes continuously monitored and any requirements for qualification specified. • Records of qualified processes/personnel/equipment maintained.				
4.10 INSPECTION AND TESTING **4.10.1 General** • Procedures for inspection/testing established/maintained/ documented in quality plan. • Procedures for keeping records identified. **4.10.2 Receiving Inspection and Testing** • Quality plan/procedures for verifying incoming product established/documented. • Procedures for handling nonconformities established. • Control procedures for incoming product established with the sub-contractor. • Procedures for product release, without incoming inspection, established.				

SYSTEM ELEMENTS	* * * *	* * *	* *	*
• Procedures for positive recall established.				
4.10.3 In-Process Inspection and Testing				
• Quality plan/procedures for in-process inspection/ testing established.				
• Product hold, release, or positive recall procedures established.				
• Procedures for handling nonconformities established.				
4.10.4 Final Inspection and Testing				
• Quality plan/procedures for final inspection established.				
• Quality plan indicates that requisite inspection/ testing carried out on receipt of product or in- process and data meets specified requirements.				
• Product not shipped unless inspection results indicate conformance.				
• Conformance results/data/documentation available and authorized.				
4.10.5 Inspection and Test Records				
• Inspection/test records established/maintained to verify conformance.				
• Acceptance criteria defined/documented/met.				
• Records identify inspection authority for product release.				
4.11 CONTROL OF INSPECTION, MEASURING AND TEST EQUIPMENT				
4.11.1 General				
• Calibration procedures established/documented/ maintained for all inspection, measuring and test equipment.				
• Calibration procedures, schedule of checks/rechecks and pertinent records established/maintained for test hardware/software.				
• Technical data pertaining to measurement devices made available to customers for verification, when required.				

SYSTEM ELEMENTS	****	***	**	*
4.11.2 Control Procedure • Measuring/test equipment selected/tested as per accuracy/precision required. • Equipment/devices calibrated at regular intervals or prior to use. • Measuring/test equipment calibrated against certified national/international standards. • Calibration status of equipment identified by a suitable indicator. • Calibration status/records maintained. • When equipment found to be out of calibration, the validity of results of previous inspections assessed/ documented. • Suitable environmental conditions/storage/ equipment established for calibration/inspections/ tests carried out. • Procedures established to guard against unauthorized tampering/adjustment.				
4.12 INSPECTION AND TEST STATUS • Procedures established for identifying inspection/test status of product. • Status of product conformance/non-conformance with regard to inspection/tests maintained throughout production cycle to ensure that only suitable product is dispatched, used or installed.				
4.13 CONTROL OF NONCONFORMING PRODUCT **4.13.1 General** • Documented control procedures established and maintained to handle nonconforming material/product.				

SYSTEM ELEMENTS	* * * * *	* * * *	* *	*
• Nonconforming material identified/documented/ segregated (if possible). • Nonconforming material prevented from use. • Nonconformities reported to functions concerned. **4.13.2 Review and Disposition of Nonconforming Products** • Personnel identified/authorized for disposition of nonconforming material/product. • Procedures established/documented for review and disposition of nonconforming product. • Action required on nonconforming product identified and reported to the customer. • Description of nonconformity recorded. • Repaired/reworked product reinspected in accordance with quality plan or documented procedures.				

4.14 CORRECTIVE AND PREVENTIVE ACTION
 	
4.14.1 General
 	
• Documented procedures established/maintained for corrective/preventive action implementation.
• Extent of corrective/preventive action is commensurate with magnitude/risk of problem.
• Changes resulting from corrective/preventive action implemented/recorded.
 	
4.14.2 Corrective Action
 	
• Corrective action procedures include:
  • handling of customer complaints
  • reports on nonconformities
  • causes of nonconformities
  • nature of corrective action
  • control of corrective action implementation/ effectiveness				

SYSTEM ELEMENTS	* * * * *	* * *	* *	*

4.14.3 Preventive Action
 	
• Preventive action procedures include:
   · analysis of potential causes of nonconformities
   · handling of problems requiring preventive action
   · control of preventive action implementation/
     effectiveness
   · management review of actions taken, procedures
     changed				

4.15 HANDLING, STORAGE, PACKAGING, PRESERVATION AND DELIVERY **4.15.1 General** • Procedures established for handling/storage/ packaging/preservation/delivery of all material. **4.15.2 Handling** • Proper procedures established for handling material to prevent damage/deterioration. **4.15.3 Storage** • Suitable storage facilities established. • Control procedures established for receipt/issue of material from stock. • Periodical review of material in stock carried out to detect deterioration. **4.15.4 Packaging** • Control procedures established for packing, packaging, marking processes to ensure conformance to specified requirements.				

SYSTEM ELEMENTS	****	***	**	*

4.15.5 Preservation

- Preservation/segregation procedures established so as to prevent damage/deterioration for the entire cycle of production to delivery.

4.15.6 Delivery

- Procedures established for protection of product after final inspection/test.
- Product quality protection provided during all phases of delivery.

4.16 CONTROL OF QUALITY RECORDS

- Documented procedures established/maintained for identification, collection, indexing, access, filing, storage, maintenance, disposition of quality records.
- Quality records, including procurement records of subcontractors, utilized to demonstrate conformance to requirements effective functioning of the quality system.
- Quality records clearly identifiable to product involved.
- Quality records stored/maintained effectively to prevent deterioration/damage/loss.
- Quality records readily retrievable.
- Procedure established to make quality records available to customer for evaluation.

4.17 INTERNAL QUALITY AUDITS

- Internal quality audit system established to verify effectiveness of quality system activities/results with planned arrangements.
- Audit schedule developed in relation to status/importance of activity.
- Audits conducted by independent staff.

SYSTEM ELEMENTS	****	***	**	*
• Audit results documented/reported to responsible personnel and management for timely corrective action. • Follow-up audit to record implementation/effectiveness of corrective action taken.				
4.18 TRAINING • Training needs identified. • Appropriate training provided. • Personnel assigned to specific tasks are qualified on the basis of education/training/experience. • Records of training activities kept.				
4.19 SERVICING • Documented procedures for providing effective service established/maintained. • Service quality effectiveness continuously verified.				
4.20 STATISTICAL TECHNIQUES **4.20.1 Identification of need** • Need for statistical techniques required to analyze/ improve operations identified. **4.20.2 Procedures** • Procedures established to implement/control application of appropriate statistical techniques.				

17

QUALITY SYSTEM AUDITING

◆ ROLE OF QUALITY AUDITS

Auditing is fundamental to quality assessment and improvement. A quality audit is an objective evaluation of the effectiveness of the quality system. It provides a timely comprehensive status report on the health of a company's quality.

Quality audits are conducted in accordance with documented procedures and they provide assurance that the implementation and maintenance of the total quality system is in concert with the stipulated quality policies, objectives, plans and procedures.

Typically, a quality audit is a verification tool that identifies system weaknesses and potential problems and, in so doing, provides avenues for corrective action and system improvement. A quality system audit offers a wide range of benefits as it:

- Helps to develop an effective total quality system
- Improves the overall management decision-making process
- Assists in the optimal allocation of resources
- Helps avoid potential problems
- Allows timely corrective action
- Reduces overhead and liability costs
- Improves productivity and morale
- Improves profitability, customer satisfaction and marketability

◆ QUALITY AUDITS AND ISO 9000 CERTIFICATION

Quality auditing is an essential and integral part of ISO 9000 certification process. There are two types of quality audits involved in ISO 9000 certification:

- Internal quality audits
- External quality audits

Internal quality audits are performed on the company's own functions by the company's own personnel. They constitute an essential requirement for ISO 9000 certification. Companies seeking ISO 9000 certification have to develop their own strategic internal quality audit plans and procedures.

External quality audits are performed either on the suppliers to assess their capabilities in meeting specified requirements or on the customers to assess their needs and expectations. As indicated earlier, for a third-party certification to ISO 9000 quality system standards, the external quality audits are performed by the accredited registrars to assess the capabilities of the supplier to meet the requirements of the chosen level of standard.

Since auditing is a subject of profound importance to quality system management, the technical committee ISO/TC 176, has developed standards on auditing to supplement the ISO 9000 series. Thus far, the following standards have been developed:

- ISO 10011: Guidelines for Auditing Quality Systems

  - Part 1: Auditing
  - Part 2: Qualification Criteria for Quality System Auditors
  - Part 3: Management of Audit Programs

This chapter, only briefly surveys the role of auditing within quality system management. For a detailed discussion on the subject, the reader is advised to consult the requisite standards or other useful sources and references.

◆ AUDITING FUNDAMENTALS

The definition of the term "Quality Audit" as given in the international standards, ISO 8402 and ISO 10011, is as follows:

> "**Quality Audit**: A systematic and independent examination to determine whether **quality** activities and related results comply with planned arrangements and whether these arrangements are implemented effectively and are suitable to achieve objectives."

Audits are normally carried out for one or more of the following purposes:

- To evaluate the effectiveness of the implemented quality system
- To assess conformance to specified requirements
- To identify shortcomings in the system
- To identify improvement opportunities

Quality system audits, whether internal or external, are performed with respect to a specific purpose and in accordance with a specified plan, procedure and criteria. There are different types of quality audits and, depending upon the need or the situation, one or several of them can be performed simultaneously. Following are the basic types of quality audits:

- System Audit: assessing how the quality management procedures are applied in practice and how effective they are.
- Product/Service Audit: evaluating the conformity of the product/service to specified technical requirements.
- Operational Audit: assessing the performance of a supplier/internal department or the needs/expectations of a customer.
- Process Audit: verifying how closely the established methods/procedures are followed in actual practice.
- Monitoring Audit: verifying the processes to confirm that all parameters are maintained within their specifications.

◆ DEVELOPING INTERNAL AUDIT SYSTEM

One of the basic requirements for any company seeking ISO 9000 certification, is the establishment and implementation of a comprehensive quality audit system to verify conformance/effectiveness of the quality activities to the planned arrangements. Following are the basic steps in developing a quality audit system:

- Define the purpose and scope of the audit.
- Establish goals and objectives.
- Identify a management commitment and focus.
- Appoint a lead auditor with designated responsibility and authority to take action.
- Establish an audit team.
- Establish an overall planning framework for the audit system.
- Define the parameters and boundaries of each activity to be audited.
- Develop implementation plans.
- Develop and document audit schedule, plans, procedures and instructions.
- Identify resources and personnel.
- Establish priorities, action plans, and carry out the audits.
- Document the audit findings.
- Bring the audit results to the attention of the personnel having responsibility in the audited area.
- Take corrective/preventive action on the deficiencies identified by the audit.
- Assess the effectiveness of corrective action.
- Assess conformance to the specified requirements.
- Assess the effectiveness of the quality system.
- Identify opportunities and initiatives for improvement.

The success of an audit program is typically dependent on the following:

- A comprehensive audit plan: needs a total understanding of the quality system requirements and team effort.
- A detailed documented set of procedures and instructions: everyone must know, understand and follow uniform procedures.
- Qualified and objective auditors: requires extensive audit training.
- Thorough and unbiased reports: requires qualified personnel, commitment, training and independence of operability.
- Documentation and communication: requires an effective documentation system and reporting of deficiencies within and across all activities.
- Timely and effective corrective action: requires management commitment, resources, authority and total cooperation.
- System elements checklist: ensures that everything which required doing has been done; Chapter 16 provides a thorough and detailed checklist for this purpose.

◆ QUALITY AUDIT FRAMEWORK

A quality audit may be required in a variety of situations, such as a process audit, supplier audit, audit of the quality system within a company, audit by an external auditor vis-à-vis accreditation requirements or at the request of company's management and/or a customer, etc. In each case, the fundamental requirement involves the establishment of a total audit procedural framework. Every audit procedure, whether for an internal audit or external audit, has a set of elements which must be addressed to develop the audit framework with an implementation plan. The following description of the quality audit system elements should provide sufficient assistance in developing an effective audit program. A flow chart of these system elements is schematically presented in Table 40.

Auditor

The effectiveness of the audit procedures and the confidence placed in them are highly dependent on the auditor's ability and expertise. The auditor must be well qualified, professionally proficient and adequately experienced in the subject. For the specific task at hand, the auditor's qualifications must be mutually acceptable to both the client requesting the audit and the auditing organization. Following are some of the general attributes that should be kept in mind in the selection of auditors:

- Competence in interpersonal and communication skills
- Ability to plan, organize, initiate, control and analyze
- Leadership abilities - to supervise, delegate, give direction and support
- Ability to work systematically, independently and judiciously
- Ability to use discretion regarding the confidentiality and proprietary of information and audit findings
- Balanced personality; absolute honesty and integrity; good attitude, conduct and appearance; self-confidence
- Ability to exercise independence of judgement

Auditee

It is the auditee's responsibility to ensure that the audit team has been provided with adequate working facilities, access to relevant information, and effective co-operation in all matters relating to the audit.

Table 40: Quality Audit System Elements

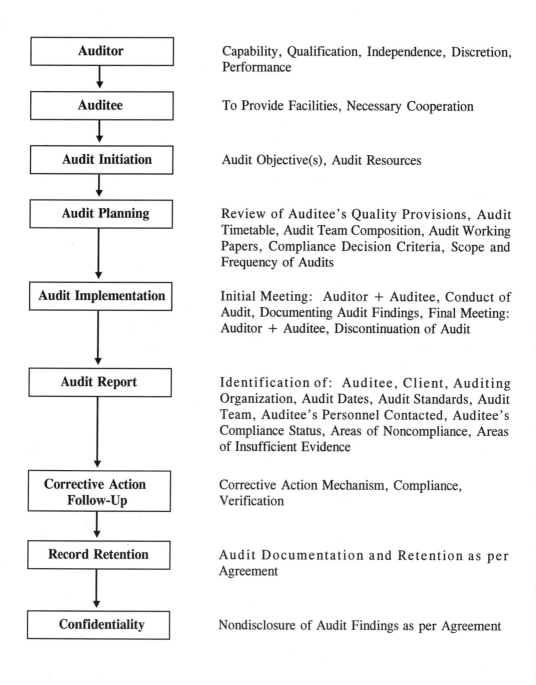

Auditor	Capability, Qualification, Independence, Discretion, Performance
Auditee	To Provide Facilities, Necessary Cooperation
Audit Initiation	Audit Objective(s), Audit Resources
Audit Planning	Review of Auditee's Quality Provisions, Audit Timetable, Audit Team Composition, Audit Working Papers, Compliance Decision Criteria, Scope and Frequency of Audits
Audit Implementation	Initial Meeting: Auditor + Auditee, Conduct of Audit, Documenting Audit Findings, Final Meeting: Auditor + Auditee, Discontinuation of Audit
Audit Report	Identification of: Auditee, Client, Auditing Organization, Audit Dates, Audit Standards, Audit Team, Auditee's Personnel Contacted, Auditee's Compliance Status, Areas of Noncompliance, Areas of Insufficient Evidence
Corrective Action Follow-Up	Corrective Action Mechanism, Compliance, Verification
Record Retention	Audit Documentation and Retention as per Agreement
Confidentiality	Nondisclosure of Audit Findings as per Agreement

Audit Initiation

Before initiating the audit, the audit objectives must be set and agreed upon by the parties. Basically, the audit objectives should centre around verifying conformance to the stated policy, objectives/goals, system procedures and processes. The auditing organization must clearly identify the requisite audit resources commensurate with the task at hand, and plan all the other administrative details necessary to carry out the audit effectively.

Audit Planning

Typically, audit planning consists of the following activities:

- Review of auditee's provisions: quality system documentation, specifications, standards, etc.
- Audit timetable: audit dates, schedule of meetings, audit team composition and structure, activities to be audited and the requisite standard against which the audit is to be conducted
- Audit working papers: all relevant forms, records, checklists, assignment sheets, agenda items, etc. necessary for the conduct of the audit
- Compliance decision criteria: all the relevant criteria used in making a decision on the conformance/nonconformance of the quality system elements to the stipulated standard

Audit Implementation

Audit implementation involves the following components:

- An initial meeting between the auditor and auditee management to clarify the overall plan for the conduct of the audit
- A detailed procedure for the conduct of the audit
- A mechanism for documenting and recording the audit findings
- A final meeting between the parties to discuss the nature and extent of noncompliance; how it shall be documented and reported; and a mutual agreement on the discontinuation of the audit.

Audit Report

The audit report is the document that formally communicates the findings of the audit to the client and the auditee. It must be prepared with great care and tenacity. It must be thorough and detailed and would normally identify the following items: the auditee, client and auditing organization, the audit dates, the audit standards, the audit team, the auditee's personnel contacted during the audit, the auditee's compliance status, the areas of noncompliance or of insufficient evidence, etc.

Corrective Action Follow-up

The objective here is to ensure that effective corrective action has been taken in every area of noncompliance. A follow-up procedure must be put in place to verify the effectiveness of the corrective action. Experience has indicated that companies who are able to develop self-correcting systems can effectively establish a constancy of compliance and improvement.

Record Retention

The objective here is to ensure that procedures have been clearly identified for the retention of audit records and documentation.

Confidentiality

Confidentiality is fundamental to all audit procedures. Consequently, a clear written agreement must be reached between the parties regarding the disclosure/non-disclosure of audit findings.

◆ AUDIT CHECKLIST: ISO 9001

Audit checklists are required to conduct the audit, whether internal or external. The external compliance/certification system audit is conducted by the Registrar and each registrar has his own audit checklist. However, the checklist given in Chapter 16, can be conveniently used to conduct a total system audit internally before getting the external audit done. For internal audit purposes, checklists have to be developed for Division-by-Division audit. Here, we are providing one such generic Divisional audit checklist that can be modified as per the Divisional needs.

Internal Audit Checklist (ISO 9001): Manufacturing

Company _____   Division _____

No.	Assessment	ISO 9001 Clause No.	Comments
1.	Request evidence of the completion of any corrective action required by a previous audit.	4.17	
2.	Determine the level of housekeeping and cleanliness.	4.9.1	
3.	Check evidence of any environmental or working conditions that may adversely affect quality.	4.9.1	
4.	Verify that general safety precautions are taken.	4.9.1	
5.	Is the Quality Policy known and understood by all?	4.1.1	
6.	Are the personnel familiar with the Quality Manual?	4.2	
7.	Assess the level of familiarity of personnel with ISO 9001 quality system requirements.	4.1.2.1	
8.	Do the personnel know their roles and responsibilities vis-à-vis ISO 9001 quality system implementation.	4.2	
9.	Are documented Procedures Manuals and /or Work Instructions available.	4.9.1	
10.	Confirm that workmanship standards, instructions and procedures are documented and consistently followed by everyone for the control of production process, inspection operations and tests.	4.9.1	
11.	Verify that the various production process steps, referenced documents and equipment correspond to the relevant documented instructions and/or flowcharts.	4.9.1	
12	Verify that correct issues of drawings, specifications and other technical data are available, properly used and documented.	4.9.1	
13.	Verify that procedures or other relevant documents are up-to-date.	4.5.1	

No.	Assessment	ISO 9001 Clause No.	Comments
14.	Check that procedures exist for the review, update and controlled issue of these instructions.	4.5.2	
15.	Is the authority and responsibility for making changes to procedures defined, documented and known to everyone.	4.1.3	
16.	Confirm that changes to procedures are notified to all concerned.	4.9.1	
17.	Verify that changes/revisions to procedures are notified to the document control system.	4.5.2	
18.	Verify that Quality Records are handled and stored properly.	4.16	
19.	Are all incoming materials, in-process product and finished goods adequately identified.	4.8	
20.	Confirm that product can be traced to components or materials from previous process steps.	4.8	
21.	Are procedures in place to monitor and control process and product characteristics.	4.9.1	
22.	Are statistical techniques used to control and analyze process capability and performance.	4.20	
23.	Are adequate instructions provided on when and how inspections and test have been carried out and results documented.	4.10	
24.	Verify that all receiving, in-process and final inspections and test have been carried out and results documented.	4.10.1-4	
25.	Do inspection and test instructions identify what test equipment is to be used and any acceptance criteria.	4.10	
26.	Determine whether product is held until required inspection and testing has been completed.	4.10.1-2	
27.	Is there defined responsibility to release product for urgent use without requisite inspections and tests.	4.10.1-2	
28.	Are product recall procedures in place.	4.10.2	

No.	Assessment	ISO 9001 Clause No.	Comments
29.	Verify whether the final product inspection has been completed by appropriate personnel prior to the final release and that product meets the defined acceptance criteria.	4.10.3	
30.	Determine whether all required inspection and test equipment is in calibration.	4.11	
31.	Are all jigs, templates, measuring devices checked for suitability of use.	4.11	
32.	Can the inspection and test status of the product be determined at each step of the process.	4.12	
33.	Check if the inspection/test status of the product is readily visible at all times.	4.12	
34.	Are procedures established to identify, document and handle nonconformities been adequately defined.	4.13	
35.	Has the responsibility to designate product conforming or nonconforming been adequately defined.	4.13.1	
36.	Has the authority to take action on nonconforming products been adequately defined.	4.13.1	
37.	Verify that nonconforming material/product is properly segregated.	4.13.1	
38.	Verify whether reworked or repaired product is reinspected.	4.13.1	
39.	Verify if documented procedures are in place for taking corrective action.	4.14	
40.	Are nonconformance reports prepared and distributed to personnel responsible for corrective action.	4.14	
41.	Are nonconformances followed up with a corrective action.	4.14	
42.	Are the corrective actions checked for effectiveness.	4.14	
43.	Are there any preventative measures to ensure non-recurrence of nonconformities.	4.14	

No.	Assessment	ISO 9001 Clause No.	Comments
44.	Are procedures in place for the handling and storing of material to prevent damage or deterioration.	4.15.1	
45.	Are contents and physical and/or chemical characteristics of material clearly identified.	4.15	
46.	Are items with a shelf-life identified as such, and periodically inspected to ensure suitability for use.	4.15.3	
47.	Check that materials are properly stored and handled to prevent damage, loss, or deterioration.	4.15.3	
48.	Confirm that the issuance of material is controlled by use of requisition, where specified.	4.15.3	
49.	Check suitability of handling equipment to ensure that they cannot cause damage and/or deterioration to product.	4.15.2	
50.	Where possible, check tag information on handling equipment (e.g. weight, size) for accuracy.	4.15.2	
51.	Determine whether department trainers communicate changes in instructions and procedures to operators and verify compliance.	4.18	
52	Inspect training records (checklists, matrices, minutes, training plan), and determine whether training needs are identified and the staff is adequately trained.	4.18	

PART FOUR

THE

QUALITY

APPLICATIONS

18

SOFTWARE QUALITY MANAGEMENT/CERTIFICATION

◆ INTRODUCTION

If there is any field that has witnessed the most rapid growth in the least amount of time, it is that of "information technology". As a result, the number of software products have also been increasing at a considerable rate. To ensure software quality, there is a need to establish guidelines for developing and implementing a quality management system. The technical committee, ISO/TC 176, has developed the following document in the ISO 9000 series which can be gainfully used to develop a software TQM model:

> "ISO 9000-3 (1991): Quality Management and Quality Assurance Standards - Part 3: Guidelines for the Application of ISO 9001 to the Development, Supply and Maintenance of Software."

The document has been based on the underlying quality system requirements of ISO 9001 and as such, sets out guidelines to facilitate the application of ISO 9001 to organizations developing, supplying and maintaining software. However, since the process of development and maintenance of software is somewhat different from that of most other types of industrial products, appropriate modifications have been incorporated to accommodate the quality aspects specific to software technology.

The nature of software development is such that some activities are related to particular phases of the development process, while others may apply throughout the process.

The guidelines in this standard have been structured to accommodate these characteristics and provide suggested controls and methods for producing software that meets purchaser's requirements.

In this chapter, we shall briefly outline how to utilize the guidelines appended in ISO 9000-3 in order to accomplish the following:

- Implementing a software TQM model
- Preparing for ISO 9001 certification for software industries

For a more comprehensive coverage of the subject, however, the reader is advised to consult the document.

◆ DEFINITIONS

Some basic definitions relating to software quality management as given in "ISO 9000-3" and "ISO 2382-1" are appended below for reference.

- **software:** Intellectual creation comprising the programs, procedures, rules and any associated documentation pertaining to the operation of a data processing system.

Note: Software is independent of the medium on which it is recorded.

- **software product:** Complete set of computer programs, procedures and associated documentation and data designated for delivery to a user.

- **software item:** Any identifiable part of software product at an intermediate step or at the final step of development.

- **development:** All activities to be carried out to create a software product.

- **phase:** Defined segment of work.

Note: A phase does not imply the use of any specific recycle model, nor does it imply a period of time in the development of a software product.

- **verification (for software):** The process of evaluating the products of a given phase to ensure correctness and consistency with respect to the products and standards provided as input to that phase.

- **validation (for software):** The process of evaluating software to ensure compliance with specified requirements.

◆ ISO 9000-3: BASIC FRAMEWORK

The overall structure of system elements for developing a software quality assurance model as outlined in ISO 9000-3 is compartmentalized into three main components:

- Quality System - Framework
- Quality System - Life Cycle Activities
- Quality System - Supporting Activities

The system aspects covered in these three components are appended in Table 41.

Table 41: ISO 9000-3: System Elements: Components

Quality System - Framework

4.1	Management responsibility
4.2	Quality system
4.3	Internal quality system audits
4.4	Corrective action

Quality System - Life Cycle Activities

5.2	Contract reviews
5.3	Purchaser's requirements specification
5.4	Development planning
5.5	Quality planning
5.6	Design and implementation
5.7	Testing and validation
5.8	Acceptance
5.9	Replication, delivery and installation
5.10	Maintenance

Quality System - Supporting Activities

6.1	Configuration management
6.2	Document control
6.3	Quality records
6.4	Measurements
6.5	Rules, practices and conventions
6.6	Tools and techniques
6.7	Purchasing
6.8	Included software product
6.9	Training

◆ DEVELOPING A SOFTWARE TQM MODEL

As indicated in the preceding chapters, the initial steps in the development of a TQM System involves strategic planning, preparation and quality orientation. The process should start as follows:

- Develop a mission statement.
- Establish a TQM Steering Committee.
- Identify the quality objectives.
- Identify the processes involved in the software production life cycle.
- Establish Process Improvement Teams.
- Delineate appropriate responsibilities and authority.
- Identify customer requirements.
- Translate customer requirements into specific tasks and projects.
- Develop a quality manual.
- Develop procedures manuals.

The next step involves the identification and implementation of all the requisite quality systems elements. Following is a brief description of the systems elements as outlined in ISO 9000-3.

Quality System - Framework

Management Responsibility
- Establish quality policy, goals and objectives.
- Establish a quality infrastructure with appropriate responsibilities and authority.
- Identify the requisite verification resources and personnel.
- Appoint a management representative to oversee the effective implementation of the quality system.
- Establish a management review process to ensure the continuing suitability and effectiveness of the quality system.
- Establish a partnership with the customer to:
  - Achieve continuous feedback - feedforward.
  - Conduct regular joint reviews of the customer's requirements vis-à-vis supplier's capability
  - Ensure conformance of the software to the customer's agreed requirements specification.
  - Verify/accept test results.

Quality System

- Establish, maintain and document an effective and integrated quality system that spans over the entire life cycle of the software production and ensures total quality.
- Document the quality system via a quality manual, procedural manuals, work instructions, etc.
- Establish a quality plan.

Internal Quality System Audits

- Establish an effective internal quality audit system to verify the quality system's effectiveness and the product conformance status.
- Take appropriate corrective action on the deficiencies identified by the audit.
- Implement preventative measures to improve quality.

Corrective Action

- Establish procedures to investigate causes of nonconforming product.
- Analyze quality records and information to detect and eliminate deficiencies.
- Apply controls to ensure that appropriate and timely corrective/preventive actions are taken and that they are effective.

Quality System - Life Cycle Activities

General

- Select an appropriate life-cycle model and organize the software development project vis-à-vis the model. The quality system life-cycle activities should include at least the following aspects.

Contract Reviews

- Establish effective contract review procedures. The supplier should review each contract to ensure that:
  - Requirements are properly defined and documented.
  - Possible risks are identified
  - Any discrepancies are resolved
  - The supplier has the capability to meet the requirements
  - The purchaser has the capability to meet contractual obligations
- Review the contract to ensure that it adequately addresses all the requisite criteria for the acceptance and handling of changes and problems, standards/procedures to be used, and the purchaser's responsibilities with regard to the requirements specification, installation, facilities, tools and software to be provided.

Purchaser's Requirements Specification

- The company (supplier) should ensure that all functional requirements for software development have been obtained from the customer. Some of these relate to performance, safety, reliability, security and privacy.
- The purchaser's requirements specification must be properly documented. The document must clearly establish and identify the appropriate responsibilities of both the supplier and the purchaser, the methods of approval for the requirements and any ensuing changes, the review procedures, the interfaces between the software product and other software or hardware products, etc.

Development Planning

- Establish a software development plan to include:
  - Project definition, objectives
  - Project organization details: resources, teams, responsibilities, subcontractors to be used, human resources, etc.
  - Project phases: development phases, required input and output for each phase, verification procedures, potential problem analysis strategy and procedures, etc.
  - Project schedule
  - Identification of requisite plans: quality plan, configuration management plan, integration plan, test plan
  - Identification of how the project will be managed
  - Development methods and tools
  - Progress control procedures
  - Documentation of inputs and outputs from each development phase
  - Verification procedures for each phase.

Quality Planning

- Establish and document a quality plan to describe the road map for the progress and development of each phase of the software development process.
- The quality plan should identify the:
  - Quality objective
  - Defined input and output criteria for each phase of the development process.
  - Details of the test verification and validation activities.
  - Specific quality responsibilities, ie., reviews and tests, change control and configuration management, defect control and corrective action, etc.

Design and Implementation

- Establish a well-structured and disciplined procedure for the software design and implementation.

- The design activities should include:
  - Proper design rules and internal interface
  - Systematic design methodology appropriate to the type of software product being developed
  - Use of past design experiences
- Design implementation activities should be in accordance with the established rules, such as the programming rules, programming languages, consistent naming and coding conventions, etc.
- Appropriate implementation methods should be used to satisfy the customer requirements.
- Establish appropriate design review procedures.

Testing and Validation

- Establish test plans and procedures for testing, validation, and field testing of the software products at each stage of their development.
- Test plans, specifications and procedures must be reviewed before starting testing activities. These should include:
  - Plans for software item, integration, system test and acceptance test
  - Test cases, test data and expected results
  - Types of tests to be performed
  - Test environment, tools and test software
  - Criteria for judging the completion of the test
  - User documentation
  - Personnel required and associated training needs
- Attention should be paid to the following aspects of testing:
  - Recording of test results
  - Identification of problems and nonconformities and reporting these to responsible personnel
  - Evaluation of test adequacy and relevancy
  - Consideration/documentation of requisite hardware/software configuration
- The supplier should validate the product at the final stage before delivery and acceptance to the purchaser.
- Establish appropriate procedures and plans for field testing whenever required.

Acceptance

- A well-defined procedure for acceptance of the final product must be established between the supplier and the purchaser.
- The acceptance procedure should take into consideration the time schedule, the procedures for evaluation, the software/hardware environments and resources, and the acceptance criteria.

Replication, Delivery and Installation

- The supplier must establish criteria for replication prior to delivery. This includes:
  - Number of copies of each software item to be delivered
  - Copyright and licensing concerns
  - Custody of the master and backup copies
  - Period of obligation for the supplier to supply copies
- Establish appropriate procedures for verifying the correctness and completeness of all copies of the delivered software product.
- The procedures for installation must be clearly established between the supplier and the purchaser.

Maintenance

- The supplier should establish procedures for maintenance of the software if required by the contract.
- Maintenance activities involve problem resolution, interface modification, and the functional expansion of performance improvement.
- Items to be maintained may include programs, data and their structures, documents for purchase and/or use, specifications, and documents for the supplier's use.
- To effectively carry out maintenance activities, the supplier should establish an appropriate maintenance plan that would encompass such activities and factors as the scope of maintenance, the identification of the initial status of the product, the support organizations, the maintenance activities and the maintenance records and reports.
- Maintenance records and reports must be kept.
- The supplier and the purchaser must establish and document procedures for incorporating changes in the software product resulting from the need to maintain performance.

Quality System - Supporting Activities
(not phase dependent)

Configuration Management

- The supplier should develop a configuration management plan and establish an appropriate system for identifying, controlling and tracking the previous versions of each software item.
- Configuration management activities may include configuration identification and traceability, the change control procedures, and the procedures for recording the status report of the software items.

Document Control

- The supplier should establish a document control system.

- Document control applies to such items as procedural documents, planning documents and product documents.
- Procedures should be established for document approval and issue and for changes to documents.

Quality Records

- The supplier should establish and maintain procedures for the identification, collection, indexing, filing, storage, maintenance and disposition of quality records.

Measurements

- As far as possible, the supplier should endeavour to develop quantitative means for measuring the quality of software products as well as the quality of the development and delivery processes.

Rules, Practices and Conventions

- The supplier should clearly identify the rules, practices and conventions employed in the established quality system and review/revise them appropriately as required.

Tools and Techniques

- The supplier should identify and use appropriate tools and techniques for the effective management of the quality system as well as for product development. These tools and techniques should be improved as required.

Purchasing

- The supplier should ensure that the purchased products or services conform to the specified requirements. To do so, the subcontractors must be effectively assessed and the purchased products verified and validated.

Included Software Product

- Where a supplier is required to include or use software products supplied by the purchaser or by a third party, he should establish and maintain effective procedures for the validation, storage, protection and maintenance of such products.

Training

- The supplier must identify training needs and provide appropriate training facilities and opportunities.
- Personnel performing specific assigned tasks should be qualified on the basis of appropriate education, training and/or experience as required.

- Subjects for training should be commensurate with the specific needs of the development and management of software products.
- Records of training activities should be maintained.

◆ ISO 9001 CERTIFICATION: SOFTWARE

Once a company has established and appropriately implemented an effective quality system for the development and production of software products, either with the help of ISO 9000-3 or otherwise, seeking accreditation/certification to ISO 9001 should be relatively easy. As indicated earlier, the quality system requirements appended in ISO 9001 series are generic in nature and as such are applicable, with suitable modifications, to any manufacturing or servicing situation. The overall process of certification has been outlined in greater details in several earlier chapters. Here, we shall recapitulate the sequence of steps as applicable to software development. Note that certification is always to either ISO 9001 or 9002 or 9003 and not to ISO 9000-3. ISO 9000-3 is simply a document that provides guidelines for establishing a TQM system for software.

Software: ISO 9001 Certification Road-Map

Step 1: TQM Implementation

- Select and/or develop a simple, user-friendly and cost-efficient TQM model.
- Stay within the bounds of your existing operatibility - systems, procedures, processes.
- Utilize the guidelines appended in ISO 9000-3 for TQM implementation. This will facilitate the preparation and implementation process for ISO 9001 certification.
- Compartmentalize the overall TQM activities appropriately and delegate/delineate implementation responsibilities to several individuals and/or groups. Involve everyone in the TQM exercise.

Step 2: Document Preparation

- The following documents have to be prepared:
  - Quality Manual
  - Procedures Manuals for ISO 9001 quality systems elements
  - Procedures Manuals or Standard Operating Procedures as used for the design, development and production of software product

- Work Instructions as used for day-to-day production work or training
- Appropriate forms, proformas, etc. as required to implement the ISO 9001 system elements
- The Quality Manual should:
  - Be brief, succinct and precise
  - Adequately outline the generic framework of the company's systems, procedures and processes
  - Adequately address all the system element of ISO 9001. Table 42 presents a cross-reference between ISO 9001 and ISO 9000-3 and should provide sufficient information about what to include in the Quality Manual against each clause. Further details on how to develop a Quality Manual are appended in Chapter 14.
- The Quality System Procedures Manuals have to be developed, as appropriate, for all the requisite ISO 9001 system elements.
- The Manufacturing Procedures Manuals are the Standard Operating Procedures the company has for carrying out their business. These procedures may have to be updated to reflect their interrelationship with the Quality Manual as well as with the generic Quality System Procedures Manuals.
- Work Instructions typically present the sequence of steps to be followed in each work area to carry out the task. These are required for the day-to-day running of the business. Many companies make these documents as part of their training manuals and use them to train/retrain workers on a continuous basis as per requirements.

Step 3: Implementing System Elements

- All the system elements and procedures as outlined in the various quality system documents have to be implemented and maintained.
- The major empahsis is on the following elements:
  - The existence of a credible quality policy and objectives
  - Proper documentation of quality plans and procedures
  - Appropriate delineation of quality responsibilities and authority
  - Quality control of incoming raw materials
  - Capability and training of workers to do the job
  - Suitable process control, production control and product verification procedures
  - Effective document control system
  - Procedures for identifying nonconformities and taking of corrective/preventive actions
  - Carrying out of scheduled internal quality audits
  - Maintenance of quality records
  - Provisions for providing effective service to customers

Step 4: Certification Process

- Select a suitable registrar and work closely with the registrar.
- Prepare all requisite documents effectively.
- Comply with the audit requirements/findings of the register.
- Achieve certification and maintain systems continuously.

Table 42: Cross-Reference Between ISO 9001 and ISO 9000-3

Clause in ISO 9001	Clause in ISO 9000-3 (note: see Table 41)
4.1 Management Responsibility	4.1
4.2 Quality System	4.2, 5.5
4.3 Contract Review	5.2, 5.3
4.4 Design Control	5.3, 5.4, 5.5, 5.6, 5.7, 6.1
4.5 Document and Data Control	6.1, 6.2
4.6 Purchasing	6.7
4.7 Control of Customer Supplied Product	6.8
4.8 Product Identification and Traceability	6.1
4.9 Process Control	5.6, 5.7, 5.9, 6.1
4.10 Inspection and Testing	5.7, 5.8, 5.9
4.11 Control of Inspection, Measuring and Test Equipment	5,7, 6.5, 6.6
4.12 Inspection and Test Status	6.1
4.13 Control of Nonconforming Product	5.6, 5.7, 5.9, 6.1
4.14 Corrective and Preventive Action	4.4
4.15 Handling, Storage, Packaging, Preservation and Delivery	5.8, 5.9
4.16 Control of Quality Records	6.3
4.17 Internal Quality Audits	4.3
4.18 Training	6.9
4.19 Servicing	5.10
4.20 Statistical Techniques	6.4

19

TQM/ISO 9000:
PROCESSED MATERIALS

◆ INTRODUCTION

As identified in Chapter 7, the Standard "ISO 9004-1: Quality Management and Quality System Elements - Guidelines" sets out a basic generic framework for developing and implementing a TQM system. With appropriate modifications, the approach outlined in the standard can be applied to any specific situation.

With increasing demands on the usability and viability of ISO 9004-1 to specific situation, the technical committee, ISO/TC 176, decided to develop a compendium standard, ISO 9004-3, with applications to "processed materials". The overall format and structure of ISO 9004-3 is virtually the same as that appended in ISO 9004-1, except for its emphasis on application to processed materials.

"**Processed materials**" refer to products (final or intermediate) prepared by transformations, consisting of solids, liquids, gases, or combinations thereof, including particulate materials, ingots, filaments or sheet structures. Processed materials are typically delivered in bulk systems such as pipelines, drums, bags, tanks, cans or rolls. Process materials come into vogue in a variety of industrial situations, including even such products as processed foods and health care products.

In this chapter, we shall present the following two aspects with regard to processed materials:

- Guidelines for implementing a TQM system vis-à-vis ISO 9004-3.
- Guidelines for ISO 9001 certification.

For a more in-depth understanding of the system elements, the reader is advised to consult the standards: "ISO 9004-3: Quality Management and Quality System Elements - Guidelines for Processed Materials".

♦ ISO 9004-3: PROCESSED MATERIALS

Much like ISO 9004-1, ISO 9004-3 also compartmentalizes the quality system elements into the following categories and provides detailed guidelines on the implementation activities associated with each element as applicable to processed materials.

ISO 9004-3: Quality System Elements

4.0	Management responsibility
5.0	Quality system principles
6.0	Economics - quality-related cost considerations
7.0	Quality in marketing
8.0	Quality in specification and design/development
9.0	Quality in procurement
10.0	Quality in production
11.0	Control of production
12.0	Product verification
13.0	Control of measuring and test equipment
14.0	Nonconformity
15.0	Corrective action
16.0	Handling and post-production functions
17.0	Quality documentation and records
18.0	Personnel
19.0	Product safety and liability
20.0	Use of statistical methods

ISO 9004-3: TQM Implementation Guidelines

- **Management Responsibility**

  - Identify management commitment to quality policy and system.
  - Develop quality policy commensurate with organization's goals and customer's expectations.
  - Develop quality objectives.
  - Establish quality system organizational structure, responsibilities, procedures, processes and resources for implementing quality system.

- **Quality System Principles**

  - Establish quality system elements identifying all phases and activities of the business; for example:
    - Marketing and market research
    - Technical research and development
    - Procurement
    - Process planning and development
    - Production process measurement, control and adjustment
    - Production
    - Process maintenance
    - Inspection, testing and examination
    - Packaging and storage
    - Sales and distribution
    - Customer use
    - Technical assistance
    - Disposal after use
  - Establish requisite quality responsibilities and authority.
  - Develop appropriate organizational infrastructure.
  - Identify requisite resources: personnel, material, financial.
  - Develop a network of operational procedure for coordinating all activities with respect to an effective quality system development, implementation and maintenance.
  - Document the quality system via:
    - Quality policies and procedures
    - Quality Manual
    - Quality plans
    - Procedures manuals/work instructions
    - Quality records
  - Establish procedures for auditing the quality system, including:
    - Audit plan
    - Audit schedule
    - Carrying out the audit
    - Reporting and follow-up of audit findings

- Establish an appropriate mechanism for a continuous review and evaluation of the quality management system.

- **Economics - Quality-Related Cost Considerations**

  - Establish procedure to collect, analyze and report all quality-related costs (such as: operating quality costs, external assurance quality costs, etc.) to management for effective functioning of the quality system.

- **Quality in Marketing**

  - Develop a framework for market needs-analysis and total product profile:
    - Product brief
    - Type/nature of product needed
    - Design/specification of product
    - Customer's requirements/expectations
    - Feedback from customer
    - Nature/extent of competition

- **Quality in Specification and Design/Development**

  - Establish plans and objectives for design/development activities. These activities will include:
    - Delineation of appropriate responsibilities
    - Establishment of time-phased design/development programs with checkpoints
    - Identification of customer needs to be accommodated in the design development process
  - Establish product testing and measurement system.
  - Define procedures for process and product design qualification and validation.
  - Establish procedures for the review of design/development activities, to include:
    - A formal documented, systematic and critical review of the design/development results at the conclusion of each phase of design development
    - Documented process/product design review elements, such as:
      - Items pertaining to customer needs and satisfaction
      - Items pertaining to product and process specifications and service requirements
  - Establish procedures for design verification.
  - Establish approval process for the total package that defines the product's quality and its manufacturing methods.
  - Conduct market readiness review to determine whether production capability and field support are adequate for the new or redesigned product.
  - Establish procedures for change control of product and process specifications.
  - Establish appropriate procedures for qualification of product and process specifications.

- **Quality in Procurement**

  - The purchasing quality program should include the following elements as a minimum:
    - Applicable issues of specifications/drawings/technical data/purchase orders
    - Selection of qualified suppliers/subcontractors
    - Agreement on quality assurance
    - Provisions for settlement of quality disputes
    - Receiving inspection planning and controls
    - Receiving quality records

- **Quality in Production**

  - Plan the production process to ensure that production operations proceed under controlled conditions in the specified manner and sequence. Controlled conditions include appropriate controls for:
    - Materials
    - Production equipment
    - Process and procedures
    - Measurements
    - Personnel
    - Associated supplies, utilities and environments
  - Conduct process capability studies to determine the potential effectiveness of all processes involved in the production operation.

- **Control of Production**

  - Establish procedures for control of production operations including:
    - Material control and traceability
    - Equipment control and maintenance
    - Control of special processes characteristics
    - Control of work instructions, specifications and drawings
    - Control of verification status
    - Control of nonconforming material

- **Product Verification**

  - Establish appropriate procedures/instructions/methods for:
    - Incoming materials and parts verification
    - In-process monitoring and control
    - Completed product verification

- **Control of Measuring and Test Equipment**

  - Establish control procedures over all measuring systems used in the development/manufacture/installation/servicing of product.

- Establish procedures to monitor the measuring process itself.
- Establish calibration procedures for all measuring and test equipment, including any test software or hardware.
- Extend the control of measuring and test equipment and procedures to all suppliers/subcontractors furnishing products and services, including any outside testing.
- Take appropriate corrective action in cases where measuring and test equipment is found to be nonconforming.

- **Nonconformity**

  - Establish procedures for identifying nonconformances and take the following action when nonconformities occur:
    - Identification
    - Segregation
    - Disposition
    - Documentation
    - Prevention of recurrence

- **Corrective Action**

  - Establish appropriate corrective/preventive action procedures, including the following:
    - Assignment of appropriate responsibilities for corrective action
    - Evaluation of significance of the problem affecting quality
    - Investigation of possible causes
    - Analysis of problem
    - Identification of potential problem and initiating preventive action
    - Measures for controlling the processes
    - Disposition of nonconforming processed materials
    - Recording of any permanent changes occurring from the corrective action into the Work Instructions and/or Procedures Manuals

- **Handling and Post-Production Functions**

  - Establish and maintain documented procedures for the following functions:
    - Handling and storage
    - Identification of product through appropriate markings, labels, etc.
    - Packaging
    - Transportation and distribution
  - Establish procedures for after-sales servicing and develop suitable methods for reporting and utilizing the feedback regarding product quality.
  - Develop an effective marketing-feedback system for reporting shortcomings and failures of product performance to ensure timely corrective/preventive action.

- **Quality Documentation and Records**

  - Establish an effective document control system for all documents affecting quality, such as: drawings, specifications, blueprints, inspection instructions, test procedures, work instructions, operation sheets, quality manual, operational procedures, quality assurance procedures, etc.
  - Maintain and control quality records, such as: inspection reports, test data, qualification reports, validation reports, audit reports, material review reports, calibration data, quality cost reports.

- **Personnel**

  - Establish procedures to control activities related to personnel, such as:
    - Training of personnel: executive, management, technical personnel, supervisors and workers
    - Qualification of personnel
    - Motivational programs

- **Product Safety and Liability**

  - The TQM system should also take into consideration the safety and liability aspects of product, such as:
    - Meeting requisite safety standards and regulations
    - Testing of design and prototypes
    - Developing/maintaining requisite safety instruction manuals and procedures
    - Developing means of product traceability and recall
    - Developing an emergency plan

- **Use of Statistical Methods**

  - Establish documented procedures for the application of statistical methods to all processes, including: market analysis; product design; reliability specification, longevity and durability predictions; process control and process capability studies; determination of quality levels/inspection plans; data analysis; process improvement; safety evaluation and risk analysis.
  - Specific statistical techniques may include: design of experiments, sampling methods, statistical process control, Pareto analysis, etc.

◆ ISO 9000 CERTIFICATION: PROCESSED MATERIALS

The process of certification to ISO 9000 for industries involved with processed materials is virtually identical to that for any other manufacturing industries. The only difference is that in this case the procedures, processes and all the quality system documentation would reflect applicability to processed materials. A detailed description of all aspects of ISO 9000 certification process has been appended in several chapters and the approach can be conveniently applied to the case of processed materials. For establishing a quality management system, or preparing for certification, companies can either develop their own quality model or utilize the approach outlined in ISO 9004-3. It must be well understood that certification is always to either ISO 9001 or 9002 or 9003 and not to ISO 9004-3. ISO 9004-3 is simply a document that provides guidelines for establishing an effective quality system. The basic structure and format of ISO 9004-3 is virtually identical to ISO 9004-1. Since ISO 9004-1 is the basis behind the development of ISO 9001, 9002 and 9003, it augments the usefulness of ISO 9004-3 for quality system implementation and certification.

As identified elsewhere, the basic steps for certification involve the following:

- Development of the following hierarchy of documentation, outlining the company's quality policies, objectives, systems, procedures and processes, in a format that accommodates the requirements of the chosen ISO 9000 model:
  - Quality Manual
  - Quality System Procedures Manual
  - Standard Operating Procedures
  - Work Instructions
- Implementation of the quality system
- Documentation of the system
- Internal quality audits
- Registration with the certification body
- Compliance with the Registrar's requirements
- Maintenance of certification status
- Continuous quality improvement

20

TQM/ISO 9000: FOOD AND HEALTHCARE SECTORS

♦ INTRODUCTION

Quality is a generic necessity for every conceivable situation. However, in food and health sectors, since the concern revolves around human health and safety, it is virtually mandatory. Both of these sectors, indeed, have their own well-established quality protocols. In this chapter, we shall describe some of these protocols and attempt to align and identify similarities with the ISO 9000 quality system framework. The following areas will be considered in this chapter:

- Food Sector
  - Hazard Analysis Critical Control Point (HACCP) System
- Healthcare Sector
  - Good Manufacturing Practices (GMP): Drugs

♦ HAZARD ANALYSIS CRITICAL CONTROL POINT (HACCP) SYSTEM

The evaluation of food operations for compliance to commercial and regulatory requirements generally involves one or more of the following:

- In-house quality assurance checks of the final product by the manufacturer
- Inspection by the regulatory authority through well-established sampling inspection protocol and/or laboratory testing
- Verification by the vendee as contractually agreed upon with the vendor
- Evaluation by a group representing the consumer

Although this traditional approach to verification is valid, useful, and sometimes the only available means of evaluation, it falls short in maximizing quality improvement efforts in the following ways:

- The available inspection resources are incapable of accommodating the ever increasing product complexity, variety and volume.
- Laboratory testing is limited to examining very small numbers of samples which may not provide sufficient meaningful information on the microbiological status of a batch of food product. Additionally, in many situations, the product may have already been distributed and consumed by the time the laboratory results are available.
- The focus of traditional methods is more on the detection of defects instead of their prevention. It lacks quality improvement emphasis.
- Today's consumers are much more concerned about the nutritional, wholesomeness and safety aspects of food. The present system is incapable of detecting deficiencies or making improvements in these areas.

Quality cannot be improved by only examining the end product. Even the detection of whether the product is safe for consumption is sometimes difficult by analyzing only the final product. Therefore, to improve the quality and safety aspects of food, it is important to have an effective on-line monitoring system that is capable of identifying the compliance status at each step of the production to allow for corrective/preventive action. Such a system helps to build-in quality and safety so that there are minimal surprises in the end product. A product that goes through a systematic step-by-step control protocol can be expected to have high compliance and to require minimal final inspection. One such protocol procedure that is gaining usage acceptance, at least in the U.S.A., Canada, U.K., Australia and New Zealand, is known as the HACCP (Hazard Analysis Critical Control Point) System.

The HACCP System

HACCP is a preventative system of food safety control. It originated with companies supplying food for U.S. space flights and is endorsed by the ICMSF (International Commission on Microbiological Specifications for Foods). It has also become incorporated in the "Recommended International Code of Hygienic Practices for Processed Meat and Poultry Products", FAO/WHO Codex Alimentarius, 1985. The HACCP concept offers a systematic and rational approach to control the microbiological hazards in food. The major emphasis of the system lies in focusing attention on those factors which directly affect the microbiological safety and quality of food.

Consequently, it avoids the many weaknesses inherent in the traditional inspection/testing approach, eliminates the wasteful use of resources on extraneous and superfluous considerations, and is, therefore, highly cost-effective. Food produced or processed in accordance with the HACCP system carries a high degree of assurance of its microbiological safety and quality and requires very little regulatory inspection.

HACCP PRINCIPLES

HACCP is a system which identifies specific hazard(s) and preventative measures for their control. The system consists of the following seven principles:

Principle 1

Identify the potential hazard(s) associated with food production at all stages, from growth, processing, manufacture and distribution, until the point of consumption. Assess the likelihood of occurrence of the hazard(s) and identify the preventative measures for their control.

Principle 2

Determine the points/procedures/operational steps that can be controlled to eliminate the hazard(s) or minimize its likelihood of occurrence - (Critical Control Point (CCP)). A "step" means any stage in food production and/or manufacture including raw materials, their receipts and/or production, harvesting, transport, formulation, processing, storage, etc.

Principle 3

Establish critical limit(s) which must be met to ensure the CCP is under control.

Principle 4

Establish a system to monitor control of the CCP by scheduled testing or observations.

Principle 5

Establish the corrective action to be taken when monitoring indicates that a particular CCP is not under control.

Principle 6

Establish procedures for verification which includes supplementary tests and procedures to confirm that the HACCP system is working effectively.

Principle 7

Establish documentation concerning all procedures and records appropriate to these principles and their application.

Application of the Principles of HACCP

The HACCP system comprises the following sequential steps:

- **Hazard Analysis:** identification of hazards and assessment of the severity of these hazards and their risks.
- **Critical Control Point (CCP):** determination of critical control points at which the identified hazards can be controlled.
- **Control Criteria:** specification of criteria that indicate whether or not an operation is under control at a particular CCP. Criteria are specified limits of characteristics of a physical (e.g., time or temperature), chemical (e.g., salt or acetic acid), or biological (e.g., sensorial or microbiological) nature.
- **Monitoring Procedures:** establishment and implementation of procedures to monitor each CCP to check that it is under control. Monitoring is the checking that a processing or handling procedure at each CCP is properly carried out and is under control. It involves the systematic observation, measurement and/or recording of the significant factors required for control. Monitoring procedures chosen must enable action to be taken to rectify an out-of-control situation, either before the start-up, or during the operation of a process.
- **Statistical Process Control:** statistical data analysis at each step of every CCP.
- **Corrective Action:** taking whatever corrective/preventive action is necessary when the monitoring results indicate that a particular CCP is not under control.
- **Verification and Audit:** implementing additional procedures to obtain supplementary information to ensure that the HACCP system is working properly.
- **Evaluation and Revision of HACCP:** continuous evaluation and revision of the HACCP system to ensure effectiveness commensurate with the changing needs and requirements of a process.

Hazard Analysis

The first major step of the HACCP system involves a complete hazard analysis of the operation under consideration. A hazard is a condition or a set of conditions in the operation of a system with the potential for initiating a defect leading to noncomformance to specified requirements. Hazard means the unacceptable contamination, growth and/or survival by micro-organisms of concern to safety and spoilage and/or unacceptable production or persistence in foods or products of microbial metabolism. Hazard analysis consists of an evaluation of all procedures concerned with the production, distribution and use of raw materials and food products to:

- Identify potentially hazardous raw materials and foods
- Identify the potential sources and specific points of contamination through an analysis of each step in the food chain
- Determine the potential for micro-organisms to survive or multiply during production, processing, distribution, storage and preparation for consumption
- Assess the risks and the severity of all identified hazards. Severity refers to the seriousness (magnitude) of the hazard, and risk is an estimate of the likely occurrence of the hazard.

Most potential hazards associated with the manufacture of food products fall into the categories of physical, biological, chemical, environmental, and transportation/ distribution/consumer abuse.

Once the potential hazards are identified, the next step is to examine their severity and conduct a risk assessment. There are several ways of rating a hazard and the rating criteria has to take into account characteristics such as product safety, purity, integrity, and effect on usage and customer relations. One simple way is to categorize the hazard as: critical, major or minor.

A critical hazard is that which could result in:

- Contamination that would be injurious to health
- Contamination by offensive or noxious matter
- Noncompliance to product definition
- Deterioration to the extent of being unusable

A major hazard is that which could result in:

- Contamination by extraneous matter
- A detrimental effect on microbiological quality
- A detrimental effect on organoleptic quality
- Documentation and production not matching (quality, type, weight)
- Impaired functional properties of the product
- Noncompliance to specified compositional standard
- Noncompliance to regulatory requirements

A minor hazard is that which could result in:

- Poorly presented product
- Non-uniform product
- Poor presentation of a manufactured unit to customers

Another commonly used approach for hazard assessment involves a two-step procedure: the first step being a risk assessment and the second step an assignment of hazard categories. This may be carried out as follows:

Risk Assessment: Evaluate a product according to the following hazard characteristics, using "+" for yes and "0" for no.

Hazard A: The product contains some "sensitive" ingredient(s).
Hazard B: The manufacturing process does not contain a controlled processing step that effectively destroys harmful bacteria.
Hazard C: There is a substantial potential for microbiological abuse in distribution or in consumer handling that could render the product harmful when consumed.

If all three hazard characteristics were present in a product, it would have a Hazard Class "+++". If a hazard is absent, a "0" would designate this as follows:

0++ - no sensitive ingredient
+0+ - product pasteurized
000 - no hazard involved

Assignment of Hazard Category: The three general food hazard characteristics stated above can be combined into a set of eight configurations (for A, B, C). The food product may be ranked according to its potential consumer health hazard as follows:

Category I: A special category that applies to non-sterile products designed and intended for consumption by infants, the aged, or the infirm.

Category II: Food products subject to all **three** general hazard characteristics.

A.   Hazard Class +++

Category III: Food products subject to **two** of the general hazard characteristics.

A.   Hazard Class +0+
B.   Hazard Class ++0
C.   Hazard Class 0++

Category IV: Food products subject to **one** of the general hazard characteristics.

    A.   Hazard Class +00
    B.   Hazard Class 0+0
    C.   Hazard Class 00+

Category V: Food products subject to **none** of the general hazard characteristics.

    A.   Hazard Class 000

Once the risk assessment and hazard category has been assigned, it is useful to take a closer look at all the intended functions collectively, e.g., the ingredients and their proportion, mixing, handling, equipment, etc.

Critical Control Points (CCP)

Once potential hazards have been identified, critical control points (CCP) have to be considered. A CCP is a location, practice, procedure, or process at which control can be exercised over one or more factors, which, if controlled, could minimize or prevent a hazard. Two types of CCP can be used: CCP1 that will ensure the control of a hazard; CCP2 that will minimize a hazard but cannot assure its control.

Critical control points provide control over microbiological, chemical and physical hazards. For example, control of the pasteurization temperature is critical to the microbiological quality of the product, i.e., the pasteurization step is a "critical control point" in the process.

A potential hazard can have more than one control point. For example, consider that a bolt on a casein wash screen or a bottler is a potential hazard; the control points for this hazard could include the equipment maintenance, metal detector, bottle scanner, magnet, sifter, and equipment design.

As indicated earlier, hazards can arise from many situations such as the physical, biological, chemical, environmental and transportation/distribution/consumer abuse. The critical control points with respect to these can be categorized as follows:

- Physical: Metal detectors, magnets, sifters/screens, thermometer calibration (not temperature), etc.

- Biological: Approved suppliers, sensitive ingredients, heat treatments, time and temperatures, holding times and temperatures, processing water, consumer abuse, etc.
- Chemical: Residues on raw materials and residues in plant (pesticides, packaging, migration, maintenance materials, processing water), etc.
- Environmental: Areas in the plant that have environments that must be controlled for product safety such as storage areas (temperature), isolation of sensitive areas (i.e., cross-contamination), general environment.
- Transportation/Distribution/Consumer Abuse: Time/temperature, instructions/labelling.

HACCP Flowchart Worksheet

Once the hazard analysis has been completed and the critical control points identified for each potential hazard, a HACCP flowchart worksheet is prepared. Efficient and accurate record keeping is essential to the application of a HACCP system. Documentation of HACCP procedures at all steps should be included and assembled in a manual. Examples are: records associated with ingredients, product safety, processing, packaging, storage and distribution, deviation file, modifications to the HACCP system, etc. An example of a HACCP worksheet format is shown as Table 43.

Monitoring HACCP with SPC

Monitoring is an integral part of the HACCP system. However, for prompt corrective/preventive action and an effective decision regarding the process, the information generated at each step of the monitoring system must be properly evaluated. The methods of Statistical Process Control (SPC) and, in particular, control chart methods provide the most effective means of monitoring critical control points. The use of control charts allows decisions to be reached with a measured degree of confidence and the risks associated with a hazard to be effectively controlled and minimized.

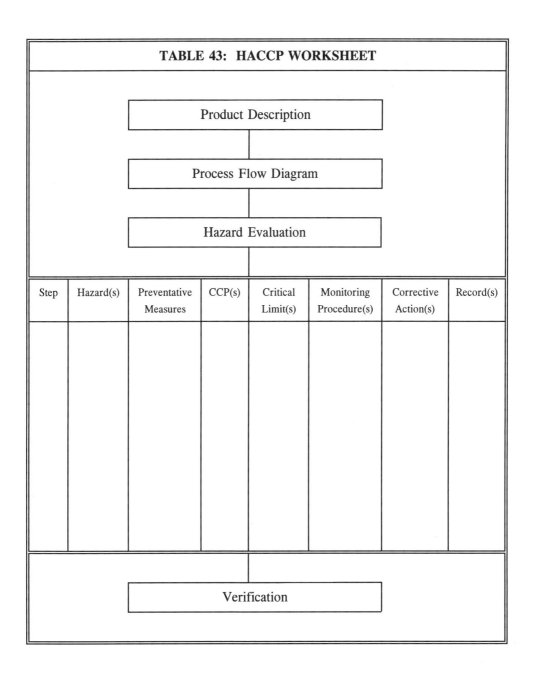

TABLE 43: HACCP WORKSHEET

Product Description

Process Flow Diagram

Hazard Evaluation

Step	Hazard(s)	Preventative Measures	CCP(s)	Critical Limit(s)	Monitoring Procedure(s)	Corrective Action(s)	Record(s)

Verification

Evaluating and Revising HACCP Systems

Although the HACCP system is continually monitored and the data analyzed through control charts, it is still important to evaluate and revise the system commensurate with changing conditions. The major purposes of revising HACCP are:

- Validation of the selection of a CCP to prevent potential hazards
- Assessment of the potential of a loss of control at any CCP that may result in an unacceptable food safety risk
- Accommodation of changing conditions, such as new potentially hazardous conditions, changes in the characteristics of a conventional food pathogen, emergence of new pathogens, changes in new materials, changes in the product flow of a plant, etc.

Thus, the key to a strong HACCP program is to anticipate change and continually identify situations that potentially increase the risk of hazards.

♦ GOOD MANUFACTURING PRACTICES (GMP)

The application of Good Manufacturing Practices for the control and assurance of quality have been in vogue for a long time. In fact, most modern day quality systems have emerged from the basic principle of GMP. The span of application of GMP principles is quite wide, ranging from food, drugs, medical devices, laboratory protocol, processed industries, cosmetic industries, etc.

To elucidate the application of GMP principles, we shall outline the key elements of the system as applicable to the production and importation of drugs for human and veterinary use.

GMP Guidelines

- **Sale**

The system starts by laying down the ground-rules that no manufacturer or importer shall sell a drug unless it has been produced in accordance with the mandated regulatory requirements.

- **Premises**

  The first consideration for the system implementation pertains to premises and maintenance of building. The premises should be designed, constructed and maintained in a manner that prevents any contamination.

- **Equipment**

  Like the premises, the equipment should also be designed, constructed, maintained, operated and arranged in a manner that permits effective sanitary conditions and prevents any contamination.

- **Personnel**

  The system emphasizes that the personnel responsible for the manufacture of drugs must be fully qualified and trained for the job.

- **Sanitation**

  The system stipulates the need for a written sanitation program for the operation of the facility.

- **Raw Material Testing**

  The raw material used for the production of a drug must meet all requisite specifications and must be properly tested prior to use.

- **Manufacturing Control**

  Manufacturing control procedures must be established and properly followed to ensure that the drug is produced as per specifications.

- **Quality Control**

  The company must have a quality control department to ensure effective implementation of quality policies, procedures and methodologies.

- **Packaging Material Testing**

  Packaging material used for packaging the drug must be examined and tested against requisite specifications prior to its use.

- **Finished Product Testing**

  The final product must be tested against the specifications of that drug prior to its availability for sale.

- **Records**

All pertinent records relating to the manufacture and quality control of the drug must be maintained.

- **Recall**

Procedures must be in place to recall either the raw material or the finished product in case of noncomformities or complaints.

- **Samples**

Under the GMP guidelines, it is required that a sample of each lot or batch of a packaged drug must be retained for a designated period, for re-examination in the event of complaint.

- **Stability**

The manufacturer should identify the normal shelf-life of the product in the package, i.e., how long the product can be expected to remain within specifications under recommended storage conditions.

- **Sterile Products**

Any drug that is intended to be sterile must be produced in separate and enclosed areas to eliminate the possibility of contamination.

- **Transportation/Storage**

Documented procedures must be established for handling, storage, packaging, preservation and delivery.

The implementation of GMP guidelines requires the following:

- Establishing and maintaining a quality manual.
- Identifying the quality policy, objectives, responsibilities, and infrastructure.
- Establishing and maintaining quality system procedures and standard operating procedures.
- Establishing all activities associated with system implementation, e.g., document control, records, internal audits, training, etc.

◆ HACCP vs GMP vs ISO 9000

With food and health-related products growing continuously in complexity, variety and volume, the concerns for human health and safety are coming to the forefront. Regulatory controls are being developed in various ways to help producers produce high quality safe products and protect consumers from any inadvertent health hazards.

One approach which is gaining wide acceptance is that of quality systems which incorporate all the principles of HACCP and/or GMP. With the acceptance of the ISO 9000 quality system standards the world over, a consensus is growing that a suitable system should incorporate the principles of ISO 9001 plus additional specific requirements pertaining to food and/or healthcare-related products.

Before we embark on outlining the procedure for extending GMP and HACCP to ISO 9001, the following should be noted:

- All three systems, GMP, HACCP and ISO 9001 have the same common fundamental purpose, viz., assurance of quality.
- GMP and HACCP are more specifically geared to the requirements of food and health sectors and their emphasis, to a greater degree, is on the product rather than the system. They are process/product control systems rather than quality management systems.
- ISO 9001 is exclusively a quality system standard and has little orientation for the product quality per sé. However, once implemented, the system generates a high quality product.
- ISO 9001 has a much broader scope than HACCP or GMP. In fact, one can consider HACCP and/or GMP as sub-sets of ISO 9001.
- If a company wishes to achieve ISO 9001 certification, it would have to identify the means by which processes are controlled. By implementing HACCP and/or GMP system, the requirement for process control would be adequately accommodated. Thus, having implemented HACCP and/or GMP guidelines, the company could be well on its way to completing the requirements of ISO 9001.

◆ EXTENDING GMP/HACCP TO ISO 9001

If a company has effectively implemented GMP/HACCP and wishes to proceed to ISO 9001 (or ISO 9002) certification, the transition and preparation is almost minimal. As a first step, the company should undertake a gap-analysis as follows:

- Make a checklist of ISO 9001 requirements.
- Identify the elements of GMP/HACCP.

- Compare the two lists to determine what additional elements/requirements are needed to be addressed to render GMP/HACCP system to meet the ISO 9001 requirements.

Table 44 presents a comparative analysis of the system requirements of the three models. Since the certification pertains to the requirements of ISO 9001, the company would, typically, have to go through the same six phases of ISO 9001 implementation, as identified in Chapter 15, i.e., Awareness, Documentation, Implementation, Audit, Certification, and Maintenance. The details of the certification process have been adequately covered in various other chapters. Recapitulating, some of the key elements are as follows:

- Development of documentation hierarchy
  - Quality Manual
  - Standard Operating Procedures
- Management responsibility
  - Quality policy, quality objectives, quality plans
  - Quality system
  - Quality responsibilities and authority .
- System implementation
  - Document control
  - Quality records
  - Internal quality audits
  - Training
- Development, alignment and implementation of GMP/HACCP standard operating procedures vis-à-vis ISO 9001 requirements.

It must be clearly understood that for ISO 9001 certification, the Quality System Registrars have to verify complete compliance to ISO 9001 requirements, irrespective of whatever systems a company is using, i.e., GMP, HACCP or any other system. Although the usage of GMP/HACCP systems would, indeed, significantly help the company to move towards meeting ISO 9001 requirements, the company would still have to revamp/realign its existing systems, operating procedures and documentation, to reflect and meet ISO 9001 requirements. The following systematic set of guidelines should facilitate the certification process:

- Conduct ISO 9001 awareness sessions in the company. Everyone should clearly understand the following:
  - Requirements of ISO 9001
  - Comparative differential between ISO 9001 and GMP/HACCP requirements

Table 44: Quality System Elements: ISO 9001, GMP, HACCP

Clause #	ISO 9001	GMP	HACCP
4.1	Management Responsibility	Sale (4.1, 4.3, 4.8, 4.19)	Management Review (4.1, 4.2)
4.2	Quality System	Premises (4.4, 4.9)	Premises (4.4, 4.9)
4.3	Contract Review	Equipment (4.1, 4.4, 4.11, 4.13)	Equipment (4.1, 4.4, 4.11, 4.13)
4.4	Design Control	Personnel (4.1, 4.18)	Personnel (4.1, 4.18)
4.5	Document and Data Control	Sanitation (4.1, 4.2, 4.8 - 4.17)	Sanitation (4.1, 4.2, 4.8 - 4.17)
4.6	Purchasing	Raw Material Testing (4.10)	Receiving/Storage (4.6, 4.10, 4.15)
4.7	Control of Customer Supplied Product	Manufacturing Control (4.9)	Verification (4.1, 4.17)
4.8	Product Identification and Traceability	Quality Control (4.1, 4.2, 4.9, 4.17)	Documentation (4.5)
4.9	Process Control	Packaging Material Testing (4.10, 4.15)	Process Control (4.9)
4.10	Inspection and Testing	Finished Product Testing (4.10)	CCP Monitoring (4.9, 4.20)
4.11	Control of Inspection, Measuring and Test Equipment	Records (4.5, 4.16)	Quality Records (4.5, 4.16)
4.12	Inspection and Test Status	Recall (4.1, 4.8, 4.12, 4.13)	Recall (4.1, 4.8, 4.12, 4.13)
4.13	Control of Nonconforming Product	Samples (4.9, 4.10)	Inspection/Testing (4.10)
4.14	Corrective and Preventive Action	Stability (4.9, 4.10, 4.15)	Nonconforming Product (4.13)
4.15	Handling, Storage, Packaging, Preservation and Delivery	Sterile Products (4.9, 4.10)	Corrective Action (4.14)
4.16	Control of Quality Records	Handling/Storage (4.15)	Quality Audits (4.17)
4.17	Internal Quality Audits		
4.18	Training		
4.19	Servicing		
4.20	Statistical Techniques		

- Develop ISO 9001 documentation:
  - Quality Manual: To address ISO 9001 elements while outlining the company's procedures, including GMP/HACCP procedures.
  - Standard Operating Procedures: To describe GMP/HACCP procedures while establishing a linkage to ISO 9001 elements.
- Implement the system
  - Elements that were not part of GMP/HACCP system, but are required vis-à-vis ISO 9001
  - Verify the effectiveness of the GMP/HACCP system elements
- Audit the system to ensure compliance to ISO 9001 requirements.
- Undergo the full certification audit and compliance with the Registrar.
- Maintain the GMP/HACCP/ISO 9001 systems.

21

LABORATORY ACCREDITATION PROTOCOL

◆ QUALITY IN THE LABORATORY

Laboratories play a vital role in the business infrastructure. Almost every aspect of business life is, in one form or another, dependent on laboratory work. The nature and extent of laboratory functions encompass a large spectrum of situations, such as: inspection, testing, calibration, research and development, regulatory compliance, forensic testing, etc.

Most sophisticated products require testing for compliance with specifications and safety regulations before release into the market and trade in many simpler commodities and products also requires supporting technical information. Test documentation has become an essential element in that trade. Even traditional products such as wool, wine, textiles and reasonably unsophisticated products and commodities are now traded almost entirely on the basis of technical specifications and objective testing, rather than - as in the previous days - on more subjective criteria. This trend to more technical information, if it is to have any value, must be supported by valid test data produced by laboratories. Lack of acceptance of laboratory test data across national borders is claimed to be a very significant barrier to trade and a number of international agreements, such as the GATT Standards Code, the OECD Code of Good Laboratory Practice and the EC and EFTA Policies on Testing and Certification here been developed in efforts to overcome this particular problem and related matters.

In most situations, products are accepted only when they are accompanied by test results. The issue here is not of acceptance of products but of the efficiency and

335

validity of test results on the basis of which the products are accepted. The reliability of these test results is, indeed, directly related to the competence of laboratories. Consequently, the major concern of most laboratories revolves around two issues:

- How to implement a credible quality assurance system?
- How to achieve accreditation for competency?

◆ LABORATORY QUALITY ASSURANCE PROTOCOLS

To address the issues of competency of laboratories, many national and international protocols have been established. In this section, we shall outline the quality requirements of the following systems. These requirements can be gainfully utilized for establishing a laboratory quality assurance system. As a matter of interest, it should be noted that all these systems have the same basic common approach to quality.

- ISO/IEC Guide 25: General Requirements for the Accreditation of Calibration and Testing Laboratories (Table 45)
- EPA (Environmental Protection Agency) Rules for Environmental Laboratories (Table 46)
- OECD (Organization for Economic Cooperation and Development) Principles of Good Laboratory Practice (Table 47)
- Federal Register (FDA): Good Laboratory Practice Regulations for Non-Clinical Laboratory Studies (Table 48)

◆ LABORATORY QUALITY ASSURANCE SYSTEM

A quality assurance system for a laboratory situation is, in basic terms, similar to any other quality system, except that it would exert more emphasis on those elements which impact the specific nature of laboratory functions. The system requires the establishment and maintenance of documented procedures, effective implementation of system requirements and continuous monitoring and control of all requisite aspects of quality.

Quality system documentation includes, as a minimum, the following:

- Quality Manual
- Quality System Procedure Manuals
- Standard Operating Procedures

Table 45: ISO/IEC Guide 25: General Requirements for the Accreditation of Calibration and Testing Laboratories

QUALITY SYSTEM ELEMENTS

- Organization and Management
- Quality System, Audit and Review
- Personnel
- Accommodation and Environment
- Equipment and Reference Materials
- Measurement Traceability and Calibration
- Calibration and Test Methods
- Handling of Calibration and Test Items
- Records
- Certificates and Reports
- Subcontracting of Calibration or Testing
- Outside Support Services and Supplies
- Complaints

Table 46: EPA Rules for Environmental Laboratories
Microbiological Analysis of Public Water Supply Samples

QUALITY SYSTEM ELEMENTS

- Personnel
- Physical Facilities
- Laboratory Equipment
- Laboratory Glassware, Plasticware and Metal Utensils
- General Laboratory Practices
- Methodology
- Sample Collecting, Handling and Preservation
- Standards for Laboratory Pure Water
- General Quality Control Procedures
- Quality Control for Media, Equipment and Supplies
- Data Handling
- Record Maintenance
- Action Response to Laboratory Results

Table 47: The OECD Principles of GLP

QUALITY SYSTEM ELEMENTS

- Test Facility Organization and Personnel
  - Management Responsibilities
  - Study Director's Responsibilities
  - Personnel Responsibilities
- Quality Assurance Program
  - General: Program
  - Responsibilities of the Quality Assurance Personnel
- Facilities
  - Test system Facilities
  - Facilities for Handling Test and Reference Substances
  - Archive Facilities
  - Waste Disposal
- Apparatus, Material, and Reagents
- Test systems
  - Physical/Chemical/Biological
- Test and Reference Substances
  - Receipt, Handling, Sampling, and Storage
  - Characterization
- Standard Operating Procedures
- Performance of the Study
- Reporting of Study Results
- Storage and Retention of Records and Material

Table 48: FDA Good Laboratory Practice

QUALITY SYSTEM ELEMENTS

- Organization and Personnel
- Facilities
- Equipment
- Testing Facilities Operation
- Test and Control Articles
- Protocol for and Conduct of a Non-Clinical Laboratory Study
- Records and Reports
- Disqualification of Testing Facilities

A brief description of the total quality system requirements for laboratories is appended below. A systematic implementation of these system elements is required for the effective functioning of the laboratory quality assurance systems.

LABORATORY QUALITY SYSTEM ELEMENTS

- **Quality Policies**
  - Quality policies are to be established by management to identify how quality objectives, regulatory/accreditation requirements and customer needs are addressed.

- **Quality Goals and Objectives**
  - To improve precision and accuracy of test results
  - To establish levels of performance for laboratory work
  - To participate in proficiency analytical testing or quality evaluation programs with other laboratories in order to achieve and maintain consistent, uniform levels of quality
  - To ensure that all personnel are adequately trained
  - To continuously improve and validate laboratory methodologies

- **Organization for Quality**
  - Identify Quality Assurance Coordinator or Manager or Director.
  - Delineate appropriate responsibilities and authority for all quality-related functions.

- **Quality system Documentation**
  - Quality Manual
  - Quality System Procedure Manuals
  - Standard Operating Procedures
  - Quality Plans
  - Quality Training Plans

- **Procurement Control**
  - Establish procedures to control purchased equipment, supplies, chemical reagents and testing materials.
  - Identify acceptable subcontractors and suppliers.
  - Extend controls exercised in the laboratory to the subcontractors also.
  - Ensure that the purchase orders, as well as the purchasing data, are adequately communicated to the suppliers.
  - Establish procedures for verification of purchased products.

- **Sample Handling, Identification, Storage and Shipping**
  - Establish adequate procedures/instructions and specifications.
  - Assign appropriate responsibilities for monitoring these functions.

- **Document Control**
  - Establish procedures for controlling documents, such as: sampling procedures; analytical and test methods; calibration procedures; auditing procedures; quality assurance manuals; standards; quality plans; computation and data validation procedures; sampling data sheets.
  - Establish procedures for document issue, approval, and change.

- **Quality Records**
  - Establish a system for monitoring quality records, such as: test and analytical results; internal/external quality audit results; instrument and gauge record cards; laboratory notebooks; reports on results of data validation; sample chain-of-custody records.

- **Chain-of-Custody Records**
  - Establish procedures for the maintenance of an unbroken record of possession of a sample from time of its collection through some analytical or testing procedure and up to and through a court proceeding, if required.

- **Control of Inspection, Measuring and Test Equipment**
  - Establish procedures for calibration, including such things as: calibration plans, quality of calibration standards, documented calibration methods, calibration source, calibration interval, environmental conditions for calibration, government/industry data exchange, labelling, etc.

- **Preventive Maintenance**
  - Develop a scheduled program of preservation and preventative maintenance.
  - Establish documented procedures for preventative maintenance of equipment, instruments.
  - Preventative maintenance schedule should relate to the purpose of the analysis or test, environmental influences, the physical location of equipment, and the level of operation skills.

- **Reference Standards and Standard Reference Material**
  - Obtain reliable reference standards for calibration.
  - Standard Reference Materials should be used from accredited sources, such as, the National Institute for Science and Technology (U.S.A.) or any other reliable source.

- **Data Validation and Analysis**
  - All information and data must be properly checked and validated; accepted/rejected as per established criteria; properly analyzed.
  - Computerized techniques should be used as much as possible.

- **Nonconformity Control**
  - Establish a set of procedures for the identification, reporting and recording of nonconformances.
  - When nonconformances occur, the work may be suspended; test and analysis may be repeated; and the results may be reported to the customer, if necessary.

- Institute a mechanism for initiating corrective action and ensuring the effectiveness of the action.

- **Corrective/Preventive Action**
  - Establish procedures for taking corrective action.
  - The document (proforma) usually employed for the system is the Corrective Action Request (CAR), which can be initiated by any individual in the laboratory who observes a major problem.
  - Corrective action process may involve: quality report compares actual results with specified results; a nonconformity is identified; Corrective Action Analyst initiates an investigation, takes an action and reports on measures taken and their impact; Quality Control Coordinator follows-up to check the effectiveness of the action; preventative measures are put into place to prevent repetitive occurrence of nonconformity.

- **Quality Cost Evaluation System**
  - Establish a quality cost system to identify and record those elements of quality assurance whose costs may be disproportionate to the benefits derived. Costs can be categorized as: Prevention Costs; Appraisal Costs; Internal-Failure Costs, External-Failure Costs.

- **Control of Subcontracting**
  - Establish procedures to control all subcontracting work. This may include:
    - · Selection of qualified laboratories
    - · Transmission of applicable technical and/or method requirements
    - · Evaluation of test and analytical reports received
    - · Partnering with suppliers and subcontractors

- **Environmental Control**
  - Effective measures must be instituted to ensure control of atmospheric conditions; working conditions; conditions relating to special tests, precision and accuracy; and in general, environmental conditions.

- **Personnel**
  - Establish procedures for the identification and provision of training needs in areas such as: quality control/quality assurance; technical; motivational and communication aspects.
  - Training and qualification records must be maintained.

- **Quality Audits**
  - Establish procedures and schedule for conducting regular audits. Audits can include: sampling audits; data processing audits; analysis or test audits; performance audits.

- **Reliability Analysis**
  - Reliability about the competency of test results is very essential. Reliability is defined as: the probability of a system performing its intended function for a prescribed period of time under specified operating conditions.

- With regard to purchase of material and equipment, reliability requirements should be specified in the contract, wherever appropriate.
- Reliability program should be planned in advance and suitable measure implemented to ensure reliability of: prediction analysis, life-testing, incoming material/equipment, operating conditions.
- Reliability program should also include: provision of adequate training of personnel, adequate preventive maintenance.

- **Statistical Methods**
  - Use of statistical methods for process capability studies, data analysis and research and development is fundamentally important for the competency and objectivity of test results.

- **Customer Complaints**
  - A suitable program must be established to handle all aspects of customer feedback and complaint resolution.

A quality system is established, documented and represented via a Quality Manual. From the quality system elements described above, we can now identify the contents of a quality manual, as appended in Table 49. The quality manual is implemented by the Standard Operating Procedures and the entire structure, thereby, forms the bulk of a laboratory quality assurance system.

◆ LABORATORY ACCREDITATION

The issue of competency of laboratories and confidence in their test results is of paramount importance whether the laboratory function is: internal to the manufacturing company; related to research and development; associated with third-party testing and calibration; related to regulatory compliance; or specified in a contract for the purpose of trade, nationally or internationally.

There is a growing realization for the need of an internationally accepted laboratory accreditation system to facilitate trade. In the absence of any such system as yet, laboratories are opting for a national laboratory accreditation system which operates in accordance with international practice as defined in various ILAC, ISO/IEC and CEN/CENELEC documents, e.g., the EN 45000 series. These systems provide efficient mechanisms to assure a high degree of reproducibility of test results.

Table 49: Laboratory Quality Manual: Format/Structure

	Section:
ABC Company, Inc.	Issue:
Lovers Lane	Page:
Quality Land	Date:
QUALITY MANUAL	Approved by:

1. Document Issue
2. Table of Contents
3. Profile of Testing Organization
4. Introduction to Quality Manual
5. Certification
6. Management of Quality Manual: Distribution/Review/Revision
7. Quality Policies, Objectives
8. Quality Organization/Responsibilities
9. Resources: Personnel and Physical
10. Quality System Review
11. Procurement Control
12. Sample Handling, Identification, Storage and Shipping
13. Document Control
14. Quality Records
15. Chain-of-Custody Procedures
16. Test Methods and Procedures
17. Reference Material and Standards
18. Control of Measuring and Test Equipment
19. Accommodation and Environmental Controls
20. Preventive Maintenance
21. Data Analysis and Validation
22. Control of Subcontracting
23. Personnel Training
24. Nonconformity Control
25. Corrective and Preventive Action
26. Quality Audits
27. Statistical Methods
28. Customer Complaints

Many countries are attempting to establish national laboratory accreditation programs based on ISO/IEC Guide 25. If laboratory accreditation bodies operate at a comparable level, if that level meets internationally agreed conditions, and if certain safeguards are in place, then assessment by one national body should meet the needs of a second national body. Acceptance of foreign test data then depends on the degree of recognition that the national accreditation body is accorded in its own country.

With the emergence of many such national systems for the accreditation of laboratories, it is becoming very easy to establish bilateral agreements by which parties in each of the signatory countries agree to recognize each other's accreditation actions and encourage the acceptance by others of test data, results, or reports issued by testing laboratories accredited under a laboratory accreditation system, administered in either countries. These agreements would reduce or eliminate unnecessary duplication of tests by laboratories in the importing countries and help to speed up the process of international trade and thereby reduce the costs of manufacturing, warehousing and selling of the products involved.

Laboratory Accreditation Process

Following is a generic sequence of steps for laboratory accreditation program vis-à-vis ISO/IEC Guide 25:

- Establish a laboratory quality assurance system.
- Identify the requirements of ISO/IEC Guide 25.
- Develop requisite documentation hierarchy: Quality Manual, Quality System Procedures Manuals, Standard Operating Procedures.
- The quality system documentation must address the system requirements of Guide 25 and adequately describe the quality system in place.
- Implement the system and internally audit it for accuracy, competency and compliance.
- Select the appropriate registrar for accreditation. This body can be the national standards organization of the country or any other accredited organization.
- Submit the quality documents to the registrar for evaluation.
- Undergo the compliance audit by the registrar.
- Achieve and maintain the certification status.

ISO Guide 25 vs. ISO 9001

With the ever increasing popularity and credibility of ISO 9000 series of quality system standards, many laboratories are showing a high degree of interest in implementing a combination of the system requirements of Guide 25 and ISO 9001 or 9002 and seek accreditation to either Guide 25 and/or ISO 9001 or 9002 (whichever is applicable). Note that, ISO 9001 is only applicable to organizations who are involved in the "Design Control" function. Before embarking on any such undertaking, it is imperative to clearly understand the protocol of each system. Table 50 presents a systematic comparison of system elements of ISO 9001 and Guide 25.

| Table 50: Quality System Elements: ISO 9001 vs. Guide 25 ||
ISO 9001	Guide 25
<ul><li>Management Responsibility</li><li>Quality System</li><li>Contract Review</li><li>Design Control</li><li>Document and Data Control</li><li>Purchasing</li><li>Control of Customer-Supplied Product</li><li>Product Identification and Traceability</li><li>Process Control</li><li>Inspection and Testing</li><li>Control of Inspection, Measuring and Test Equipment</li><li>Inspection and Test Status</li><li>Control of Nonconforming Product</li><li>Corrective and Preventive Action</li><li>Handling, Storage, Packaging, Preservation and Delivery</li><li>Control of Quality Records</li><li>Internal Quality Audits</li><li>Training</li><li>Servicing</li><li>Statistical Techniques</li></ul>	<ul><li>Organization and Management</li><li>Quality System, Audit and Review</li><li>Personnel</li><li>Accommodation and Environment</li><li>Equipment and Reference Materials</li><li>Measurement Traceability and Calibration</li><li>Calibration and Test Methods</li><li>Handling of Calibration and Test Items</li><li>Records</li><li>Certificates and Reports</li><li>Subcontracting of Calibration or Testing</li><li>Outside Support Services and Suppliers</li><li>Complaints</li></ul>

The ISO 9000 series of standards provides a generic system for quality management of an organization, irrespective of its actual function. ISO Guide 25 is a document developed specifically to give guidance to laboratory proprietors and managers on both quality management, in a laboratory environment, and technical requirements for the proper operation of a testing laboratory. To the extent that the documents address quality management, Guide 25 can be regarded as a version of ISO 9001 or 9002 written in terms most understandable by laboratory managers. When interpreted in a laboratory context, the system elements of the two documents are almost identical.

The essential differences between Guide 25 and ISO 9001 are as follows:

- Technical Requirements

  Guide 25 requires: specific technical competence on the part of all senior laboratory personnel; rigid adherence to specified test methodology; participation in proficiency testing programs, where possible.

- Auditing

  Quality system auditors for ISO 9000 are individuals who normally possess formal education and training in auditing techniques with a deep and thorough knowledge of system standards. They, however, do not require any more than a passing knowledge of the specific technology of the organization under evaluation.

  Laboratory accreditation is based on the notion of "peer review", that is, the assessors must be as experts or more so, in the technical as well as management skills, than the staff of the laboratory under assessment.

- Certification/Assessment Approach

  Quality management system audit attempts to assess compliance with a particular designated system standard without attempting to identify the suitability of that standard for a particular organization. An assessment of a laboratory for compliance with Guide 25, on the other hand, requires: assessment of the compliance with the system elements plus assessment of the technical knowledge of the personnel and also some other aspects, such as: evaluation of the suitability of the test selected, its implementation, calibration and maintenance of equipment and provision of suitable accommodation. Also, in the laboratories, there is a specific need to monitor performance by any objective means of inter-laboratory test-proficiency testing.

- General

  ISO 9000 is a bit more broad in the overall management aspect of quality and is, typically, a system standard.

  Guide 25 is concerned about the specific aspects relating to quality in the laboratory context, such as: assessment of technical competence of personnel; specific requirements of particular products or measurements; potentials for performing a quality job (quality system) as well as technical competence (ability to achieve a technical result).

Preparing for Guide 25 and ISO 9001

Preparing for the combined set of requirements of ISO 9001 and Guide 25, is not too difficult. The Quality Manual must be prepared so as to address the elements of both documents. The same holds for the other tiers of documents, viz., Quality System Procedures and Standard Operating Procedures.

However, it must be clearly understood that the certification/accreditation process of ISO 9001 and Guide 25 is different. The ISO certifications are carried out by independent registrars. These registrars can conduct an ISO 9000 certification for a laboratory but not a laboratory accreditation vis-à-vis Guide 25. Laboratory accreditations vis-à-vis guide 25 are carried out by either the national standard bodies or other accredited organizations specifically designated for this purpose. Therefore, if a laboratory wishes to achieve laboratory accreditation to Guide 25 as well as ISO 9000 certification, it has to undergo two separate sets of processes. The only thing common to the two processes is the preparation and documentation of the system which can be accommodated through a single set of documentation.

The overall process of certification/accreditation to ISO 9000 and/or Guide 25 is almost the same. This process has been substantially elucidated in the other chapters.

♦ ISO 10012: Q.A. REQUIREMENTS FOR MEASURING EQUIPMENT

The ISO technical committee, ISO/TC 176, has developed the following two standards in the ISO 10000 series to address the need for quality assurance of measuring equipment as applicable to all manufacturing situations, including testing and calibration laboratories.

- ISO 10012: Quality Assurance Requirements for Measuring Equipment:

  - Part 1: Metrological Confirmation System for Measuring Equipment
  - Part 2: Measurement Process Control

The documents provide quality assurance requirements for measuring equipment that can be gainfully used in a laboratory context. In this section, we are only providing the overall structural framework of these requirements; for more details, the reader should consult the international standards.

Part 1: Metrological Confirmation System for Measuring Equipment

Following is a list of elements that needs to be addressed through documented procedures:

- Measuring equipment suitability for intended use
- Confirmation system
- Periodic audit and review of the confirmation system
- Planning
- Uncertainty of measurement
- Documented confirmation procedures
- Records
- Nonconforming measuring equipment
- Confirmation labelling
- Intervals of confirmation
- Sealing for integrity
- Use of outside products and services
- Storage and handling
- Traceability

Part 2: Measurement Process Control

As of this writing, Part 2 is still in the draft stage. The document emphasizes the establishment and documentation of objective performance criteria and procedures for measurement processes and measurement process controls. The following system elements needs to be addressed through documented procedures:

- Documentation
- Measurement processes
- Measurement process set-up and design
- Metrological confirmation system
- Measurement process control system
- Analysis of measurement process control data
- Surveillance of the measurement process
- Intervals of surveillance
- Control of the measurement process
- Failure of the measurement process control system
- Verification of the measurement process
- Identification of verified measurement processes
- Measurement process control records
- Personnel
- Periodic audit and review of the measurement process control system

22

ISO 14000: ENVIRONMENTAL MANAGEMENT SYSTEMS

♦ INTRODUCTION

There is a growing public concern about the depleting quality of our environment. Organizations all over the world are becoming cognizant of this fact, and they are attempting to pay serious attention to the matter. While the regulators are considering imposition of stringent rules and regulations for the protection of environmental quality, the manufacturing organizations are organizing themselves to voluntarily take the responsibility for self-regulating their functions through the implementation of effective Environmental Management Systems (EMS).

The quality of our environment is virtually dependent on the way we utilize our materials, products, and manufacturing processes. Most products, processes, and services follow a life-cycle pattern and, depending on their nature and complexity, each stage of their life-cycle has some impact on the environment. The loadings on the environment can be in the form of gaseous emissions to the air or as liquid or solid wastes discharged to the soil or water. The failure to effectively control these entities is resulting in the loss of natural resources and decreased biodiversity, degradation of water and air quality, and dumps and landfills that hold recyclable and usable materials that can be easily brought into operation in one form or another.

What is needed for achieving and maintaining sustainable environmental quality levels? The answer to this question is by no means easy. There are a host of divergent factors that impact environmental quality. Notwithstanding however, a good starting point is to:

- Develop viable environmental quality designs
- Implement well-structured environmental quality management systems

The success of these undertakings would, indeed, depend on the commitment and extent to which organizations would be prepared to provide requisite management, technical, and financial resources and support systems.

The concern for the environment is reaching a critical point and, consequently, it is now commanding global attention. Many concerned organizations have issued guiding principles for environmental management and business charters for sustainable development. Some of the major ones are as follows:

- The United Nations Rio Declaration on Environment and Development
- International Chamber of Commerce (ICC) Business Charter for Sustainable Development
- Coalition for Environmentally Responsible Economies (CERES) Principles (formerly the Valdez Principles)
- Keidanren Global Environment Charter: Japan Federation of Economic Organizations
- Environmental Guiding Principles: European Petroleum Industry Association (EUROPIA)
- Objectives for Sustainable Development: National Round Table on the Environment and the Economy (NRTEE)
- Business Principles for a Sustainable and Competitive Future: Business Council on National Issues

In line with these emerging initiatives, another important development has been set into motion. The international Organization for Standardization (ISO) has created a new technical committee, ISO/TC207, to address these issues and develop international standards on environmental management systems. The committee has already developed drafts of the following two standards:

- ISO 14001: Environmental Management Systems - Specification
- ISO 14xxx: Guide to Environmental Management Principles, Systems and Supporting Techniques

In the next few sections, we shall outline the basic framework of the systems elements of these two standards. As a long-term perspective, the committee is considering the development of additional related documents on the following subjects:

- Environmental Auditing and Related Investigations
- Environmental Labelling
- Environmental Performance Evaluation
- Life-Cycle Assessment

As of this writing, the exact titles and the numbering system for these documents have not been finalized; however, it is expected that these documents will be issued under the 14000 series of standards. This series is intended to be in conformity with the ISO 9000 series of quality system standards.

♦ ENVIRONMENTAL MANAGEMENT SYSTEMS: DESIGN

As indicated above, the first important step for an effective EMS is its design. If a system is designed properly in the first place, it would have high chance of success and sustainability. The design process starts by taking a comprehensive look at all aspects of the life-cycle stages of products, processes and materials that impact on environment. Typically, the life-cycle stages involve the following:

- Acquisition of raw materials
- Manufacturing processes
- Use, reuse, maintenance, and application
- Waste management, recycling, and disposal

The life-cycle inventory identifies and quantifies the material, energy, and water inputs and the generation of environmental loadings or wastes throughout the product life. The design process integrates the life-cycle inventory with other measures and criteria of environmental burdens associated with the products, such as performance, cost, cultural, legal and technical aspects. A comprehensive evaluation and integration of all of these elements results into an effective design model for the environment. An important thing to keep in mind is that the design must always be generated on a well-structured and disciplined approach rather than a piece-meal crisis-oriented response approach.

Although the design process and methodology may differ from one organization to the other, there are some general core principles that every designer and organization is expected to follow, such as:

- Commitment to do good to the environment
- Protection of the biosphere
- Minimization of environmental risks
- Sustainable utilization of natural resources
- Conservation of energy
- Effective waste management
- Continuous product/process improvement

Finally, it is important to mention that a well-designed Environmental Management System renders many benefits for the organization, including:

- Disciplined approach to doing business
- System uniformity and efficiency
- Optimal utilization of resources
- Effective anticipation and compliance of regulatory requirements
- Cost control
- Competitive advantage
- Meeting customer's environmental expectations
- Enhancing image and market share

◆ ENVIRONMENTAL MANAGEMENT SYSTEMS: SPECIFICATIONS

In this section, we shall outline the basic framework of system elements addressed in the forthcoming international standard: "ISO 14001: Environmental Management Systems - Specifications". The standard specifies some elements of the environmental management systems that can be applicable to all types and sizes of organizations and can accommodate diverse geographical, cultural and social conditions.

The specifications are prescriptive in nature and are intended to provide guidelines for establishing an effective EMS which can be integrated with other existing management system elements. The standard does not establish mandatory requirements for environmental performance beyond commitment, in the policy, to compliance with applicable regulatory requirements, and to continual improvement.

The standard shares common management system principles with ISO 9000 quality system standards, and therefore, if an organization has already developed a quality management system in conformity with ISO 9000 standards, it can easily utilize this framework for environmental management.

In this section, we shall briefly outline the basic framework of system elements of ISO 14001. For a more extensive coverage of the subject, the reader is advised to consult the standard as and when it is ready and available.

ISO 14001: Environmental Management systems: Specifications

4.1 Environmental Policy

Define and document environmental policy. The policy should:

- Be relevant to the nature, scale and environmental impacts of activities, products and services.
- Include a commitment to continual improvement.
- Be in compliance with environmental legislative and regulatory requirements.
- Provide framework for establishing environmental objectives and goals.
- Be communicated to everyone concerned.

4.2 Planning

4.2.1 Environmental Aspects

Establish and maintain procedures to identify environmental aspects of activities, products, and services that the organization shall control.

4.2.2 Legal and other Requirements

Establish and maintain procedures to ensure compliance to legislative and regulatory requirements.

4.2.3 Objectives and Targets

Establish and maintain documented environmental objectives and targets at all levels within the organization that are:

- Commensurate with the legislative and regulatory requirements, environmental aspects, the technological, financial, operational and business requirements of the organization and interested parties.

- Consistent with the environmental policy.

4.2.4 Environmental Management Program

Establish and maintain a program for achieving the objectives and targets. It should include:

- Designation of appropriate responsibilities
- Means and timeframe for achieving the objectives
- Mechanisms to ensure that the program shall also apply to projects relating to new or modified developments, activities, products and services.

4.3 Implementation and Operation

4.3.1 Structure and Responsibility

- Define, document and communicate roles, responsibilities and accountability for the management of environmental issues.
- Provide requisite personnel, technical and financial resources for the implementation and verification of environmental policies and objectives.
- Appoint a management representative to ensure:
  - Effective system implementation
  - Reporting on the performance of the system to the management for review and improvement

4.3.2 Training, Awareness and Competence

- Identify training needs and provide appropriate training to personnel whose work may create a significant impact upon the environment.
- Employees, at all levels, should be trained to be aware of:
  - Importance of conformance to the policy, procedures and system
  - Significance of their work activities and environmental benefits of improved personal performance
  - Potential consequences of departure from specified procedures
- Personnel for specific assigned tasks should be selected on the basis of their training, knowledge and experience.

4.3.3 Communications

Establish and maintain suitable means of communication for receiving and relaying relevant information and data internally and externally.

4.3.4 Environmental Documentation

Establish and maintain an effective documented information system for the EMS.

4.3.5 Document control

Establish and maintain a document control system to ensure that all requisite documents are:

- Properly identified
- Periodically reviewed/revised and approved by authorized personnel prior to use
- Available at all appropriate locations
- Promptly removed when they become obsolete
- Legible, readily identifiable and effectively maintained

4.3.6 Control Procedures for Routine Operations

Ensure that the EMS activities are carried out under controlled procedures by:

- Preparing appropriate documented procedures
- Establishing criteria for capability and acceptance of operating controls.

4.3.7 Emergency Preparedness

Establish and maintain procedures for responding to emergency situations. These procedures should be revised and updated as appropriate.

4.4 Checking and Corrective Action

4.4.1 Monitoring and Measurement

- Establish procedures to monitor key characteristics of processes.
- Establish procedures for calibration of monitoring equipment and maintenance of calibration records.

4.4.2 Nonconformance and Corrective and Preventive Action

Establish procedures for the identification of nonconformance and initiation of corrective and preventive action. The corrective/preventive action should be commensurate with the magnitude of the risk encountered.

4.4.3 Records

Establish procedures for the effective maintenance of all requisite EMS records.

4.4.4 Environmental Management System Audit

Establish and maintain a program and procedures for audit to ensure that:

- The EMS conforms to the requirements of this standard.
- The system has been effectively implemented and maintained.

4.5 Management Review

The management shall review the EMS, at regular intervals, to ensure its continuing suitability and effectiveness. Records of reviews shall be maintained.

◆ EMS: PRINCIPLES AND SUPPORTING TECHNIQUES

The technical committee. ISO/TC207, has developed another standard: "ISO 14xxx: Guide to Environmental Management Principles, Systems and Supporting Techniques", as a follow-up and supplement to the "ISO 14001: EMS Specifications" standard. As of this writing, the standard has not been assigned a number. This guideline builds on the core elements of EMS and provides methodology for initiating, implementing and improving the environmental management system. The standard also stresses the fact that an environmental management system cannot be a totally independent system; its components will be inextricably interwoven with most of the organizations' overall management system.

The basic key principles of an Environmental Management System include the following:

- Putting environmental management as top priority for the organization.
- Identifying and developing management and employee commitment to the protection of the environment.
- Delineation of appropriate responsibilities.
- Identification of activities, products and service which may have an impact on the environment.
- Identification of any legislative or regulatory requirements.
- Establishment of two-way communications with internal and external stakeholders.
- Development of policies, objectives, targets and strategies.
- Development of disciplined methodologies and management processes for achieving targeted performance levels.
- Coordination of EMS with other management systems.
- Provision for appropriate resources and training.
- Methods of monitoring and assessing performance.
- Review and audit of the system.
- Focus on continuous improvement.

The standard stipulates core elements of the EMS model, via the following building blocks:

- **Define Purpose/Establish Plan**
  - Identification and evaluation of environmental aspects and risks
  - Environmental Policy
  - Internal standards of performance
  - Environmental objectives and targets
  - Environmental strategic plan
  - Environmental management program

- **Implement - Building Capability**
  - Resources - human, physical, and financial
  - Organizational - alignment and integration
  - Accountability and responsibility
  - Environmental values and motivation
  - Knowledge, skill and training

- **Implement - Support Action**
  - Operational control
  - Emergency planning and response
  - EMS documentation
  - EMS records and information management
  - Communication and reporting

- **Measure and Improve**
  - Measuring and improving
  - Audits and reviews of the EMS
  - Corrective and preventive action
  - Continual improvement

♦ ENVIRONMENTAL MANAGEMENT: SYPNOSIS

The beginnings of a revolution for the protection of the environment can be vividly seen at the horizon. The activities of the next century would be overwhelmingly engrossed around the issues of environmental management. Human health and safety is of paramount importance. But, it is intricately interwoven with our ecosystem. Consequently, environmental quality is one issue that commands everyone's unequivocal attention. Organizations who undertake activities, produce products or deliver services that have an impact on the environment must clearly understand the roles and responsibilities that they have to accept in ensuring environmental quality and safety. They have a responsibility toward society - the society in which they themselves exist.

Notwithstanding the societal obligation, there are many tangible and intangible benefits for the organizations to have effective environmental management systems. Excellent companies are cognizant of these economic benefits and they always will operate in a proactive rather than reactive mode in addressing these important issues. Some of the benefits associated with a proactive EMS include:

- Achieving significant competitive advantage through operational and production efficiencies
- Increased acceptability of products and services
- Cost control and minimization of losses
- Optimal utilization of resources through linking of environmental objective and targets with specific financial outcomes
- Meeting customers' and stakeholders' expectations
- Enhanced market credibility and market share
- Effective waste management
- Reduction in liabilities
- Improved industry/government relations
- Opportunities for improved technology
- Service to society

PART FIVE

THE

QUALITY

IMPROVEMENT

23

QUALITY IMPROVEMENT TOOLS

◆ INTRODUCTION

As repeatedly indicated earlier, quality improvement starts at the process level. The final product is simply a sum total of several processes spread over the life cycle of the product. To expect to achieve higher levels of product quality, therefore, requires continuous monitoring, control and improvement of the processes. The basic sequence of steps for a typical process improvement program involves the following:

- Identify the process for improvement.
- Identify process characteristics and boundaries.
- Evaluate the current state of control and capability of the process vis-à-vis the specified requirements.
- Challenge the existing assumptions and accepted procedures.
- Identify improvement opportunities.
- Flow chart the process.
- Implement new procedures and initiatives.
- Gather and analyze data through statistical methods.
- Monitor and control the process.
- Analyze problems.
- Eliminate deficiencies and implement improvements.
- Re-evaluate and redefine the new process.
- Assess the performance and identify the improvement achieved.
- Repeat the cycle of continuous improvement.

Process improvement comes through a continuous evaluation of the process performance. There are several excellent analytical tools available for problem identification/analysis and process improvement. These were identified in Chapter 5 and are presented here in Table 51. Some of these tools have been popularly categorized into two groups as follows:

7 Traditional Tools	7 New Tools
• Cause-Effect Diagram	• Relations Diagram
• Pareto Chart	• Affinity Diagram/KJ Method
• Checksheet	• Systematic/Tree Diagram
• Histogram	• Matrix Diagram
• Scatter Diagram	• Matrix Data-Analysis Method
• Control Chart	• Process Decision Program Chart (PDPC)
• Flow Chart	• Arrow Diagram

Both sets of tools are equally and effectively used for various aspects of process improvement. As an example, Table 52 presents a schematic of the sequence of steps for process improvement with an appropriate application of some of the traditional tools. The emergence of new tools is in consequence of the more recent expanded focus on total quality management. In this chapter, we shall only provide a brief description of some of these tools. For a more extensive application of these techniques, the reader is advised to consult other useful sources and references.

◆ BRAINSTORMING

Brainstorming is a process designed to generate ideas from the collective knowledge of a group of people. It is a problem-solving technique used to expand one's thinking to include all the dimensions of a particular topic at hand. The method can be used for:

• Identifying process problems.
• Identifying causes of process problems.
• Generating process improvement ideas.
• Generating improvement implementation ideas.

Tools and Methodologies	Quality Improvement Activities		
	Problem Identification	Problem Analysis	Planning and Implementation
Brainstorming	✓		✓
Flow Chart	✓		✓
Checksheet	✓		
The Visual Factory	✓	✓	✓
Cause-Effect Diagram	✓	✓	✓
Pareto Chart	✓	✓	✓
Just-in-Time	✓	✓	✓
"PURI" Process Enhancement Wheel	✓	✓	✓
Quality Function Deployment	✓	✓	✓
Force Field Analysis		✓	✓
Shewhart-Deming Cycle		✓	✓
Nominal Group Technique	✓		✓
Benchmarking	✓		✓
Block Diagram	✓	✓	✓
Relations Diagram	✓	✓	
Control Charts	✓	✓	✓
Statistical Process Control	✓	✓	✓
Design of Experiments		✓	
Systematic/Tree Diagram	✓		✓
Arrow Diagram		✓	✓
Affinity Diagram/KJ Method	✓		✓
Matrix Diagram	✓		✓
Matrix Data - Analysis		✓	
Process Decision Program Chart (PDPC)	✓	✓	✓
Concurrent Engineering	✓		✓

Table 51. Quality Improvement Tools

Table 52. Process Improvement Steps

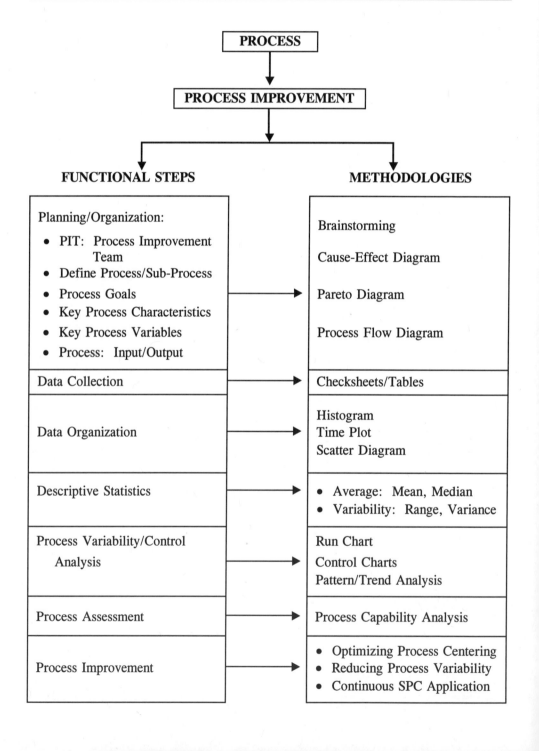

The brainstorming process can be structured or unstructured in design. In the structured approach, each person in the group shares an idea as his/her turn comes around or passes until the next turn. The process continues until all the members have run out of ideas. This method facilitates effective participation by everyone involved. The unstructured brainstorming process allows the group members to express their ideas as they come to mind. Although this tends to create a more relaxed setting, it also runs the risk of the session being dominated by the most vocal participants in the group.

Procedure

- Clearly identify the problem on a flip chart.
- State the purpose and objective.
- Each person takes a turn, in sequence, to offer a single idea at a time.
- Record ideas on the flip chart exactly as they are reported.
- Do not interrupt, censor or criticize ideas. Allow for a free and creative flow of thoughts and ideas.
- Do not discuss ideas; questions may be asked for clarification of an idea.
- Encourage participation.
- No individual person should be judged as an expert.
- All ideas are acceptable.
- Ideas can evolve from other people's ideas.
- Allow members to pass when it is their turn but yet contribute further ideas on future turns.
- When everyone passes on a complete turn, the brainstorming session ceases and the list of ideas is turned over to the problem-solving team.

◆ CHECKSHEET

Checksheets are tools that help to collect information and data in an easy and systematic format for compilation and analysis. To effectively use the checksheet, it is important to have a clear understanding of the purpose of data collection and the final results which may be gained from it. Checksheets are generally useful in identifying the:

- Location of defects or parts
- Performance of operations in a sequence
- Reasons for noncompliance
- Process distribution and behaviour
- Defect causes and maintenance checks

Procedure

- Identify the data to be collected.
- Design a checksheet to compile this data.
- Collect the data.
- Tabulate the results.

Table 53 provides an example of a checksheet monitoring various types of defects.

Table 53. Checksheet for Types of Defects		
Process _____ Date _____		
Specification _____ Operator _____		
Defect Type	Tally	Frequency
Crack	### ### ### ### ### //	27
Pinhole	### ### ///	13
Cold Lap	### /	6
Surface Finish	////	4
Miscellaneous	### ###	10
Total		60

◆ QUALITY FUNCTION DEPLOYMENT (QFD)

As defined by Professor Yoji Akado of Japan, Quality Function Deployment means "converting the consumer's requirements into substitute characteristics and setting the designed quality of the finished products by deploying the relationships systematically, starting with the quality of each functional component to the quality of each part and process." Basically, QFD is a means of obtaining a clear understanding of the customer's requirements, translating them into quantitative engineering terms and working together through cross-functional teams, from marketing, design, manufacture and procurement, to meet the customer's needs and requirements. The idea is to incorporate directly into the design of the product the engineering characteristics that match the customer's wants (attributes) and priorities. By doing so, the company can:

- Reduce product introduction time, engineering changes and overall costs.
- Improve cross-functional planning and communication.
- Improve quality, reliability and customer satisfaction.

Procedure

- Establish a well-trained and knowledgeable cross-functional team.
- The team must clearly understand the:
  - Required quality by the customer
  - Designed quality by the management
  - Offered quality by the staff
- Gather complete data/information on the customer requirements.
- Prepare a QFD matrix chart consisting of the:
  - Required quality elements
  - Deployment of quality elements
  - Function deployment
  - Unit parts deployment
  - Technical deployment
  - Deployment with regard to cost and reliability considerations
- The QFD matrix is used to develop an optimal product design that accommodates the customer's priorities and requirements, product/process alternatives, market needs, and available technologies.

◆ FORCE FIELD ANALYSIS

Force Field Analysis is a technique for identifying problems, their causes and the driving forces that help or obstruct a change which affects process improvement. In every situation requiring change or improvement, there is a conjunction of forces which help as well as hinder the process. By identifying both types of forces, an overall strategy can be developed to tackle the change.

Procedure

- Identify the problem.
- Establish a Process Improvement Team.
- Perform a Cause and Effect Analysis.
- Identify all the forces; classify the positive and negative forces separately.
- Prepare the Force Field Diagram (see Figure 6 for example).
- Evaluate the forces with respect to "ease of change" and "impact" on the process.
- Perform a Force Field Analysis:
    - The "restraining forces" are those keeping the problem at its current level (the cause of the problem).
    - The "driving forces" are those pushing the problem toward improvement (the solution to the problem).
- The team develops a strategy to minimize or eliminate the restraining forces and augment the effect of the driving forces to achieve process improvement.

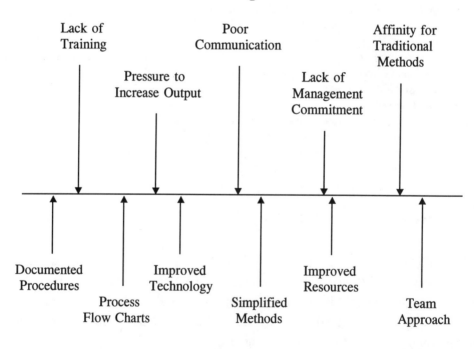

Restraining Forces

Lack of Training   Poor Communication   Affinity for Traditional Methods

Pressure to Increase Output   Lack of Management Commitment

Documented Procedures   Improved Technology   Improved Resources

Process Flow Charts   Simplified Methods   Team Approach

Driving Forces

Figure 6: Force Field Analysis for Implementing a Process Change

◆ "PURI" PROCESS ENHANCEMENT WHEEL

P-U-R-I: Plan - Upgrade - Record - Improve

A system is simply a sum total of processes. To improve the system, it is imperative to improve the individual process. Process improvement is only feasible and meaningful when the team can clearly develop a sense of direction with regard to the following:

- What needs to be improved?
- What is the current best?
- What is the goal?
- How would the goal be achieved?
- How would the achievement be measured?

The PURI Process Enhancement Wheel, outlined in Figure 2, Chapter 3, provides simple cyclic guidelines for continuous process quality improvement.

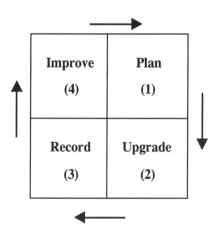

Procedure and Target

- Identify the characteristics/variables/attributes of the process that need to be improved.
- Identify the state of their current level of excellence.
- Define a goal for enhancement for each or all of the characteristics.
- Establish a strategy for implementing the improvement effort.
- Identify improvement initiatives/projects.
- Implement the improvement plan.

- Monitor and control the improvement efforts.
- Identify deficiencies of the improvement initiatives.
- Take corrective/preventive action.
- Continue monitoring the performance.
- Evaluate results.
- Identify the improvements achieved.
- Standardize the achieved improvements.
- Adjust the process to the new standards/aims.
- Continue the cyclic process of improvement.

◆ THE VISUAL FACTORY

The Visual Factory Technique can, typically, be considered as an extension of the childhood school activity of "show and tell". It is a powerful means of pictorially communicating essential messages to improve the overall business quality environment in the organization. The method consists of exhibiting and displaying, at key locations in the organization, various key results, significant accomplishments and essential quality/productivity enhancement exhortations. some of the items amenable to the visual display are as follows:

- Quality policy, objectives, goals, operating plans
- Vision/mission statement
- Track records regarding: safety, defect prevention, yields, process control activities, etc.
- Activity profile regarding: training, team work, empowerment, etc.
- Profile of planned improvements and their results
- Focus on customer satisfaction
- Daily/weekly news: internal as well as external
- Market trends and company standing
- Profile of process improvement initiatives such as: Statistical Process Control (SPC), Just-in-Time (JIT), Design of Experiments (DOE), etc.
- Improvement profile of key quality characteristics
- Activities of employee groups
- Recognition and reward of employees

Organizations with a long-term vision and mission for establishing a sustainable quality culture and a performance mindset would drive enormous benefits from the visual factory approach. Some of the spin-offs of the technique are:

- Improved communications
- Transparency of operations
- Improved employee moral
- Visibility of empowerment
- Visibility of the company's health status
- Tangible improvements in quality of products and services
- Improved flow of information

Procedure

- Develop a master list of entities to be displayed.
- Develop and organize the format and structure of display.
- Design the content for display.
- Identify key locations for display.
- Optimize the plan through Process Management Teams.
- Implement the plan.
- Monitor schedule, results, and feedback.
- Continuously rejuvenate and reenergize the technique.

◆ SHEWHART - DEMING CYCLE

PDSA: Plan-Do-Study-Act

The Shewhart-Deming cycle is a cyclic process for continuous quality improvement. The method is most effective for planning and testing improvement activities prior to full-scale implementation.

Procedure

- Identify opportunities for improvement.
- Identify improvement initiatives.
- Plan and develop a theory to be tested.
- Carry out the trial.
- Collect all relevant data.
- Statistically analyze the results.
- Compare the results with the theory.
- Implement improvement.
- Revise the theory commensurate with this additional knowledge.
- Identify new opportunities for improvement.
- Repeat the continuous improvement cycle.

◆ NOMINAL GROUP TECHNIQUE

The Nominal Group Technique is a problem-solving method that involves identifying a problem, developing possible solutions, rank ordering the priorities and selecting the most optimal solution through group consensus.

Procedure

- Identify the problem.
- Gather a team.
- Limit the discussion to one topic per meeting.
- Generate ideas in writing.
- Record ideas without discussion or comments.
- Conduct group discussion to clarify the ideas.
- Do not allow argumentation or criticism of ideas.
- Vote on the results of the discussion.
- Discuss and clarify the vote.
- Establish a final consensus.
- Identify the solution.
- Implement the solution.

◆ BENCHMARKING

Benchmarking is a process in which companies improve their products and services by targeting against and adopting industry's best practices. Whenever a company decides to implement a quality improvement system, it has two options: to reinvent the wheel and develop its own system or to adopt, with or without modification, a system used by another company which has achieved excellence in that area. The latter option is generally more viable, more effective, simpler, less demanding and cost-effective.

Procedure

- Identify the process to be benchmarked.
- Establish a Process Improvement Team.
- Understand the process characteristics and boundaries.
- Identify which companies to benchmark, ie. those with an excellent track record in the area of processes similar to yours or different from yours.
- Establish a relationship with the company and collect and share information.

- Identify the benchmarks by collecting data through surveys, professional contacts, interviews, journals, advertisements, etc.
- Analyze the benchmark data and information.
- Implement and monitor improvement initiatives.
- Evaluate the process performance.
- Continue the cycle of improvement.

◆ STATISTICAL PROCESS CONTROL (SPC)

Statistical Process Control (SPC) is a technique employed to control by means of statistical methods the system of causes and their variability in a process. The basic quality factors of interest in a process are accuracy, precision, bias, process stability, process conformance, uniformity, repeatability and reproducibility. The fundamental characteristic to be controlled is the variability in the process. Variability comes from several sources, such as man, machine, material, method, measurement, money and management. Variability in the process can be measured, evaluated and controlled. To do this, data is collected at critical control points for each process and analyzed through statistical methods. The analysis indicates whether the process is under control or requires a corrective/preventive action. This continuous analysis of on-line process control data helps diagnose and correct problems which otherwise would go unnoticed and become part and parcel of the final product. A product which is well controlled during the process stages with SPC methods will require minimal final inspection and verification.

Procedure

- Identify the process.
- Establish a Process Improvement Team (PIT).
- Establish goals.
- Develop a process flow chart.
- Identify the process inputs and outputs.
- Identify the key process characteristics.
- Brainstorm and prioritize the process characteristics.
- Identify the key process variables.
- Collect process data.
- Analyze process variability.
- Take corrective action.
- Bring the process under statistical control.
- Study the process capability.

- Improve the process through proper experimental design.
- Continue SPC analysis for ongoing improvement.

◆ AFFINITY DIAGRAM/KJ METHOD

The affinity diagram of the KJ (Kawakita Jiro) method is another brainstorming tool to gather ideas, facts and opinions about an unexplored area and organize them into interrelated subgroupings having mutual affinity. This method is most useful in situations where the problem is magnanimous and complex while a simple implementable solution is required. The KJ method stimulates creativity and ensures full team participation.

Procedure

- Identify the problem and state the issue.
- Collect narrative data and record individual responses on small cards.
- Mix the cards and spread them randomly on a large table.
- Sort and group the cards that seem to have mutual affinity. Avoid having too many groups as much as possible.
- Specify a header card that captures the essence of the grouping and place it on top for each group of cards.
- Transfer the information from the cards onto paper with lines surrounding the groupings most closely related.
- The information obtained from this brainstorming exercise helps to identify and highlight improvement opportunities and initiatives.

◆ SYSTEMATIC/TREE DIAGRAM

A tree diagram provides a systematic approach in developing the most appropriate and effective means of accomplishing a given set of objectives. A typical application of a systematic diagram involves:

- Identifying the causes of a problem.
- Refining continuous improvement strategies to achieve excellence.
- Developing objectivity for goals and actions.
- Developing and improving the quality of design for new products.

The systematic diagram is typically an "objective-means" diagram. For each objective, various possible means for achieving it are developed and itemized. The means are then evaluated and prioritized and the objectives are confirmed.

Procedure

- State the objective or goal.
- Generate all possible means or causes.
- Continue the tree diagram by generating further causes or means until all ideas are exhausted.
- Systematize the causes or means.
- Review and confirm the objective.

Figure 7 displays a tree diagram for producing a quality manual.

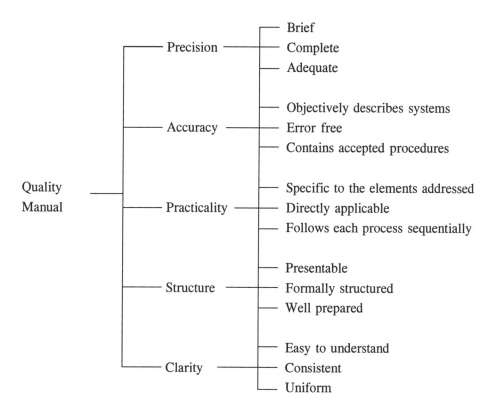

Figure 7: Systematic/Tree Diagram for Producing a Quality Manual

◆ CONCURRENT ENGINEERING (CE)

The traditional approach to design development entailed having individuals or groups in each engineering speciality area work on the design in isolation. Today products have a much higher level of design complexity and sophistication which requires an effective and timely contribution from all responsible participants in the product life cycle to collectively evolve a suitable design.

Concurrent Engineering is the process of developing a viable, suitable and effective design in an optimal time frame through the collective effort of several interrelated crossfunctional units. The process necessitates the concurrent application of various engineering specialities and expertise to produce an appropriate design without "stopover" delays. The key elements of a CE process are as follows:

- Total cultural and management transformation from the traditional approach to the new teamwork approach
- Multi-discipline teamwork
- Integrated multi-functional participation
- Disciplined methodology
- Continuous inter and intra-functional interface and communication
- Effective problem-solving and conflict resolution
- Continuous development and improvement of design to satisfy customer requirements and expectations
- Optimization of product/process design, support systems, resources and time constraints

Procedure

- Identify and develop a comprehensive understanding of the customer's requirements and priorities.
- Establish multi-functional teams.
- Identify the total elements and requirements of the product's life cycle.
- Develop an optimal design.
- Test the design.
- Measure performance.
- Institute improvement initiatives.
- Continuously improve the design.

24

CHANGE MANAGEMENT

◆ CHANGE - A REALITY CHECK

Change is a perpetual and interminable phenomenon. It is a virtual reality of life. Change is inevitable - it is all around us and we are immersed in it. There is little or no escape from change.

Change has eternal life. Change manifests itself in a variety of ways in varying degrees at every step of our life. In the present era, we are witnessing far more rapid streams of changes than ever before. Unlike our simplistic ancestors fighting for survival, today our lives are plagued by abundance rather than absence - surplus rather than scarcity. It is not the sparse simplicity of too little but the crowded complexity of too much too quickly, that affects our lives.

The global order is changing faster then we can comprehend. The rapidity and voluminosity with which changes are encompassing almost every conceivable aspect of our lives - technological, political, economic, social, cultural and personal, is profoundly superabundant. More changes have been induced in our societal infrastructure in one century alone, than the cumulative changes witnessed over the past several centuries. We have almost radically reshaped the environment we live in. Perhaps, the most significant change we are facing today is change itself. We are going through the age of instability.

With the globalization of the marketplace, the economic order is continuously undergoing rapid changes. Almost every day, organizations are being hammered and challenged by abrupt economic fluctuations, intense competitive pressures, and new paradigmatic shifts. This volatility virtually forces the organization to continuously adapt their strategies and systems to the shocks and forces of time. To remain viable in the marketplace, organizations have no choice but to accept and institute changes and continue the reengineering process.

Change portrays two distinctly different facets - it represents growth, opportunity and innovation, as well as threat, disorientation and upheaval. With the paradigm shift that accompanies the change, organizations experience altered states of cultural behaviour, thought processes, judgement value, and to some extent the basic rules and regulations. Even when changing, adapting and evolving is a normal part of life, human attitude and adaptive capabilities are intensely influenced by the rate and extent of change. If controlled properly, change can be pleasantly challenging and invigorating - otherwise, it can be demeaning and dehumanizing.

Change is indispensable for circumventing and preventing stagnation. Most organizations are cognizant of the fact that, to succeed they have to persistently disturb the present. The paradigms of the quiet past shall not work in the turbulent future. With new demands, organizations have to think and act anew.

◆ ANATOMY OF CHANGE

Whenever an organization initiates changes, it does so for a valid and compelling reason - financial, technological, competition, productivity enhancement, changing customer demands, or market pressures. The change process can culminate into either a minor adjustment, reshuffling or reengineering or a major overhauling, restructuring or downsizing of the organization. Depending on how change is managed, minor changes may or may not create any significant impediments in the change process. However, irreversible radical structural changes must be carefully handled because they can polarize the organization creating high levels of fear, uncertainty and demoralization of the workplace that can be damaging to the organization's credibility and profitability.

Notwithstanding the magnitude of change, most change processes are characterized by behaviourial changes of some sort or the other. Generally speaking, an individual goes through some or all of the following stages of behaviourial change during the process of change.

Behavioural Stages of Change

- Apprehension
- Denial
- Anger
- Negotiation
- Resentment
- Depression
- Cognitive Dissonance
- Compliance

What is fundamental to change management is the ability of the organization to short-circuit these stages and achieve an individual's unequivocal acceptance as early as possible. The process of managing organizational change is a complex subject, and needs to be tailored specifically to the particular situation, culture and people who are affected by the change. Any good change management strategy assesses why individuals resist change and tailors a strategy to address each factor.

Change is a people-dependent phenomenon. Change brings about cognitive dissonance (psychological turmoil). For change to be accepted wholeheartedly, people must perceive a congruence among their feelings, beliefs and behaviour. Real change occurs only from the integrated personality of the person. Managers must be sensitive to the value system of the individual to bring about effective and lasting change. For this, the management must provide appropriate support systems that are congruent with the behaviourial stages of change.

The major task in any change process is overcoming resistance to change. Different people react differently to change. Each person sees the change through a personal crystal ball. Some of the basic reasons why people resist change are as follows:

- Change represents unpredictability. It inculcates a fear of the future. People resist change not because they love the past, but because they are uncertain of the future.
- When change is not born out of the shared vision, people do not perceive a congruence between their beliefs and the nature of change.
- Change means giving up something - foregoing the familiar, snugly routine.
- Change implies instability, disorientation and loss of control.
- Most people consider change to be unnecessary, ill-conceived and detriment to the interests of the organization.

◆ CHANGE MANAGEMENT - A COGNITIVE APPROACH

In recent years, there has been a growing trend towards studying human behaviour from the *cognitive* standpoint to improve human performance. The "science of cognition" is a relatively new subject area, however, it is gaining momentum and credibility in many diverse fields of study, including quality control. In this chapter, we are attempting to introduce the applications of cognitive approach to change management. We are hoping that managers can gainfully utilize this new, hitherto untapped, concept to manage change effectively.

As we can realize, an individual's attitude and behaviour patterns have the greatest impact on the change process. Attitude formation is a resultant of the cognitive processes. If we can succeed in tapping the cognitive psyche of the individual to generate a positive mindset, we can expect to achieve acceptance to change more quickly and enthusiastically.

Cognition pertains to awareness, judgement, perception of reality without subjective bias. Cognitive processes occur in the neocortex region of our brain. The cognitive process begins when a person perceives a given situation and makes a subjective evaluation of what it is and what it means in relationship to his circumstances, beliefs, and values. The judgements, of course, are subject to continuous review in the light of changing events.

In addition to the thought processes coursing though our cognition, there are also other forces at play that impact our behaviour and attitude. These are the emotional feelings generated by the limbic system of the brain that lies just below the cerebral cortex where cognition resides.

There is a certain degree of correlational inter-dependence between our cognition and the emotive reactions of the limbic system. That is to say, our cognitive perceptual analysis can influence our emotional feelings and, thereby, determine our behaviour patterns. On the other hand, if we approach a situation with our limbic system already in some emotional state, as a result of prior thoughts, this will tend to colour the interpretation our cognition shall make of the new situation being faced.

Let us consider some examples to elucidate this delicate relationship between our cognition (neocortex) and the emotional feelings (limbic system).

Consider, first, the physiological dependence of emotions on cognition. When we perceive a situation, the cognition draws-up some conclusions. These conclusions are matched against our beliefs. If there is a high degree of congruence between the two, we accept the situation with a positive attitude. Since the cognitive process operates on a continuum, our perceptual analysis is subject to revision and, consequently, so is our emotive reaction. To give you a real-life personal example, I remember, at one time, having a buffet lunch with some of my friends at a restaurant. I was thoroughly enjoying what I was eating. Suddenly, my friend Paul turned around and asked me if I knew what I was eating. Obviously, what I thought was chicken legs were really frog legs. Instantaneously, my feelings of enjoyment changed to disgust (I hate frog legs). Thus, you can see that my cognitive appraisal of the situation (chicken legs) was positive and, consequently, my emotive and behaviourial reaction was in harmony with my value system. However, with additional factual information, my revised cognitive judgement was unfavourable to my emotional feelings and, therefore, my behaviour was altered.

Now, consider the reverse cycle - the impact of emotions on cognition. If our limbic system is preoccupied with some emotional state, as a result of prior thoughts or events, we would tend to perceive the new situation in a less realistic manner. How often, for example, we carry our anger and frustration from events that transpire at home, onto our working environment and indiscriminantly show our anger on our colleagues for no obvious fault of theirs.

Let us now examine how cognition operates during the change processes. The way we perceive a situation, make a mental picture and draw conclusions - determines how we react to organizational change. Our thoughts, attitude and behaviour patterns can cause us to resist, or it can cause us to embrace and support the change. When change transpires in an organization, each person attempts to seek as much available information as possible about the situation. The cognition evaluates this information against personal needs, experiences, fears , expectations and beliefs and draws conclusions about the viability and receptability of change. If there is a high degree of compatibility between our cognitive perception and beliefs, we shall formulate a positive mindset and our behaviour stages of change would move faster towards acceptance of change. Many a times, of course, our judgements are biased in favour of our own interests. It's human nature to filter the information, through selective perception, in a personal way and draw conclusions that reflect our own viewpoint.

The magnitude and power of cognitive processes have a phenomenal impact on events. Just imagine how many different ways an individual can draw his or her own conclusions in a change process:

- If the available information is insufficient or unreliable, the individual's cognition is bound to make faulty assumptions.
- If there is a lack of operational transparency vis-à-vis the change process, the individual will formulate a sense of distrust, fear, and uncooperativeness.
- Even if the available information is reliable, the cognition can draw faulty assumptions and misinterpretations because of some preconceived emotional reactions and would, consequently, develop a negative mindset.

Undoubtedly, therefore, the speed at which an individual will accept change is highly dependent on the judiciousness and efficacy of his cognitive evaluations and emotive reactions to change. For change to be accepted wholeheartedly, both the individual as well as the manager have an important role to play. The manager must provide meaningful input about change and be sensitive to the value system of the individual. The individual must also endeavour to formulate unbiased and realistic evaluation of the total change process and must perceive a congruence between his perception and feelings.

◆ MANAGERS AS CHANGE AGENTS

From the above discussion, let us draw some fundamental conclusions about the change process, as follows:

- Change is inevitable and indispensable.
- During the process of change, people go through a variety of behaviourial changes.
- Attitude to change is a resultant of an inter-play between cognitive processes and emotional feelings.
- Acceptance of change comes through a clear understanding of the change process, balancing of cognitive and emotive reactions, and developing a positive mindset.

What role can the management play in facilitating the change process? Change can be brought about quickly and harmoniously, but it requires management's ingenuity, patience and dedication. Effective change management starts with understanding the process of change, identifying the factors that impact the change process, and developing suitable framework to facilitate the change process.

As a first step, organizations should endeavour to bring about change in a slow and systematic manner. Sudden and drastic changes create confusion, fear, apprehension and resistance. For instance, neither sudden empire-building is a wise strategy when profits are up, nor drastic downsizing is a panacea for all ills during market volatility and declining profits. Functioning under vacillating and inconsistent operational framework can rarely bring sustainable success. Constancy and stability are the most powerful tools for effective change management.

Secondly, it must be understood that change is a people-dependent phenomenon. Most people perceive change to be a negative entity. Change cannot be brought about by dictate. Compliance by dictate only brings about short-lived and cosmetic change. Real change occurs only from the integrated personality of the person. Consequently, organizations must clearly understand the needs, expectations and cognitive value-system of the people and develop appropriate framework to facilitate the acceptance process. The basic requirements of people during a change process can, typically, be characterized as follows:

- Clear picture of the change process
- Complete, reliable information
- Transparency of operations
- Cognitive Congruence
  - Unbiased, realistic evaluation of change process
  - Congruence with emotional feelings
  - Affinity with needs, expectations and beliefs
  - Positive attitude
- Management Support
  - Encouragement, support for personal role change
  - Maintenance of control, responsibility
  - Appropriate resources, opportunities
  - Involvement and empowerment
- Personal Growth
  - Personal suitability/capability for midcourse correction
  - Cross-functional interface impact
  - Long-term impact of change on personal growth

Finally, effective planning is fundamental to change management. Organization should not start swinging at the task of change without proper planning. Some of the essential elements of planning include the following:

- Identification of means of effective dissemination of information
- Development of proper communication network
- Preparation of managers to handle change
- Involvement of employees in the change process
- Transparency of operational framework

Road Map for Change Management

- Develop a plan for the change process, to include:
  - Purpose of change
  - Type and nature of change
  - Magnitude of change
  - Areas/units subject to change
  - Time schedule for change
  - Impact of change on units/individuals
- Develop a profile of change process.
- Identify channels of dissemination of information.
- Select and prepare capable managers to handle and coordinate the change process.
- Provide training to managers, if necessary, on behaviourial aspects of human undertaking.
- Establish groups and encourage group discussions on the change process.
- Involve everyone in the change process.
- Clearly identify: nature of change; impact; benefits to the reorganization and individuals.
- Managers should utilize cognitive approach to change management and identify:
  - What information is available to the individuals?
  - How the individuals perceive the change process?
  - What are the individual's emotive reactions?
  - How does the individual evaluate the change process?
  - Is the change process compatible with the individual's beliefs and expectations?
  - What are the individual's perceptions about the long-term impact of change on the organization as well as himself?
  - What judgements and attitude the individual is forming about the change process?
- Managers should help individuals, in every possible way, to make the transition as smooth as possible.
- Develop a step-by-step plan for implementing the change.
- Develop a suitable infrastructure.
- Identify and provide the requisite resources.
- Monitor progress.
- Review/revise/reset priorities.

Making change happen seems awfully difficult. Sometimes it seems to take forever; sometimes it does not happen. In fact, the more successful the organization, the more difficulty it has changing. To turn around a negative change into a propitiously positive proposition, a manager must know when to implement a change, how much and how. In addition, managers must exhibit commitment, dedication and exemplary working attitude and behaviour towards change. More succinctly speaking, managers must act as change agents.

◆ INDIVIDUALS AS CHANGE AGENTS

Although management plays a paramount role throughout the process of change, no amount of meaningful and sustainable organizational changes can transpire without an unqualified and unequivocal participation and acceptance of change by the individuals. Individuals can make substantial contributions in more than one of the following ways:

- Understanding the importance of change
- Alleviating any skepticism about the change process
- Assisting in implementing change with a positive mindset
- Becoming an instrument of change
- Becoming a change agent

The first most important thing for any individual is to understand the nature, reality and importance of change. Following are some of the essential elements of the change process:

- If the organization is instituting changes, it must be doing so for a good reason.
- Changes are not always a bad idea; changes also connote progress.
- Management has to make tough decisions to keep the company afloat.
- If the company is changing, the individual really has no choice but to change.
- Change does not come by easily; it brings with it difficulties, problems and disorientation.
- Management has neither all the answers, nor have the entire capability to make it happen. It's too big a job for the management to handle alone. They need help.
- Individuals are also part of the organization and it is their duty to facilitate any process which the management deem important for the success of the organization. In fact, individuals are paid to handle problems, provide solutions and support the management. They are not paid to cause problems or resist the requisite changes.

We shall now append some guidelines on how individuals can make significant positive contributions to the change process:

- When changes transpire in the organization, try to be an active participant to the process.
- Seek reliable information and try to understand the true nature and impact of changes.
- Try to understand the organization's mandate and need towards the change process.
- Make a realistic cognitive evaluation of the changes.
- If the changes are for a worthy cause, try to develop a positive mindset and help facilitate the implementation process.
- If the changes are detrimental to the interests of the organization, present your viewpoint to the management and establish a positive rapport.
- Recognize and appreciate the managements's perspective:
  - Management has a specific responsibility towards the organization.
  - If changes are necessary, they shall have to be made. It's their responsibility to ensure that changes are implemented harmoniously and effectively.
  - Management have some idea how the changes will be implemented, but they don't have all the answers. They are themselves trying to discover the most optimal solution.
  - Change process is not the exclusive domain of management alone; it's everyone's responsibility.
  - Management, like anyone else, is also prone to making mistakes.
- Be tolerant of management's mistakes. Management is genuinely seeking for your help. Instead of making their job difficult, try to help simplify the process and support management's efforts.
- Don't resist change. You can be singled out and accused of causing trouble and getting in the way of progress. Anger, frustration and resentment can offer no benefits.
- Consider change as a new challenge. Look for new opportunities in the change process. Expend your energies and efforts in making the change work rather than resenting and fighting the change.
- Grab hold of the opportunity and reinvent the future rather than redesigning the past.

"BE THE CHANGE YOU'RE TRYING TO CREATE."

MAHATMA GANDHI

25

SELF-DIRECTED WORK TEAMS

◆ THE AGE OF TEAMWORK

Perpetual changes are a normal part of business life. Businesses must continually change and evolve, vis-à-vis market demands, in order to survive and prosper. Most successful businesses are aware of this fact, and they continually reengineer their operations to remain viably competitive. The reengineering process can involve a variety of actions, including:

- Realignment of functions
- Organizational restructuring
- Development of new models/methods
- Introduction of new systems/operating procedures

Within the past few years, we have witnessed innumerable paradigm shifts in the business circles. The most noticeable one has been what we will term as the "people revolution" - a growing realization of the fact that human contribution and commitment is the most fundamental driving force for any organization. This appreciation of human potential paved the way for accentuated democratization of the workplace. As a consequence, people were empowered with greater control to achieve excellence. The means to achieve these ends involved the concepts and processes of teamwork, quality circles, high-involvement workforce, etc. This modus operandi provided the workers with more responsibility, authority, information, training, and decision-making power. The resultant output of these efforts proved to be highly beneficial for both the worker and the organization. It provided the workers both the intrinsic (work-related) and extrinsic (recognition) rewards. For the organization, it amounted to higher performance, better market share, superior quality, technological innovativeness, and greater profits.

The teamwork process is a valuable tool, but like all other tools and techniques, it requires continuous augmentation. A model is effective only if it has the capability of accommodating changing requirements. Situations in today's marketplace are not static; they are highly dynamic and fluid in nature. New demands and priorities are a virtual reality of today's scenario. Organizations have to have the capability to proactively respond to these changing demands. Consequently, the means and operational framework and methodology has also to undergo perpetual redesigning and enhancement. Today's concept of Self-Directed Work Teams (SDWT) is one such redesign of teamwork concept that was born out of a necessity to address the changing and evolving marketplace needs.

◆ SELF-DIRECTED WORK TEAM: THE CONCEPT

The concept and process of teamwork is indeed a well understood entity. The basic difference between various team approaches is reflected by the way a team is structured and how it functions. To clearly understand this new concept of self-directed teams, we shall first describe the role and process of traditional teams.

In the traditional teamwork model, the manager or supervisor identifies a corporate objective or project; a team is created; the team works together under the direct responsibility of the supervisor and develops solutions to the problem; when the task is completed, the team may be dissolved. Thus, traditional teams have, at least, the following distinctive characteristics:

- They are created in response to a specific issue or project.
- They function under the traditional hierarchical structure.
- They may have a limited shelf-life.
- Their orientation is task-specific and management controlled.

In contrast, a Self-Directed Work Team (SDWT) is not necessarily formed in response to a specific task or project. A unit or division may create one or several SDWTs and these teams become responsible for the management of the overall work profile of their unit. The team consists of a group of 7 to 10 people, who has the complete responsibility for planning, performing, managing and controlling all work processes assigned to them. The teams develop their own objectives, commensurate with the corporate objectives, and they work together to address all relevant issues for the effective functioning of the unit. There is no vertical hierarchy or any boss/worker relationship. Although hierarchical structure may be present in the organization for administrative purposes, workers in a self-directed team share equal responsibility and authority to accomplish the task. The team members are selected on the basis of their ability for the task at hand. The team selects its own leader, on a rotational basis, to facilitate the process.

A self-directed team, generally, operates at the system level and not at the process level. For specific process improvement needs, there can be one or more Process Improvement Teams (PITs) operating under the umbrella of an SDWT. Notwithstanding however, an SDWT can also be created for a special project, if needed. Typically, an SDWT undertakes the responsibility for the entire work profile of the unit. The team works together on an ongoing, day to day, basis and the work is usually designed to give the team ownership of a product or service. The team functions as a high-involvement team with the freedom, responsibility and authority to self-manage their work and performance. They plan, manage, and control their own work processes; they set their own goals, commensurate with corporate goals; they establish their own schedules and functional procedures; and they are accountable for the quality of their work. Typical characteristics of a self-directed team include the following:

- Participation/cooperation
- Absence of hierarchy
- Decision-making by consensus
- Operational flexibility
- Continuous learning/improvement
- Commitment to teamwork
- Responsible empowerment
- Effective change management
- Effective response capability

◆ SELF-DIRECTED VERSUS TRADITIONAL TEAMS

Before embarking on implementing the self-directed team model, it is imperative to clearly understand the comparative strengths and weaknesses of the two approaches. Following is a highlight of salient features of the two models:

Traditional Team Model

Strengths

- Quick decision-making due to central control
- Little employee resistance
- Little need for specialized training
- Faster acceptance of results

Weaknesses

- Authoritative and autocratic
- Little empowerment and freedom
- Restrain on input and participation
- Lack of creativity and innovativeness
- Little opportunity for personal growth

Self-Directed Team Model

Strengths

- High involvement and cooperation
- Commitment to teamwork
- Flexibility and freedom of operation
- No fear of hierarchy
- Decision-making by consensus
- Generation of creative/innovative ideas
- High empowerment
- Pride of ownership
- High accountability/responsibility
- Opportunity for continuous learning and personal growth
- High response capability to change
- Focus on continuous improvement

Weaknesses

- Resistance from middle management
- Requires extensive start-up planning
- Involves high training costs
- Slow decision making

In light of the above discussion, it is evident that this new concept of self-directed teams is a viable and efficacious extension and augmentation of the traditional team model. The most outstanding contribution of the SDWT model is in its capability to respond to changing needs.

The traditional teams are more static and structured in nature. Since they are generally created in response to a specific issue or project, they don't have the capability and flexibility to respond to any major changes in the project or accommodate any other pressing issue within the project phase. When the project is completed, the team may be dissolved.

The self-directed teams are created as an entity to address any or all issues requiring resolution. They are more dynamic and flexible enough to be able to undertake one or several tasks or accommodate any other issue requiring immediate attention. The team can have an eternal life unless required otherwise. This unique structural and functional framework of the SDWT is most suitable for:

- Continuous improvement focus
- Continuous reengineering
- Continuous information flow
- Continuous training and development
- Continuous opportunities for personal growth
- Continuous environmental scanning
- Continuous response capability

Notwithstanding the obvious superiority of the SDWT model, organizations must always carefully evaluate each situation individually and its viability for self-directed team approach. In respect of this caution, the following points should be borne in mind:

- There is a distinct possibility that the self-directed team approach may not be either applicable or suitable for every situation. For example, it is believed that the SDWT model is most suitable for manufacturing situations and may be a risky venture for situations where there are task/organizational limitations or low group interdependence or situations separated by geographical distances and boundaries.
- The SDWT concept creates high levels of anxiety and tension among the middle management for fear of loss of control. Seemingly, the premise of self-directed teams is the elimination of the middle management.
- The SDWT concept can send alarm signals for impending drastic organizational changes and can, therefore, inculcate a sense of fear, uncertainty and disorientation in the workforce.

- At the individual level, it can create apprehensions about individual recognition and acceptance as team members or leaders.

◆ SDWT: DESIGN AND IMPLEMENTATION

No two companies are alike. The design and implementation of a self-directed team must uniquely fit the profile and infrastructure of the company. Below, we are appending some general guidelines that could be used to develop a road map for implementing a self-directed team model:

- Someone in the organization (typically a member of the executive management) starts the process by identifying the possibility of using self-directed team approach for enhancing the quality and productivity of the company's functions and operations.
- The management supports the idea and commits to provide requisite resources for its execution.
- A Steering Committee is appointed, made-up of top management and other key personnel (managers, supervisors, workers, engineers, etc.).
- The steering committee conducts a thorough literature search on the subject, identifies benchmarks, and develops a framework by which SDWT concept can be implemented.
- The steering committee identifies a particular unit or division in the organization where the SDWT model can be implemented. The area identified should be such that it has a specific need for improvement and carries a high chance of success for the new process.
- A self-directed work team consisting of between 7 to 10 members is established in the chosen unit. The team members should include personnel from the steering committee, key managers and supervisors, key functional people with technical expertise, and personnel responsible for the work processes.
- The team selects a leader to facilitate the functional process.
- Typically, the team does the following:
  - Looks at the overall functional profile and work processes of the unit to identify where improvements can be made.
  - Evaluates all specific functions, such as: customer needs/satisfaction; current processes and how they address customer needs; the inputs into the unit; the in-process activities; the outputs; people involvement, empowerment, and contribution; the overall current system for hiring, firing, training, planning, scheduling, compensating, and a host of other related aspects, including job satisfaction, opportunities for improvement, etc.
- The team selects an appropriate pilot project to start the teamwork process.
- The team works over the project until its completion.

- The team can start another project or undertake the task of planning and improving the total functions and work processes of the unit. Typically, a self-directed team can be annotated as a management body responsible for the effective management of the unit.

In the process outlined above, there are some specific functional aspects of teamwork that need to be further elucidated. They relate to the following:

- Role and responsibilities of:
  - Team leader
  - Team members
- Developmental aspects of SDWTs.

Team Leader

The role of a team leader in a self-directed team is that of a facilitator. He does not supervise people. He becomes instrumental in the team's search for viable solutions and effective and speedy decision-making. Leadership is shared by the members of the group. Generally, the team appoints a leader for a term of 2 to 4 months. Some teams rotate leadership roles at every project or every meeting. In some cases, the leader amy be appointed by the executive management, in the initial stages, from among former supervisors or managers who hold the management vision, mission, values and objectives. Leadership is not defined by position, but by function and competence. Typically, while the SDWT is responsible for managing within the boundary, the leader manages the boundary itself.

The skill, ability, and competence of a leader are of paramount importance for the successful functioning of the team. It is the responsibility of the leader to:

- Generate a climate of trust and cooperation
- Balance appropriate levels of participation
- Ensure that every team member has an opportunity to provide input
- Support, protect, and defend everyone equally
- Understand members' needs, beliefs and value-system
- Handle conflicts positively, constructively, and effectively
- Respect and maintain confidentiality
- Encourage growth and development
- Ensure team regulations and decorum
- Move from managing people to managing ideas and tasks

Team Members

Membership to the team is voluntary. Generally, members are selected on the basis of their expertise and suitability in relation to the nature of the task at hand. Like the leader, members have as much or more responsibility in effective functioning of the team. Following are some of the basic characteristics of team members:

- They should be genuinely interested in the welfare of the group, the unit and the organization.
- They should share a common vision and value-system with the management.
- They should be honest, open and proactive.
- They should be sensitive to the needs, opinions, ideas and feelings of others.
- They should respect the team rules and support the leader.
- They should accept ownership, responsibility and accountability for team decisions.
- They should participate freely, willingly, and constructively.
- They should be prompt, regular and active participants to the team.
- They should help build the team for success.
- They should facilitate, rather than hinder, the decision-making process.
- They should see that everyone has an equal opportunity for growth and development.

Self-directed teams are successful when:

- They are receptive to management's goals and priorities.
- They share a common mission and commitment.
- They are responsive to changing needs and requirements.
- They operate in a climate of trust, openness and togetherness.
- Roles are balanced and shared to facilitate growth and development.
- Opinions and ideas are expressed freely.
- Creativity and risk taking is a normal part of the process.
- There are opportunities for continuous training, development, and growth.
- People feel a sense of belonging and congruence among their feelings, beliefs, and value-system.
- Decision-making is through consensus.

SDWT: Developmental Aspects

Traditional teams are task-oriented. They do not go through any rigorous developmental process. Their operability is simple and structured. Self-directed teams, on the other hand, are management-oriented. They involve new operating principles, diversified structures, empowered responsibility, and drastic organizational realignment. Extreme care should be exercised, at least in the initial stages, to ensure proper design, implementation, and functioning of the team. Typically, a SDWT undergoes the following stages of development to maturation:

- **Passive Apprehension**

At the initial team formation stage, there is always a general sense of confusion and apprehension among people. No one knows what to expect. Structures, roles and responsibilities are changing. Team members and leaders are learning to cope with new realities, functions, team concept, and self-directed mode of operation. This stage can be facilitated through acquisition and provision of requisite information and awareness training.

- **Participative Interdependence**

As the team starts functioning, a different set of anxieties creep in. People are now moving from dependence to interdependence. Personal beliefs and controls are being challenged. Some members may experience anxiety and frustration while others may feel excited and energized with the new challenge. There can be some loss of productivity in this phase. This is where the leader's abilities come into play - to provide support, to ensure balanced levels of participation and control, to facilitate and create harmony out of diversity of opinions, ideas and beliefs.

- **Role Maturation**

The team has now reached a stage where the roles and responsibilities are clear but members are adjusting to the new status quo. A sense of integration, unity, and self confidence is beginning to permeate in the team operability.

- **Self-Direction**

The team now reaches the level of maturity to function as a self-directed team. The dominant characteristics of this stage include: sense of empowerment, responsibility and accountability; ownership of processes; feelings of trust, respect, and support; feeling of accomplishment, and pride; a surge of rejuvenation.

◆ SDWT: SYPNOSIS

Teamwork is a way of life in today's business world. High-involvement/high-performance self-directed work team model presents a viable option for the effective functioning of the workplace. The SDWT approach furnishes many benefits for the organization as well as to the individuals. Some of these benefits include the following:

Benefits to the Organization

- Helps to achieve greater output with less resources
- Makes organizational realignment/restructuring process easy
- Provides quick response capability to changing needs
- Enhances worker motivation, satisfaction, and performance
- Provides opportunities for continuous learning, development, and growth
- Helps deliver high quality products and services to the customer with speed, accuracy and precision
- Supports continuous improvement focus

Benefits to Individuals

- Greater empowerment and involvement in the decision-making process
- More opportunities for individual growth and development
- More support, recognition, and reward
- Greater control over changing environment
- Greater variety, challenge and job satisfaction
- Opportunities for creativity, innovativeness and fulfilment
- More information and control over organizational operatibility

Finally, we shall recapitulate and summarize the self-directed team implementation process with the following implementation checklist.

Implementation Checklist

- Identify management commitment for the implementation of the SDWT system.
- Establish a steering committee.
- Develop a strategic plan.
- Identify a pilot project.
- Design a self-directed team.
- Implement the SDWT process.
- Establish common mission and objectives.
- Allocate appropriate resources.
- Provide adequate training, education, and cross-functional training.
- Develop communication strategy.
- Empower the workforce.
- Monitor and measure progress and performance.
- Recognize achievements and reward the workforce.
- Maintain continuous improvement focus.

BIBLIOGRAPHY

●

REFERENCES

A. BIBLIOGRAPHY

1. Ackerman, R.B. et al (1987): "Process Quality Management and Improvement Guidelines". AT&T Bell Laboratories, P.O. Box 19901, Indianapolis, Indiana.

2. Belasco, J.A. (1990): "Teaching the Elephant to Dance". Crown Publishers, New York

3. Canadian Standards Association: National Standard of Canada: "CAN-Q395-81: Quality Audits". Canadian Standards Association, Rexdale, Ontario, Canada.

4. Crosby, P.B. (1979): "Quality is Free.": McGraw-Hill Book Company, New York, U.S.A.

5. Deming, W. E. (1982): "Out of the Crisis": Massachusetts Institute of Technology, Massachussets, U.S.A.

6. Felkins, P.K., Chakiris, B.J. and Chakiris, K.N. (1993): "Change Management - A Model for Effective Organizational Performance".

7. Juran, J.M. (1986): "The Quality Trilogy": Quality Progress - American Society for Quality Control, August 1986, pp. 19-24.

8. Juran, J.M. (1989): "Leadership for Quality": Free Press, New York.

9. Mills, C.A. (1989): "The Quality Audit: A Management Evaluation Tool,": ASQC Quality Process, Milwaukee and McGraw-Hill Book Co., New York.

10. Miuro, Akio (1989): "Don't Suffer Through Bad Manuals": Quality Progress - American Society for Quality Control, December 1989, pp. 96.

11. Mizuno, Shigeru (1988): "Management for Quality Improvement - The Seven New QC Tools". Productivity Press, Cambridge, Massachussetts.

12. Orsburn, J. et al (1990): "Self-Directed Work Teams". Business One Irwin, Homewood, Illinois.

13.   Rosander, A.C. (1991): "Deming's 14 Points Applied to Services". Marcel Dekker, Inc., New York and ASQC Quality Press, Milwaukee, Wisconsin.

14.   Wellins, R., Byham, W. and Wilson, J. (1991): "Empowered Teams". Jossey-Bass Publishers, San Fransisco, California

B. AUTHOR'S REFERENCES

A large part of the material presented in this book has been extracted from the author's teaching and consulting notes, published books and professional papers. A selected list of references is as follows:

PUBLISHED BOOKS

1. Puri, S.C. (1994): "ISO 9000 Certifcation and Total Quality Management", 1st ed. (Portuguese language). Qualitymark Editora Ltda., Rua Felipe Camaráo, 73 - Maracaná, 20511-010 - Rio de Janeiro, Brazil.

2. Puri, S.C. (1984): "Statistical Process Quality Control - Key to Productivity". Standards-Quality Management Group, P.O. Box 30051, 250 Greenbank Road, Nepean, Canada.

3. Puri, S.C. and Mullen, K. (1980): "Applied Statistics for Food and Agricultural Scientists". G.K. Hall & Co., Boston, Massachussets.

4. Puri, S.C., Ennis, D. and Mullen, K. (1979): "Statistical Quality Control for Food and Agricultural Scientists". G.K. Hall & Co., Boston, Massachusetts.

5. Puri, S.C. (1989): "Statistical Methods for Food Quality Management". Publication number A73-5268. Agriculture Canada, Ottawa, Canada.

6. Puri, S.C. (1981): "Statistical Aspects of Food Quality Assurance." Publication Number 5140. Agriculture Canada, Ottawa, Canada.

TECHNICAL PAPERS

1. Puri, S.C. (1995): "TQM/ISO 9000/SPC: Why Do Systems Fail": Transactions, 49th Annual Quality Congress - American Society for Quality Control, Cincinnati, Ohio.

2. Puri, S.C. (1995): "TQM plus ISO plus HACCP - The Trilogical Connection": 79th Annual Conference of the Central Atlantic States Association, Baltimore, Maryland.

3.   Puri, S.C. (1993): "Extending GMP and HACCP to ISO 9000: Guidelines for the Health Care and Food Sectors": Annual Qualtiy Forum - Ontario Food Protection Association, Toronto, Canada.

4.   Puri, S.C. (1993): "TQM + ISO 9000 - The Next Strategic Imperative": Transactions, 32nd Annual Conference of Mettallurgical Society of CIM, Québec City, Canada.

5.   Puri, S.C. (1993): "Service TQM Model via ISO 9004-2": Transactions, 47th Annual Quality Congress - American Society for Quality Control, Boston, Massachussetts.

6.   Puri, S.C. (1992): "The ABC's of Implementing ISO-9000": Transactions, 46th Annual Quality Congress - American Society for Qaulity Control, Nashville, Tennessee.

7.   Puri, S.C. (1991): "Deming and ISO 9000: A Deadly Combination for Quality Revolution": Transactions, 45th Annual Quality Congress - American Society for Quality Control, Milwaukee, Wisconsin.

8.   Puri, S.C. (1990): "Food Safety and Quality Control: SPC with HACCP": Transactions, 44th Annual Quality Congress - American Society for Quality Control, San Fransico, California.

9.   Puri, S.C. (1989): "Genesis of Statistical Process Control": Transactions, Update 89 Seminar. The Institute of Environmental Science and the Society of Reliability Engineers, Ottawa, Canada.

10.   Puri, S.C. (1989): "Continuous Improvement: Master Check-list": Transaction, 43rd Annual Quality Congress - American Society for Quality Control, Toronto, Canada.

11.   Puri, S.C. (1988): "Applied SPC and the Taguchi Approach": Transactions, 19th International Symposium on Applied Technology and Automation, Monte Carlo, Monaco.

12.   Puri, S.C. (1988): "International Perspectives on Quality and Standardization": Transactions, 34th Annual Quality Forum - American Society for Quality Control, Toronto Section, Toronto, Canada.

13.   Puri, S.C. (1987): "Agri-Food Business: The Years Ahead": Transactions, 2nd Seminar of the European Organization for Quality Control - Section for QC in the Food Industry, Zurich, Switzerland.

14. Puri, S.C. (1987): "Developing Countries - A National Plan for Quality-Productivity": Transactions, International Conference - International Association of Science and Technology for Development, Paris, France.

15. Puri, S.C. (1987): "Management of Food Quality: Issues and Trends": Transactions, 33rd Annual Quality Forum - American Society for Quality Control, Toronto Section, Toronto, Canada.

16. Puri, S.C. (1987): "Quality Challenges and Opportunities for Developing Countries": Transactions, 31st Annual Conference - European Organization for Quality Control, Munich, W. Germany.

17. Puri, S.C. (1987): "A Plan of Excellence for a Regulatory Agency": Transactions, 41st Annual Quality Congress - American Society for Quality Control, Minneapolis, Minnesota.

18. Puri, S.C. (1987): "Estimation of Weibull Distribution Parameters for Failure Analysis": Transactions, International Conference - International Association of Science and Technology for Development, Los Angeles, California.

19. Puri, S.C. (1986): "A Master Plan for Quality-Productivity": Transactions, 7th Latin American Quality Control Congress, Saltillo, Mexico.

20. Puri, S.C. (1985): "Quality and Deregulation": Transactions, 40th Annual Quality Congress - American Society for Quality Control, Anaheim, California.

21. Puri, S.C. (1984): "Quality Registration Programs": Transactions, World Quality Congress - European Organization for Quality Control, Brighton, U.K.

22. Puri, S.C. (1983): "Quality, Standardization and Developing Countries": Transactions, II-Asia Pacific Congress, Mexico City, Mexico.

23. Puri, S.C. (1983): "Quality Indicators for Corporate Management": Transactions, 37th Annual Quality Congress - American Society for Quality Control, Boston, Massachusetts.

24. Puri, S.C. (1983): "Quality Management and Cost-Recovery": Transactions, 37th Annual Quality Congress - American Society for Quality Control, Boston, Massachusetts.

25.   Puri, S.C. and McWhinnie, J. (1981): "Quality Management Through Quality Indicators - A New Approach": Quality Assurance - Methods, Management and Motivation. Society of Manufacturing Engineers and American Society for Quality Control, U.S.A.

26.   Puri, S.C. (1980): "The Role of Standardization in the Manufacturing of Products, Goods, Exchange, and Services": Transactions, 24th European Organization for Quality Control, Warsaw, Poland.

27.   Puri, S.C. (1979): "Management of Total Reliability": Microelectronics and Reliability, Vol. 19, No. 1/2, pp. 7-10.

28.   Puri, S.C. (1978): "Quality Control and Reliability": Engineering and Statistical Research Institute, Agriculture Canada, Ottawa, Report q-58, pp. 6-7.

29.   Puri, S.C. (1976): "Application of MINQUE Procedures to Block Designs": Communications in Statistics. Vol. 5, No. 2, pp. 191-196.

30.   Puri, S.C. (1974): "Panel Grading of Butter - a Feasibility Study": Proceedings XIX International Dairy Congress, New Delhi, India.

INDEX

The Author

Subhash C. Puri is an internationally renowned author, lecturer and consultant on the subject of quality. As principal of Standards-Quality Management Group, an Ottawa (Canada) based consulting company, he provides training and consultation on a variety of subjects such as: TQM, ISO 9000 Certification, Quality System Auditing, SPC, Business Process Reengineering, etc. Prior to starting his own consulting and training activities, he served as Director and Chief Statistician at Agriculture Canada and taught at several universities in Canada and abroad.

As one of the leading authorities on the subject, he has been a keynote speaker and lecturer for many associations and organizations in several countries. For over two decades, he has provided extensive training and consultation to numerous organizations and companies in the manufacturing, service and public sectors at the national and international levels, for implementing TQM and ISO 9000 systems.

Being actively involved in the national and international standardization activities, he has made significant contributions to the development of statistical and quality standards. He is the chairman of CAC/ISO/TC69, member of CAC/ISO/TC176 and has served as chairman/member on many other standards committees. He is the author of several books and has published numerous professional papers on the subject.